KENT AND EUROPE, 1450–1640

KENT AND EUROPE, 1450–1640

MERCHANTS, MARINERS, SHIPPING AND DEFENCE

Edited by
Robert Blackmore and Craig Lambert

THE BOYDELL PRESS

First published 2025
The Boydell Press, Woodbridge

ISBN 978-1-83765-150-4

The Boydell Press is an imprint of Boydell & Brewer Ltd
PO Box 9, Woodbridge, Suffolk IP12 3DF, UK
and of Boydell & Brewer Inc.
668 Mt Hope Avenue, Rochester, NY 14620-2731, USA
website: www.boydellandbrewer.com

Our Authorised Representative for product safety in the EU is Easy Access System Europe – Mustamäe tee 50, 10621 Tallinn, Estonia, gpsr.requests@easproject.com

A CIP catalogue record for this book is available from the British Library

CONTENTS

TABLES

NOTES ON THE EDITORS AND CONTRIBUTORS

Robert Blackmore is a Visiting Fellow at the University of Southampton. He is the author of *Government and Merchant Finance in Anglo-Gascon Trade* (Palgrave, 2020), and regularly contributes to *BBC History Magazine.*

Craig Lambert is Professor of Maritime History at the University of Southampton, author of *Shipping the Medieval Military* (Boydell, 2011), co-editor of *Military Communities in Late Medieval England* (Boydell, 2018), co-editor of *The Routledge Companion to Marine and Maritime Worlds, 1400–1800* (Routledge, 2020), and co-author of 'William Fowler, Sir William Garrard, Sir John Hawkins and the Sixteenth-Century Atlantic Slave Trade', *English Historical Review*, 139 (2024), 680–714.

Gary Baker is a Senior Research Fellow at the University of Southampton. He is co-author of 'William Fowler, Sir William Garrard, Sir John Hawkins and the Sixteenth-Century Atlantic Slave Trade', *English Historical Review*, 139 (2024), 680–714, and author of 'Domestic Maritime Trade in Late Tudor England c.1565–85: A Case Study of King's Lynn and Plymouth', in Claire Jowitt, Craig Lambert and Steve Mentz (eds), *The Routledge Companion to Marine and Maritime Worlds, 1400–1800* (Routledge, 2020), 95–124.

Sheila Sweetinburgh is a Specialist Associate Lecturer in Medieval and Early Modern Studies at the University of Kent and a Trustee of the Canterbury Association for Medieval and Early Modern Studies (CAMEMS). She has published widely on late medieval and early modern Kent and recently co-edited a major book on Kent's maritime history: *Maritime Kent through the Ages: Gateway to the Sea* (Boydell, 2021).

ABBREVIATIONS

BL	The British Library
CCAL	Canterbury Cathedral Archives and Library
CCCC	Corpus Christi College, Cambridge
KHLC	Kent History and Library Centre
TNA	The National Archives

Introduction

ROBERT BLACKMORE

This book explores Kent's history from the mid-fifteenth to mid-seventeenth centuries, emphasising its relationship with Europe. The main concerns of the volume's chapters are often, like those of so many of the region's inhabitants – then as now – affixed on the sea. As an appeal to Elizabeth I, in search of a reduction in their contribution to the support of the royal household, articulated in 1593:

> First Kent is a marytime contrye, and is not only vpon euery occasion compelled to watche the beacons and to keepe watche and warde at the coaste of the sea, but is also vpon euery approche or showe of thenemye dryven to put on armes and to keepe the fielde more often and more chargeable then any inland cowntie and any other marytime shieres of the realme […] This shiere is in manor the onlye highe streate and waye by the wch all commers and goers into and out of the Realme for matters of state doe passe and repasse.[1]

The twin features of Kent and its environs are clearly expressed here: that this was a hotly contested frontier zone, while – simultaneously – also being a dynamic thoroughfare. It is a duality that permeates this book: which, first and foremost, seeks to explain how such a perplexing situation could have functioned. What were the connections across the Channel and adjacent North Sea, the so-called 'Narrow Seas'? How did they change? Most importantly, it asks: how was this experienced by those at the time? What roles did people from Kent's towns and villages, and their European counterparts, perform in them? How did they impact their lives? To answer such questions, this book focuses on the reciprocal movement of people and goods through the county's ports, the merchant fleets and the maritime workforce that facilitated this interchange, as well as the military communities that defended it.

1 London, The National Archives (hereafter TNA), SP 12/245, fol. 106.

In discussing the characteristics of Kent, however, there is one critical problem: the impulse to cite the physical environment, principally geography, as the key explanatory factor in its history. This is especially so when dealing with the interdependent relationship between two places. Whilst often simplistic, with the case of Kent it is at least understandable. Its geography is noteworthy enough. Situated in the extreme southeast of the British Isles, it is the nearest English county to the European mainland, just 21 miles away. Kent is bounded by water on three sides. It is a place where the Thames Estuary in the north and the Channel in the south meet the North Sea. Thus, it had easy access to all these, as well as onward access to the Baltic and the Atlantic Ocean.

The interaction between humans and their surroundings is complex. The presence of physical thoroughfares may have been a necessary precondition for Kent's long maritime history. Yet, some go so far as to present its geography as genuinely deterministic: as leading to causally inevitable outcomes. Even Alfred North Whitehead, the philosopher, mathematician and native of Ramsgate, did so as he discussed the historical importance of the waters around his childhood home in his 1927 essay 'England and the Narrow Seas'. 'The history of the world depends on a lot of little things', he argued, 'apart from which events would have happened differently'. This is true enough, but he added that 'London would never have been heard of as a great centre of commerce unless just to the north of the Straits of Dover there had been a magnificent anchorage off Deal'.[2]

Certainly, such features must have contributed to it being a crossing point to and from the continent for millennia. Two brief Roman military expeditions arrived there in 55 and 54 BCE. Julius Caesar (100–44 BCE), who led them and provided our oldest first-hand testimony about Britain, asserted that no one, 'besides merchants generally go there', and even they only knew of the 'coast and the regions which are opposite Gaul'.[3] Yet, when he first arrived, he found the 'nature of the place' also made it a natural fortress, where 'the sea was confined by mountains', the White Cliffs, 'so near to it that a missile could be thrown from their summit onto the shore'.[4] Moreover, though the Romans later found a seemingly favourable harbour, their first

2 Alfred North Whitehead, 'England and the Narrow Seas', *The Atlantic* (June 1927), 791–8, at p. 793.

3 T. Rice Holmes (ed.), *C. Julius Caesar, Commentarii Rerum in Gallia Gestarum VII A. Hirti Commentarius VII* (Oxford, 1914), 4.20.3: 'Neque enim temere praeter mercatores illo adit quisquam, neque his ipsis quicquam praeter oram maritimam atque eas regiones quae sunt contra Galliam notum est.'

4 *Ibid.*, 4.23.3: 'Cuius loci haec erat natura atque ita montibus angustis mare continebatur, uti ex locis superioribus in litus telum adigi posset.'

foray almost ended in disaster, when their fleet encountered a sudden storm at anchor and many ships were lost.[5]

So, even with this earliest of examples, Kent's geography played an altogether indeterminate role. Its advantageous geographical position might allow it to serve as a link to the continent, but this could be offset by countervailing environmental factors. The missing element is the people. They were the key variable which influenced whether the county was a conduit or barrier. Human geography might add further to a tendency towards determinisms, especially in Kent's social and economic history. For, through the medieval and early modern periods about which this study is concerned, the county was positioned precisely between the rapidly growing city of London and the wealthy and populous cities of the Low Countries. Yet, these too need not have developed where or how they did. In short, while geography is a powerful explanatory tool, it should be used sparingly. How humans chose to use nature's endowments, or not, how our behaviour and knowledge, our social and economic organisation, evolved with them and very often, in turn, were used to change them, are just as important factors in shaping the history of a place – perhaps more so.

All these diverse elements should become apparent as we set the scene for this book. For – as the Middle Ages gradually transformed into the Early Modern period – there were a bewildering array of changes and continuities. The European discovery of the Americas from 1492, and the rise of the Spanish and Portuguese empires, were slow to make a serious impact in England. Rather, the internal politics of the kingdom and that of neighbouring parts of Europe form the shifting background. There was the appearance of successive new dynasties. The last Plantagenet kings, Henry VI (r. 1422–61, 1470–71), Edward IV (r. 1461–70, 1471–83), and Richard III (r. 1483–85), gave way to the Tudors in 1485 with the rule of Henry VII (r. 1485–1509). Europe was rocked by the Protestant Reformation from 1517 and Henry VIII (r. 1509–47) broke with the Roman Catholic Church in the 1530s. His children, Edward VI (r. 1547–53), Mary I (r. 1553–58), and Elizabeth I (r. 1558–1603), each successively pursued their own divergent domestic and overseas policies concerning England's continental neighbours and religion. James VI & I (r. 1603–25) merged the Crowns of Scotland and England into a personal union under a new Stuart dynasty. Then, finally, the reign of his son Charles I (r. 1625–49) saw the British Isles slide into civil war.

Alongside tempestuous politics and religious change inside and outside England, the period 1450–1640 saw a profound socioeconomic transformation take place across Europe.[6] These two centuries brought a surge in economic growth, with an increase in the scale and complexity of economies and improved

5 *Ibid.*, 4.28–9.

6 Henry Kamen, *European Society 1500–1700* (London, 1984).

integration of markets. In England, agricultural production expanded considerably, a result of a rise in both the extent of cultivation – as more land was brought under the plough – and its intensity, as new farming techniques were applied. The persistent enclosure of common land, and later the Dissolution of the Monasteries (1536–41) – with its redistribution of monastic property – benefited the gentry and a class of yeoman farmers. This encouraged further commercialisation and specialisation of agriculture, particularly where production was encouraged by the proximity of urban markets, especially London. At the same time, there was some substantive industrial development. Historic manufacturing industries, such as clothmaking, were changing, with the 'old draperies' gradually supplanted by finer 'new draperies'; at the same time new domestic manufacture grew, often of goods that had previously been imported, such as household goods. There was increased iron production, and the burning of coal in domestic and industrial settings greatly expanded.[7]

Kent experienced these changes like any other place – oftentimes more so.[8] The county's vibrant land market was enhanced by the Dissolution.[9] The east of the county specialised in grain production to be sold onto an increasingly commercialised market.[10] There was likewise concurrent commercialisation of the brewing industry.[11] Grander textiles were increasingly produced around Sandwich and Canterbury.[12] There was expanding iron production in the Weald.[13] Maritime industries such as shipbuilding grew.[14] These are just a few examples, but the sum result was that – throughout the period – the

7 Keith Wrightson, *Earthly Necessities: Economic Lives in Early Modern Britain* (New Haven, 2000). Wrightson provides an excellent broad overview of economic and social change in Britain during this period.

8 For region-specific overviews, see, for example: Mavis E. Mate, *Trade and Economic Developments, 1450–1550: The Experience of Kent, Surrey and Sussex* (Woodbridge, 2006); C. W. Chalklin, *Seventeenth-Century Kent: A Social and Economic History* (London, 1965).

9 Michael Zell, 'Landholding and the Land Market in Early Modern Kent', in Michael Zell (ed.), *Early Modern Kent 1540–1640* (Woodbridge, 2000), pp. 39–74.

10 Stephen Hipkin, 'The Structure, Development, and Politics of the Kent Grain Trade, 1552–1647', *Economic History Review*, 2nd series, 61:S1 (August 2008), 99–139.

11 Mate, *Trade*, pp. 60–80.

12 Jane Andrewes, 'The Early Modern Period 1500–1700: Trade and Industry', in Stuart Bligh, Elizabeth Edwards and Sheila Sweetinburgh (eds), *Maritime Kent through the Ages: Gateway to the Sea* (Woodbridge, 2021), pp. 235–52, at 245–7; Jane Andrewes, 'Industries in Kent, *c.* 1500–1640, in Zell (ed.), *Early Modern Kent*, pp. 105–39.

13 Henry Cleere, David Crossley, Jeremy Hodgkinson and Bernard Charles Worssam, *The Iron Industry of the Weald* (Cardiff, 1995); Jeremy Hodgkinson, *The Wealden Iron Industry* (Cheltenham, 2008).

14 Andrewes, 'Trade and Industry', pp. 235–52, at pp. 128–31.

county was a comparatively rich place. In 1524–25, the lay subsidy returned a higher level of tax per square mile in Kent than everywhere else apart from Middlesex.[15] Past commentators have, yet again, put this down to geography. Edward Hasted wrote in his *History and Topographical Survey* of the county at the end of the eighteenth century, that 'to its situation, this county owes, in a great measure, that wealth and abundance which is so lavishly diffused over every part of it'. Furthermore, he specifically cited its natural endowment of waterways and access to maritime shipping lanes: 'the sea-coast, and the rivers Thames and Medway, furnish employments so various and lucrative to all ranks of people, and cause such an accumulation of trade and riches'.[16] In such ways, Kent's prosperity has long been associated with waterborne commerce, an economic activity that linked the county's urban and rural communities through the exchange of their respective surplus production, and tied both – in turn – to the rest of the country – London in particular – and also to Europe.

Strangely enough, however, in a 1574 survey of the kingdom, the list of Kent's ports, creeks, and landing-places numbered just 18. Even if augmented by adding those that were missed, it would still be a distinctly average quantity for an English coastal county. Cornwall, by contrast, had 43, Hampshire 66 and Essex an astonishing 131.[17] Perhaps it is pertinent here that Kent's endowment included the Downs, the 'magnificent anchorage off Deal' which Whitehead considered so crucial.[18] Likewise, despite the impact of the often-cited longshore drift – that silted harbours and produced an unremitting flow of complaints from contemporaries – important ports like Sandwich and Dover remained usable; the latter especially so once royal work on its harbour was finally completed under Elizabeth I.[19] Kent's coastal towns also enjoyed strong overland transport links with London that allowed for reliable communication. A government postal service was established by Mary I in 1558.[20] The 1574 survey noted the posts across 56 miles from London to Dover,

15 Zell, 'Landholding', pp. 39–74, at p. 47ff. This was despite the fact that the Cinque Ports were exempt from this taxation.

16 Edward Hasted, *The History and Topographical Survey of the County of Kent: Volume 1* (Canterbury, 1797), pp. 1–13.

17 TNA, SP 12/96, fols 213–27. The ports, creeks, and landing-places named in the survey are Deal, Dover, Faversham, Folkestone, Fordwich, Heathe, Hythe, Lydd, Margate, Milton, Queenborough, Reculver, Romney, Sandwich, Tennet, Tenterden, The Downs, Whitstable. This would seem to exclude a number of busy harbours, e.g. Rochester.

18 Whitehead, 'England and the Narrow Seas', p. 793.

19 Andrew Margetts, Giles Dawkes, Damian Goodburn, Lucy Allott, Stacey Adams and Alice Dowsett, 'What "Incomparable Jewells Havens, and Sure Harbours Are": The Remains of Late 16th Century Dover Harbour and Their Wider Significance', *Post-Medieval Archaeology*, 57:1 (2023), 177–98.

20 TNA, SP 11/14, fol. 32.

via Dartford, Rochester, Sittingbourne and Canterbury.[21] This made Kent's harbours attractive ports-of-call, particularly in the event of an unpropitious wind or tide. There would even be a brief period from the early 1620s to 1640s when Dover became a considerable international entrepôt.[22]

Despite such a positive description of late medieval and early modern Kent, it should be emphasised that any prosperity was unevenly distributed – even by the standards of the time. Wealth inequality was higher in the county than everywhere in England, except London, in both 1327–32 and 1524–25.[23] Whilst not the only factor, a lot came down to demography. There had been a prolonged phase of population stagnation across Europe since the fourteenth century, caused by – among other factors – the advent of plague (*Yersinia pestis*) which reduced the population by up to half. With the onset of early modern economic expansion, however, particularly the increase in food production, this trend came to an end. The population of England experienced a significant increase, especially in the sixteenth century, rising – according to one estimate – from approximately 2.4 million people in 1520 to about 3.9 million in 1591.[24] The population of Kent likewise saw substantial growth, increasing from around 75,000 people in the mid-sixteenth century to nearly 130,000 by 1600, a rate that slightly surpassed the national average.[25] Urban areas, particularly London, witnessed exceptional rises in population, and many of Kent's towns also grew.[26] The population of Dover, for example, is estimated to have multiplied more than four times from the start of the sixteenth century to the middle of the seventeenth century. The number of residents increased from fewer than 1,000 in 1500 to between 1,200 and 1,900 in 1562, and possibly reached between 4,000 and 6,000 by the late 1630s.[27]

21 TNA, SP 12/96, fol. 103.

22 J. S. Kepler, *The Exchange of Christendom: The International Entrepôt at Dover 1622–1651* (Leicester, 1976).

23 G. Alfani and H. García Montero, 'Wealth Inequality in Pre-Industrial England: A Long-Term View (Late Thirteenth to Sixteenth Centuries)', *Economic History Review*, 2nd series, 75:4 (November 2022), 1314–48, at p. 1330. Alfani and García Montero calculated that the Gini index for Kent was 0.798 in 1327–32, compared with 0.455 in Devon and 0.953 in London. By 1524–25, Kent's had increased to 0.833, considerably greater than Buckinghamshire's on 0.597 and very close to London's, which then stood at 0.839.

24 E. A. Wrigley and R. S. Schofield, *The Population History of England 1541–1871: A Reconstruction* (London, 1981), pp. 183, 528.

25 Patricia Hyde and Michael Zell, 'Governing the County', in Zell (ed.), *Early Modern Kent*, pp. 7–38, at p. 7; Chalklin, *Seventeenth-Century Kent*, p. 27.

26 Jacqueline Bower, 'Kent Towns, 1540–1640', in Zell (ed.), *Early Modern Kent*, pp. 141–76, at p. 160ff.

27 Mary Dixon, 'Economy and Society in Dover 1509–1640' (unpublished Ph.D. thesis, University of Kent, 1992), pp. xi, 359–75.

In general, economic growth did not keep up with the rise in population. Prices, which had fallen after the mid-fourteenth century, also began to rise considerably, and with this inflation, the value of real wages fell. Average real income in England dropped by almost all measures between 1500 and 1640.[28] Even as the economy grew in size and complexity, the income created simply generated intensified social stratification. This seems to have occurred more in Kent than almost anywhere else. There was the potential for increased wealth for the county's producers, who could do well from rising prices. Merchants and mariners could be especially prosperous with rising profits to be made from trade, which in turn they could then re-invest.

Kent's communities would nevertheless face considerable challenges, not least the frequency of war. This study is itself bookended by conflict: from the purported end of the Hundred Years' War (1337–1453), oftentimes marked by the English defeat at the Battle of Castillon in 1453 – with the loss of the final remnants of England's Plantagenet kings' twelfth-century continental empire – through to the Wars of the Three Kingdoms which tore apart the British Isles (1639–53). The years in between were likewise interspersed with violent confrontations. Indeed, at the beginning of the timeframe of this book, on 28 August 1457, a French army under Pierre de Brézé sacked and burned Sandwich.[29] This very much set the tone for subsequent centuries. There were no fewer than seven further confrontations with France, in 1496–98, 1512–14, 1522–26, 1542–46, 1557–59, 1562–63 and 1627–29. Some of these would involve Kent more than others. Certainly, a critical moment came in 1558, when the French finally re-took Calais, and its pale, which had, since 1347, been in English hands just a short distance from Kent's coast. The county also featured when Elizabeth I intervened in the French Wars of Religion (1562–98), sending, among others, Kentish troops from Kent's ports to Normandy.[30]

As powers struggled for political supremacy, the centres of the European economy would shift. Once, the great Italian trading cities of Genoa or Venice, and the northern group of trading towns, the Hanseatic League, dominated commerce. Thanks to trade and industry, especially in cloth, cities of the Low Countries, such as Bruges, Ghent and Tournai, were amongst the wealthiest places anywhere in the Middle Ages. In this, English wool had been the key raw material. Yet the commercial history of much of Europe in this period

28 Henry Phelps Brown and Sheila Hopkins, *A Perspective of Wages and Prices* (London, 1981), pp. 28–31; Gregory Clark, 'The Condition of the Working Class in England, 1209–2004', *Journal of Political Economy*, 113:6 (December 2005), 1307–40, at p. 1311; Wrightson, *Earthly Necessities*, pp. 116–31.

29 William Boys, *Collections for an history of Sandwich in Kent: With notices of the other Cinque Ports and members, and of Richborough* (Canterbury, 1792), p. 674.

30 TNA, SP 12/226, fol. 38.

revolved around the rise and fall of the great entrepôt at Antwerp.[31] In the first half of the sixteenth century no other city could challenge this great hub of trade and culture in the Habsburg-ruled Low Countries, especially during the reign of the Holy Roman Emperor Charles V (r. 1519–56). As a result, perhaps the most defining conflict of the era, for both Kent and Europe, began with the 'Dutch Revolt' against his son, the King of Spain, Philip II (r. 1556–98), in the 1560s, which became the Eighty Years' War (1568–1648).

Antwerp's status would begin to decline after the mid-sixteenth century, but this trend was cemented by the city's sack by mutinous Spanish forces in November 1576 – the infamous 'Spanish Fury' – and later the blockade of the Scheldt river. The centre of trade moved elsewhere, particularly to a new polity born of the revolt, the Republic of the Seven United Netherlands (the United Provinces). The rise of the Dutch Republic in the sixteenth and seventeenth centuries into an economic and military superpower has long fascinated economic historians. It defied geographical determinism, whether through the reclamation of large areas of land from the sea using a network of pumps and dikes, or the building of the largest merchant fleet in seventeenth-century Europe despite having negligible timber-bearing forests.[32] Its trading companies, especially the Dutch East India Company, the *Verenigde Oostindische Compagnie* (VOC), established 1602, brought in the wealth of Asia. The Protestant-dominated polity would also become a significant trading partner for England and a military ally when Elizabeth I went to war with Spain in 1585. The Treaty of Nonsuch that year granted Elizabeth control over three 'Cautionary Towns' in the Netherlands: Brielle, Fort Rammekens, and Vlissingen, which remained in English hands until sold back in 1616. Even after the defeat of the famous 1588 Spanish Armada adjacent to Kent's coast, conflict with Spain continued until the 1604 Treaty of London. This peace lasted only a generation, however, and a further indecisive Anglo-Spanish war took place in 1625–30, early in the reign of Charles I, while a far larger – and more destructive – confrontation, the Thirty Years' War (1618–48), gathered pace in Central Europe. Conflict, particularly that with a religious dimension, displaced waves of refugees alongside economic migrants. Though these were, it should be said, often overlapping groups.

In keeping with their proximity to the European continent, this book shows how Kent's communities had a ringside view of events. Migrants would frequently arrive on its shores, being 'in manor the onlye highe streate

31 Herman Van der Wee, *The Growth of the Antwerp Market and the European Economy: Fourteenth-Sixteenth Centuries* (The Hague, 1963).

32 Christiaan van Bochove, *The Economic Consequences of the Dutch: Economic Integration around the North Sea, 1500–1800* (Amsterdam, 2008), particularly pp. 186–95.

and waye'.[33] Likewise, the county's merchants and mariners would have to pursue their seaborne activities in what was a constantly changing, oftentimes dangerous, maritime world. Piracy and the aggression of enemy ships were persistent threats. Kent's ships and other military assets would be regularly called upon for defensive or offensive action.

Many might contend that these things had long been the case – and might argue that this was, in part, because of where Kent was situated. This may at least have been why the county was dominated by the Cinque Ports. The confederation of coastal towns had survived from at least as far back as the eleventh century. Four of the five original head ports, Sandwich, Dover, Hythe and New Romney, were in the county, as were the majority of its 'limbs', places such as Faversham. While a political, social and economic institution, the main reasons for its existence were arguably geographic and military.[34] It was the Cinque Ports' strategic position at the closest crossing point from England to the continent that long made their mandated provision of fifty-seven ships for fifteen days valuable to the Crown. Whether for defensive coastal protection, the delivery of military force or diplomatic expeditions, they were in the right place, and – in exchange – the Cinque Ports gained a raft of privileges, not least considerable legal and administrative autonomy as well as tax advantages.[35]

Investment by the English Crown in Kent's physical defences likewise occurred in both the medieval and early modern contexts 'to keepe watche and warde at the coaste'.[36] Impressive royal castles were developed from the eleventh century at key strategic locations at Dover – again to guard the short crossing to Europe – and at Rochester, on the Medway, near the approach to London by land and sea.[37] Successively, during 1539–47 Henry VIII expended considerable royal funds constructing his Device Forts. Many of these fortifications – designed to house modern gunpowder weaponry – were placed around Kent, such as that built at Sandgate, near Folkestone, those at Deal,

33 TNA, SP 12/245, fol. 106.

34 For a discussion on this topic, see C. Lambert, 'Naval Service and the Cinque Ports, 1322–1453', in Gary P. Baker, Craig Lambert and David Simpkin (eds), *Military Communities in Late Medieval England. Essays in Honour of Andrew Ayton* (Woodbridge, 2018), 211–36.

35 Felix Hull (ed.), *A Calendar of the White and Black Books of the Cinque Ports, 1432–1955* (London, 1966), pp. ix–xlii; Graham Brindle, 'A Social and Economic Study of the Cinque Ports Region, 1450–1600' (unpublished Ph.D. thesis, University of St Andrews, 1979).

36 TNA, SP 12/245, fol. 106.

37 John H. Beeler, 'Castles and Strategy in Norman and Early Angevin England', *Speculum*, 31:4 (1956), 581–601, particularly at p. 595; R. Allen Brown, 'Royal Castle-Building in England, 1154–1216', *The English Historical Review*, 70:276 (1955), 353–98.

Walmer and Sandown, to guard the Downs anchorage, and a blockhouse at Milton-next-Gravesend on the Thames to the north of the county, again to defend the way to London.[38]

This brief introduction has endeavoured to establish the backdrop for a study of Kent and Europe during the years 1450–1640. It has contextualised and extended the county's stated dualities: how the county and its surrounding area looks to have been both a bridge and a barrier, a thoroughfare and theatre of war. Kent was wealthy but unequal, it was dynamic and changing but with one foot in its medieval past. The problem of the implicit role of geography remains, but clearly historical change could occur in a multiplicity of ways. Any explanations for that change need, therefore, to be more sophisticated. The county sat, partly through geographic happenstance, at the nexus of northern European maritime trade links at precisely the time that these were pushed back and forth by political contention and the fortunes of war. It is the condition and behaviour of the people of Kent and Europe in this challenging context that is of interest in this book's five substantive chapters.

The first, titled 'Late Medieval Kent, *c*.1450–*c*.1550, delves straight into the socioeconomic, political, and religious history of the county in the fifteenth and sixteenth centuries. The second chapter, titled 'Maritime Trade and Kent's Ports, *c*.1540–*c*.1640', explores the commercial activity of the county's port towns and their communities. It assesses their roles in the English and wider European economy, the impact of England's political relationships and the role of migration in building social and human capital. The third chapter, 'The Merchant Fleet and Maritime Community of Kent, 1580–1630', explores the size, structure and spatial distribution of Kent's merchant fleet during an often-overlooked period and offers a reconstruction of the careers of Kent's maritime community. The fourth chapter, titled 'The Defence of Kent, *c*.1540–*c*.1640', traces the county's military strength across the period, its significance as a naval hub and centre of coastal defence. The fifth and final chapter, 'Maritime Predation in the Narrow Seas, *c*.1540–*c*.1640', explores predatory maritime activities in the waters around Kent across the same period, with an emphasis on those actions undertaken under private initiative rather than by government. It addresses both theft at sea and the acquisition of goods from wrecks or ships in distress by salvage. It questions the apparent lack of emphasis on this region in past scholarship and underlines the normalcy of aggressive predatory behaviours, especially in regions with two adjacent coasts.

38 B. M. Morley, *Henry VIII and the Development of Coastal Defence* (London, 1976).

1

Late Medieval Kent, *c.*1450–*c.*1550

SHEILA SWEETINBURGH

Even though it is unlikely any of those living in late medieval Kent would have seen a copy of what has come to be known as the Gough Map, they would have recognised their 'country' due to its position between the great walled city of London (to the northwest) at the head of the Thames Estuary and English Calais across the Narrow Seas (to the east). For any potential Kent audience, the key features would have been the named coastal and riverine towns across the county and the dominance of the river systems that fed into the Thames Estuary and by extension the North Sea. While it is likely the map's early London provenance may explain this apparent topographical emphasis on the relationship between Kent and the capital (and its river), politically, economically and even socially this would have been viewed as appropriate by many in Kent, especially among the leading citizens of the various towns and cities and their rural peers. For even though there are no roads shown as passing through Kent, the marking of the recently rebuilt Rochester Bridge across the Medway would have been sufficient for those familiar with the county to denote the importance of the ancient route from London to Dover via the two episcopal cities of Rochester and Canterbury.

Therefore, the Gough Map is a helpful entry into this contextual exploration of Kent's history during a period that saw a complex mix of continuity and change in all aspects of society. Although much of the emphasis here will be on the maritime communities, as Gough highlights, inland urban communities were similarly part of this network of waterborne commerce. As a case in point, the stone from the quarries near Maidstone was carried from there via the River Medway and the Thames Estuary to Whitstable, and thence from that port by cart to Canterbury for the rebuilding of the city's Newingate in the late fifteenth century. For while in this instance the materials were transported within the county, the impetus for the work on the city's defences had been initiated by and remained important to the Crown.

The gate, like its earlier 'twin', the city's Westgate, marking the road from London to Dover (and Calais).[1]

Research on this period has benefited from several initiatives, not least the continuing output of scholarly work in national and regional journals, as well as *Archaeologia Cantiana*, the long-running annual journal of the Kent Archaeological Society, two volumes, in particular, as part of the Kent History Project: *Later Medieval Kent, 1220–1540* (2010) and *Early Modern Kent, 1540–1660* (2000); doctoral research, primarily, but not exclusively, at the two Canterbury-based universities; the recently edited collection on *Maritime Kent through the Ages*, published in 2020, and the forthcoming 'Immigration and Emigration in Kent', both of which have benefited from symposia over the last decade. Other initiatives include the Romney Marsh Research Trust which has published numerous studies on this period based on research relating to the history of the 'Romney Marshes'. Among the distinguished contributors to debates concerning the county's late medieval economy have been Maryanne Kowaleski and Mavis Mate whose prodigious outputs have covered a host of topics, from the relative importance of sea fishing in eastern ports vis-à-vis the growth of such activities by West Country fishermen, to the transition from ale to beer and the role of immigrants in the beer brewing industry that was beginning to take place from the early fifteenth century.[2]

Nor has such scholarship been confined to what might be viewed as traditional historical areas of research because matters relating to Kentish book culture and the provision of education in the county have demonstrated higher levels of literacy and numeracy than are normally associated with this period. Furthermore, as Gillian Draper has shown for the Romney Marshes, this was not solely an urban phenomenon, which is seemingly in part a product of the particularity of agrarian tenures and peasant farming practices, as well as the high level of interconnections and networks between the countryside and the town. Equally, at times, these are seen to go beyond what has been labelled pragmatic literacy and demonstrate, especially but not exclusively in urban communities, an understanding of the role and value of written documents and how they might be deployed in the sometimes centuries-long battle for greater civic autonomy. Even though such ideas seem to have started taking shape in the thirteenth century, especially among the Cinque Ports, they remained pertinent, as Justin Croft has shown, into the later Middle Ages. Indeed, for some maritime and inland towns, full corporate status would not

1 Canterbury Cathedral Archives and Library (hereafter CCAL), CC/FA/7, fol. 10r.

2 Maryanne Kowaleski, 'The Expansion of the South-Western Fisheries in Late Medieval England', *Economic History Review*, 2nd series, 53 (2000), 429–54; Mate, *Trade*, ch. 5.

be fully realised until the later Tudors, for example, the charter New Romney received from Elizabeth I in 1563.

Moreover, the movement of people, goods and ideas within and beyond the county boundary, which is one of the underpinning themes of this volume, was not confined to secular society. In addition to the long history of episcopal engagement in national and international affairs, many of the numerous religious houses, some of which were exceedingly ancient and wealthy, as well as the late medieval secular colleges, were involved in such interchanges that, in turn, at times drew in members of the parish and stipendiary clergy. As David Rundle has highlighted, certain Christ Church Priory priors during the fifteenth century were early and active supporters of new palaeographical developments in the production of manuscripts that have in previous scholarship been viewed as almost solely Italian with England on the barbaric periphery.[3] Thus, the activities of monastic and secular churchmen, including parish clergy in both dioceses, and in part illustrated through book ownership in wills and other sources, have produced an indication about the extent and scale of religious and intellectual networks in late medieval Kent. Furthermore, some of the ideas adopted by certain of these clerics, as well as members of the laity, may have affected expressions of late medieval piety and thus the place of heterodoxy, as well as orthodoxy, in the parish and elsewhere, topics that have been explored by Robert Lutton and Paul Lee amongst others.[4]

Notwithstanding this wide-ranging and extensive scholarship on late medieval Kent, London has cast a long shadow in academic terms, just as it did economically and socially during the fifteenth and sixteenth centuries. Yet, as many of the scholars noted above have shown, the extensive national records point to the significance of Kent's medieval and early modern history not only nationally but internationally, and that this can be enhanced through the deployment of locally produced sources, many of which are in the county itself. The presence of a considerable number of towns from the Cinque Ports confederation with their remarkable civic archives, the Canterbury city archives, the two diocesan archives and the archives of certain religious houses have received varying degrees of academic attention with the potential to reveal more about a wide range of topics.

As the author of *The Lybelle of Englysche Polycye* noted in the second quarter of the fifteenth century, peace in the seas between England and her continental neighbours was paramount for trade to prosper. One of the key

[3] David Rundle, *The Renaissance Reform of the Book and Britain: The English Quattrocento* (Cambridge, 2019), pp. 136–42.

[4] Robert Lutton, 'Heresy and Heterodoxy in Late Medieval Kent', in Sheila Sweetinburgh (ed.), *Later Medieval Kent 1220–1540* (Woodbridge, 2010), pp. 167–87; Paul Lee, 'Monastic and Secular Religion and Devotional Reading in Late Medieval Dartford and West Kent' (unpublished Ph.D. thesis, University of Kent, 1998).

ways to ensure this was to safeguard the 'tweyne eyne' of the kingdom: Dover and English Calais as they 'kepe the narowe see'.[5] However, while this did not mean the cessation of piracy by certain mariners from ports such as Dover and Sandwich, which was seemingly viewed at the local level, even if not by the Crown, as acceptable, of far greater interest and then concern to most in Kent was the renewal of the Hundred Years' War, first successfully under Henry V but during the minority and subsequent rule of his son, Henry VI, increasingly disastrously.

For early fifteenth-century Kent, probably the high point was Becket's Jubilee year of 1420, when the Canterbury bailiffs congratulated themselves on the exceedingly large number of pilgrims who had been successfully catered for when they visited the city.[6] What percentage came from overseas is unknown but the promotional activities by both city and priory, as well as the presence of the king and emperor, presumably drew in some from the continental mainland, especially through Dover which continued to press its official monopoly of passage traffic from Calais. This support for Becket, as well as the cathedral and religious community more broadly, by all the Lancastrian kings offered the priors considerable links to the royal court, and the priory similarly benefited from its London properties, both from the rents collected from lawyers, merchants and others and the help such professionals could provide.[7]

A likely further marker of this success in 1420 is the peak of new *intrantes* or independent artisans/traders as annual licence payers in Canterbury that year because thereafter the trend was downwards, albeit with some variation year on year. Whether this reflects the arrival of fewer immigrants specifically to Canterbury in the second quarter of the century is unclear. During the same period at Sandwich, for example, the port benefited from the arrival of foreign merchants, primarily the Genoese and Venetians, the factors of some merchant families of the former residing in the town, while Hanseatic merchants also used the port, and those from the Low Countries shipped in a range of commodities. Local shipmasters and owners also gained from this

5 George Warner (ed.), *The Lybelle of Englysche Polycye: A Poem on the Use of Sea Power* (Oxford, 1926), p. 2.

6 CCAL, CC/OA/1, fol. 34v; William Urry, 'The Jubilee of St Thomas, 1420: Billeting and Rationing Problems in the Fifteenth Century', *Canterbury Cathedral Chronicle*, 42 (1947), 26; Sheila Sweetinburgh, 'Pilgrimage in "An Age of Plague": Seeking Canterbury's "Hooly Blisful Martir"', in Linda Clark and Carole Rawcliffe (eds), *The Fifteenth Century XII: Society in an Age of Plague* (Woodbridge, 2013), pp. 68, 74, 76.

7 Meriel Connor, 'The Priory of Christ Church Canterbury and Its Connections with London in the Late Middle Ages', *Archaeologia Cantiana*, 135 (2014), 34–7, 40–2.

overseas trade, not least from goods transhipped to their smaller, shallower draught vessels that could negotiate the Wantsum Channel and then the Thames Estuary to London. On the return voyage, they brought goods destined for export, as well as supplying Calais with goods and other provisions including livestock. Nor was such cross-Channel and coastal trade solely conducted from Sandwich, as mariners from the south coast ports between Dover and Rye, just over the Sussex border, similarly engaged in shipping commodities, including sea coal from Newcastle.

Moreover, the earlier innovative agrarian policies of the great ecclesiastical landholders, especially in east and central Kent, continued to be emulated by peasant farmers, some of whom were now leasing manorial demesnes in addition to tenant lands. Some of those who benefited from Kent's extensive and active land market, in large part a consequence of the prevalence of gavelkind tenure, were Cinque Port townsmen. Like the Honywood brothers from Hythe, Andrew Bate of Lydd was a butcher-grazier who sought to capitalise on the demand generated by English Calais as well as good local markets for meat.[8] Yet Bate's tactics to enhance his growing landholdings were, as Spencer Dimmock has shown, largely at the expense of his poorer neighbours whose holdings comprised only a few acres.[9] A disparity among landholders was similarly noted by Mate for Otford in 1440, but while for some this would have reflected hardship, in broad terms wages were higher than in other parts of the country. This meant that those with smallholdings were often able to supplement their incomes, especially because rents were falling, and towards the mid-century in many manors they were not being collected at all.[10] Consequently, for the more prosperous peasantry, their urban peers, as well as members of Kent's gentry families, the earliest decades of the fifteenth century were broadly good, even though plague and uncertain harvests continued to cause difficulties.

However, within a short time conditions began to deteriorate, heralding the mid-fifteenth-century depression, which was catastrophic and long-lasting. Albeit, like any such widespread calamity, some were able to take advantage of the situation, as is evident from the increasing number of surviving wills from Kentish testators and the bequests listed. These challenging circumstances were a complex product of continuing plague outbreaks – at least

8 Sheila Sweetinburgh, 'Hythe's Butcher-Graziers: Their Rôle in Town and Country in Late Medieval Kent', in Christopher Dyer, Andrew Hopper, Evelyn Lord and Nigel Tringham (eds), *New Directions in Local History since Hoskins* (Hatfield, 2011), pp. 103–13.

9 Spencer Dimmock, 'English Small Towns and the Emergence of Capitalist Relations, c.1450–1550', *Urban History*, 28 (2001), 16–20.

10 Mavis Mate, 'The Economy of Kent, 1200–1500: The Aftermath of the Black Death', in Sweetinburgh (ed.), *Later Medieval Kent*, p. 18.

one of country-wide importance per decade – further issues concerning grain harvests, and the financial and other difficulties producers faced from royal purveyance. To these were added problems concerning the supply of bullion for coinage, which compounded the deflation caused by population decline: when the market could not absorb the crops and wool clip being produced. Likewise, ongoing disasters in the war with France, including a French raid on Queenborough, meant expensive requirements in manpower and resources to guard the coast, as well as the return of large numbers of disillusioned soldiers following defeat in Normandy and perceived mismanagement and corruption by those seen as closest to the king.[11]

Against this backdrop, the county rose in revolt. Even though men from Sandwich, Dover and the villages around seem to have been implicated in the initial rising led by the 'Hermit Blewbeard', this was easily quashed and his severed head displayed on Canterbury's Westgate. In contrast, the main rebellion under Jack Cade a few months later involved far more insurgents, drawing men in large numbers from the cloth-manufacturing Wealden parishes that had suffered from disruption to the overseas cloth trade. Drapers and others involved in this trade from places like Maidstone were similarly among the rebels, and more generally there were many from central and western Kent, but seemingly fewer from the east of the county. Furthermore, even after Cade's capture, dissent was not quelled and further disturbances took place in the Medway valley and Weald in the autumn of 1450. Indeed, the name Jack Cade remained a rallying cry for a further six years.

Thereafter, even though Grummitt sees little evidence of 'any Yorkist-Lancastrian rivalry in Kent before 1459', he accepts that the raid on Sandwich by the French two years earlier 'encouraged local men, especially the barons of the Cinque Ports, to look to [the earl of] Warwick for protection'.[12] The earl had been appointed captain of Calais in 1456, where he began to build his power base, and one of the expectations was that he would safeguard English maritime interests in the Channel. This he sought to do by attacking enemy shipping as well as ensuring he had a means of communication with support in England through Sandwich. Such tactics were sufficient to provoke the French raid, and while it is unclear how much damage the town sustained, it was seen as symptomatic of the Lancastrians' inability to protect the town.

Political stability returned in 1461 with the success of the Yorkists and the reign of Edward IV. Within Kent, the earl of Warwick continued to enjoy considerable support, further enhanced by his appointment as constable of Dover Castle and Warden of the Cinque Ports in 1460. This was presumably of benefit to Kent society while the Yorkists were united. But the period

[11] *Ibid.*, p. 19; David Grummitt, 'Kent and National Politics, 1399–1461', in Sweetinburgh (ed.), *Later Medieval Kent*, p. 245.

[12] Grummitt, 'Kent', pp. 248, 249.

before the restoration of Henry VI, and the Readeption of 1470–71 itself, although short-lived, did cause problems for those in the county. Especially so at Canterbury and several of the Cinque Ports, because in continuing to support Warwick against Edward IV, they found themselves on the losing side in 1471.[13] Even though such involvement in national politics does not appear to have had major long-term implications for the economy of Canterbury or for several of the Cinque Ports that were similarly implicated, in the short term it did require the civic authorities at Canterbury to buy back royal favour following the execution of the city's mayor.[14] Presumably, it also had a detrimental effect on the 1470 Jubilee, albeit the offer of a papal indulgence to pilgrims was expanded to include the feast at Michaelmas in 1471.[15]

For Canterbury, the later fifteenth century does appear to have been especially challenging. As Andrew Butcher has shown, Christ Church Priory found it increasingly difficult to find tenants, leading to empty properties and some dilapidation, while the corporation's far more limited property portfolio was similarly in trouble as the need for repairs rose, but rents did not – even if tenants could be found.[16] Such problems, although not unknown, were far less acute in most other late medieval Kentish towns but those at Canterbury may have been compounded by a reduction in the number of pilgrims visiting Becket's shrine. Yet the change in the accounting system by the priory hinders a full assessment of any downturn in the level of offerings received and therefore any assessment of pilgrim numbers. Perhaps more importantly, the corporation was deeply concerned about the reduction in clothmaking in the city, leading to the introduction of measures to try to halt the decline. These proved insufficient, however, and the centre of the county's cloth production for much of the next century was the Weald until the arrival of religious refugees in Elizabeth's reign to first Sandwich and then Canterbury and their introduction of the new draperies.

For the county's southern and eastern ports, the later Middle Ages brought other difficulties. While the repercussions of national political instability were a part of this, of greater concern to the local civic authorities were matters of outside lordship and physical geography. For the former, while the Cinque Ports individually had gained varying degrees of autonomy during the Middle Ages, the process had often been protracted and uneven across the confederation. Lydd's leading citizens, for example, had received permission from the town's lord, the archbishop of Canterbury, to elect annually the town's

[13] Malcolm Mercer, 'Kent and National Politics, 1461–1509', in Sweetinburgh (ed.), *Later Medieval Kent*, pp. 255–7.

[14] CCAL, CC/FA/5, fol. 131r.

[15] Sweetinburgh, 'Pilgrimage', pp. 74, 76.

[16] Andrew Butcher, 'Rent and the Urban Economy: Oxford and Canterbury in the Later Middle Ages', *Southern History*, 1 (1979), 39–43.

bailiff, but the abbot of Battle Abbey, who held Dungeness as part of the great manor of Wye, carefully guarded his rights concerning wrecks and matters of salvage from the sea. Even more tenacious were the abbots of Faversham Abbey. Their far more extensive rights continued to include the choice of the town's mayor from the three candidates nominated by the townsmen, as well as some responsibility for the town jail, rights over the local fishing weirs and market dues. The abbey also held much of the property in the town.[17] Attempts to engage in negotiations with outside institutions were not confined to the Cinque Ports, and at Canterbury, the corporation had battled intermittently since the thirteenth century over what it saw as the city's rights in Longport against St Augustine's Abbey. This long-running dispute drew in the abbey's daughter house of St Lawrence's Hospital, and it was possibly only the Crown's insistence on arbitration in the last decades of the fifteenth century that led to an agreement. Nonetheless, even though this matter was resolved, there were problems within the corporate body, which led to the issuing of a charter by Henry VII which stipulated the format of the civic government thereafter. Then, in the years around 1500, members of the corporation became embroiled in a dispute with Christ Church Priory over matters of jurisdiction. The situation at Maidstone was more akin to Faversham because the town was under archiepiscopal lordship, and, like Bury St Edmunds, the leading citizens' Corpus Christi guild, which had its own guildhall and almshouse, seemingly sought to act as the 'civic government in waiting', albeit its religious services were held at the church of All Saints' College.

Turning to geographical matters, often cited in the historiography are the disastrous consequences of the late thirteenth-century 'Great Storms' that New Romney, in particular, experienced. But in the fifteenth century, Dover witnessed the similarly serious effects of storm damage on the town's harbour and inundation of coastal marshlands. Meanwhile, the long-term, cumulative effects of longshore drift and the silting up of the various harbours are viewed as critical by the late fifteenth and early sixteenth centuries. The local civic authorities shared this assessment and were prepared to expend considerable sums to counter the problem using a mix of digging and diverting streams to clear their harbours of sand and shingle. Yet for some towns, their resources were increasingly insufficient. At the end of the fifteenth century the mayor of Sandwich approached Cardinal Morton and Henry VII for financial assistance, and twenty years later Dover asked for help from the London Merchant Adventurers towards covering the costs; both were equally unsuccessful.[18]

17 Justin Croft, 'The Custumals of the Cinque Ports c.1290–c.1599: Studies in the Cultural Production of the Unban Record' (unpublished Ph.D. thesis, University of Kent, 1997), ch. 4.

18 Maidstone, Kent, Kent History and Library Centre (hereafter KHLC), Sa/Fat/12. London, British Library (hereafter BL), Egerton MS 2093, fols 44r–45r. The letter

There was a willingness to look overseas to find the right expertise, and New Romney, Hythe and Sandwich were among the towns prepared to employ men from the Low Countries when required.[19] This trust of outside knowledge may be seen as a byproduct of the overseas trading links all these ports enjoyed with Flanders, Holland and Zeeland and would again be deployed by Thomas Digges in the 1580s when he managed the new harbour works at Dover on behalf of Elizabeth's privy council.

Notwithstanding this narrative of decline, as Susan Rose for Sandwich, or Kowaleski and Mate more broadly have noted, while this did increasingly curtail the use of such ports for larger ships – which in the case of Sandwich haven included its use as a place to muster large royal expeditionary forces – maritime activities involving shallower draft vessels continued to be important.[20] Meanwhile, as Robert Blackmore has discussed, the value of the Downs as a safe anchorage would remain a key factor in the longevity of Kent's maritime history for centuries.[21] Furthermore, in the shorter term, the ports demonstrated considerable adaptability and resilience. Even though Sandwich was no longer used by the Venetian galleys and Spanish trade was erratic, until the mid-sixteenth century, the port continued to handle wine from Bordeaux and a range of imports from the Low Countries, as well as shipping raw wool to the Staple in Calais. Indeed, the cross-Channel supply route to Calais was a major boon throughout the period discussed, especially for Dover and Sandwich. In addition, other local portsmen continued to participate in this and coastal trade. At Hythe, as well as the Honywood brothers, who remained extremely successful butcher-graziers into the later decades of the fifteenth century, other local butchers including Robert and later John Hooker probably similarly benefited from the Calais market. Among those from the port who shipped cattle, and more occasionally horses, in the early 1480s were Nicholas Aulisforde, John Fraryk and Nicholas John.[22] Equally, their contemporary who attracted the attention of the Hythe chamberlains for his maritime trading activities was Thomas Stace. Among the cargoes he carried

to the Merchant Adventurers was taken on the town's behalf by Sir John Clerke, the master at the Maison Dieu who was also one of the harbour wardens at Dover.

19 Gillian Draper and Frank Meddens, *The Sea and the Marsh: The Medieval Cinque Port of New Romney*, Pre-Construct Archaeology monograph (London, 2009), pp. 34–5; James Holman, *Medieval New Romney: A Town Shaped by Water*, Canterbury Archaeological Trust monograph (Canterbury, 2020), p. 60.

20 Susan Rose, 'The Port of Sandwich in the Later Middle Ages', in Bligh, Edwards and Sweetinburgh (eds), *Maritime Kent*, pp. 371–86, at p. 382; Maryanne Kowaleski, 'Maritime Trade and Industry in Medieval Kent', in Bligh, Edwards and Sweetinburgh (eds), *Maritime Kent*, pp. 215–34, at p. 220; Mate, 'Economy of Kent', p. 24.

21 See Introduction, this volume.

22 Sweetinburgh, 'Hythe's Butcher-Graziers', pp. 103–6.

were red and other processed herring, sea coal, iron and gunpowder, while the selling of salt, wine, figs and raisins points to his overseas trading activities.[23]

Additionally, the transport of passengers and mail across the Channel was beneficial for Dover's local economy. Those involved included mariners, local hostellers and others active in the town's victualling industries, whose potential customers had to wait for favourable tides and weather conditions.[24] As well as Dover's bakers, brewers and butchers, the town's fishermen similarly supplied those providing hospitality at a price through the fish market. Among Kent's maritime communities, fishing continued to be a significant industry during this period and, for the Cinque Ports, remained a central aspect of their confederation's identity. For even though Kowaleski is right to highlight the growth of sea fishing among the West Country ports, the range of fish species available to Kentish fishermen during the different fishing seasons offered major opportunities. Consequently, these fishermen, while presumably encountering competition from the larger boats and innovative curing methods of their Low Countries counterparts, still maintained their identity as fishermen. In addition to the Hythe fifteenth-century local taxation records, the late medieval and early Tudor testamentary sources from maritime settlements on the south, east and north coasts of Kent demonstrate the strategies fishermen, and their families, adopted successfully to safeguard their fishing communities. For example, at Folkestone, even though sons were the most frequent beneficiaries of fishing gear in the form of nets, capstans, lines and hooks, and boats, the high proportion of testators with young children meant that testators' wives were seen as conduits to aid the next generation of fishermen.[25] However, nets were only rarely intended to form all or part of the dowry for the daughters of fishermen. This may reflect the versatility of cash or other objects rather than a reluctance to marry fishermen.[26] Nonetheless, the dangerous nature of the industry was recognised, as had been apparent in early fifteenth-century Hythe when a hundred mariners were lost. Consequently, there was an understanding of the need to mitigate risk, and the use of boat shares was employed by fishermen across Kent.

Yet not all fishing in Kent was conducted from boats. The use of fish weirs or kiddles had been a feature of both the south and north coastal communities

23 Sheila Sweetinburgh, '"Ready for to go to the Sea": Maintaining Fishing Families in Late Medieval Hythe', in Bligh, Edwards and Sweetinburgh (eds), *Maritime Kent*, pp. 387–400, at pp. 396–7.

24 Rose, 'Port of Sandwich', pp. 382–3; Kowaleski, 'Maritime Trade', pp. 221–2.

25 Sheila Sweetinburgh, 'Strategies of Inheritance among Kentish Fishing Communities in the Later Middle Ages', *The History of the Family*, 11 (2006), 98–102.

26 Among the examples are testators from Deal and Lydd; John Salmon (Deal) KHLC, PRC 32/13, fol. 138r; John Owter (Deal) PRC 32/14, fol. 17r; Adrian Dyne (Lydd) PRC 32/12, fol. 171r.

for centuries, including on the Isle of Sheppey.[27] Equally, fishermen had dredged for oysters and other shellfish, to supply the local and London market. The continuing value placed on this industry is evident from the way the late Elizabethan oystermen of Faversham pursued their case in the royal courts against their counterparts at neighbouring Milton Regis, as well as similar intermittent disputes over rights between Faversham and Whitstable. Perhaps the nature of the industry, the use of the foreshore as the location of the weirs, meant that it was especially compatible with farming. One family who held both fish weirs and farmland were the Swanton family from Whitstable/Seasalter whose members were active for at least three generations in this way. Indeed, the frequency of the fisherman-farmer is noted in the historiography through to modern times, yet some sea fishermen in Kent also successfully combined fishing and trading.[28]

The manufacture of salt was a coastal industry which was reliant on the region's physical geography, albeit by the fifteenth century few of these salt works were still functioning and instead the county's mariners were more involved in the shipping of salt from Bourgneuf Bay, on the French Atlantic coast.[29] However, shipbuilding and repairing remained important. To reduce the danger of exposure to storms and enemy raids the most important sites were away from the coast, on the Thames (Deptford, Greenwich, Woolwich and Erith), Medway (New Hythe) and Rother (Small Hythe) estuaries. As Kowaleski has noted, Crown records provide most of the evidence for these works, but recent archaeological excavations at Small Hythe have located several mud docks where ships were constructed before being taken to the coast for fitting. Even though ships were still being constructed at Small Hythe in the early sixteenth century, the focus in Kent was the shipyards of the Thames Estuary, and of these Woolwich was the most important, while on the English south coast Southampton and Portsmouth became the favoured locations for the construction of vessels for the Crown by the later fifteenth century.[30] In addition to master shipwrights such as Robert Brekynden of Small Hythe, a considerable team covering a wide range of skills was required and the nature of the contracts meant that these craftsmen moved between shipyards. For example, Brekynden and his team were required to work at Portsmouth as well as their home base at Small Hythe. At the Woolwich

27 Melanie Caiazza, 'Saints and Weirs: Late Medieval and Early Modern Communities within a Small Island Landscape in North Kent', in Bligh, Edwards and Sweetinburgh (eds), *Maritime Kent*, pp. 401–16, at pp. 412–15.

28 Sweetinburgh, 'Maintaining Fishing Families', pp. 396–7.

29 William Kirk, 'Development of a Medieval Industry: The Emergence and Decline of Coastal Salt Production in East Kent' (unpublished MA dissertation, University of Kent, 1999), pp. 39–45.

30 Kowaleski, 'Maritime Trade', pp. 229–31.

shipyard in the early sixteenth century, skilled workers from counties such as Cornwall and Yorkshire were retained to construct the thousand-ton *Henri Grâce à Dieu*.[31]

As well as fulfilling short-term contracts, migration into and out of the county might involve a wide range of scenarios, from resettlement to the annual visits of the Westermen, fishermen from Devon and Cornwall, who were allowed to join their Lydd counterparts fishing off Dungeness and to use the local fish market. Yet, while such movement of people was seemingly common in the fifteenth century, whether from countryside to town or between towns, the numbers involved had apparently declined by the last decades of the century due to economic and other pressures outlined above.[32] Nonetheless, for some individuals, migration to enhance their socioeconomic position remained an option even during this period, as noted by Butcher in his assessment of the New Romney freemen's lists and from the *intrantes*' and freemen's records from Canterbury.[33] For example, this form of 'betterment' migration, a term used by Peter Clark in 1972, is evident among some New Romney migrants, although the Stuppeny family was one of the few whose advancement took them to the pinnacle of the town's civic elite within a couple of generations and they were similarly successful at the neighbouring port of Lydd.[34]

These families benefited from the social links they cultivated through kinship and marriage, as well as commercial or other networks. For the Drylond gentry family of Faversham, there was at least one branch of the family in London, and William Drylond, a parishioner of St Mary's in Faversham, in 1492, wished to be buried in the church of St Margaret in Bredstrete and one of his executors was Richard Knyght, a London fishmonger.[35] In addition to their mercantile activities, other family members had advanced their status through the acquisition of both rural and urban property, as well as advantageous marriages for their offspring. James Drylond's daughter Constance had married Thomas Walsingham, the son of a wealthy London merchant, the elder Thomas having bought the manor of Scadbury near Orpington in northwest

31 *Ibid.*, p. 231.

32 Nonetheless, the Westermen were still coming to Lydd in the 1570s; KHLC, Ly/FAc/3, fols 240r, 243r, 245r. Some of these fishermen occasionally went as far east as Dover; KHLC, Do/FCa/1, fol. 222r.

33 Andrew Butcher, 'The Origins of Romney Freemen, 1433–1523', *Economic History Review*, 2nd series, 27 (1974), 16–27; Sheila Sweetinburgh, 'Starting a New Life as Artisans and Traders in Ricardian and Henrician Canterbury', *Archaeologia Cantiana*, 143 (2022), 33–50.

34 Sheila Sweetinburgh, 'Eternal Town Servants: Civic Elections and the Stuppeny Tombs of New Romney and Lydd', in Mette Bruun and Stephanie Glaser (eds), *Negotiating Heritage: Memories of the Middle Ages* (Turnhout, 2008), pp. 149–72.

35 TNA, PROB 11/10/170.

Kent for a hundred marks in 1424.[36] Although slightly pre-dating this study, John Philipot's fourteenth-century career demonstrates such links between London, Kent and mainland Europe. Born in Kent, he became a London citizen and later mayor, successfully dealing in a range of commodities though his primary business was exporting wool to Calais. His marriages were equally successful and through his first wife he acquired Grange manor. Located on the Medway Estuary and therefore useful as an intermediary between London and east Kent ports, Grange was also a Cinque Port – thereby providing Philipot with certain royal tax exemptions as a merchant and wool exporter.[37] Nor in some families were such holdings confined to Kent or neighbouring counties, and among those with landed interests in the Calais area was William Waren of Dover. In 1506 he bequeathed to his wife Joan all his lands and tenements in Calais and all those in the lordship of Marke and Eye within the Marches of the town.[38]

According to the *England's Immigrants* project database, Flemish and Scottish immigrants were the most numerous in 1480s Kent.[39] Flemings exclusively moved to Canterbury, as did many of the Scots, though a couple were resident in Dover. Of the remainder, almost all resided in towns not far from the north Kent coast. Canterbury's dominance as a destination for those coming from overseas is also reflected in the total figures that include those for whom place of origin is unknown, although from this total (238) some aliens settled in Sandwich (27), New Romney (23), Dover (16), Hythe (13) and Tenterden (10). In Canterbury, under 10 per cent were listed as servants but all were said to be Flemings. Among these, two were in the household of their fellow countryman Cornelius Jonson while six were in service to Gerard Jonson, including Herman Jonson, who may have been a relative learning his trade from his kinsman. According to the city's *intrantes*' lists, both Cornelius and Gerard were shoemakers, the former first appearing in 1474 and trading in the city's Burgate ward until at least 1487, becoming a Canterbury freeman by redemption in February two years later. However, there is far less information concerning female immigrants, albeit there are two references to alewives from overseas. In 1484, Ida Duchewoman was fined 16d for selling half a barrel of ale per week in the city's Westgate ward and two years later Anisia Duchewoman was fined 8d similarly in the same ward. Yet some of their

36 TNA, PROB 11/5/213; https://blogs.canterbury.ac.uk/kenthistory/thomas-walsingham-and-scadbury/ (accessed 14 March 2025).

37 Frank Meddens and Gillian Draper, '"Out on a Limb": Insights into Grange, a Small Member of the Cinque Ports Confederation', *Archaeologia Cantiana*, 135 (2014), 8–9, 24–5.

38 KHLC, PRC 32/9, fol. 104v.

39 See *England's Immigrants 1330–1550*, https://www.englandsimmigrants.com (accessed 14 March 2025).

compatriots seemingly struggled and Elizabeth Sare of St George's parish, Canterbury, bequeathed a smock to Joan, 'a Douchwoman', in 1514.

As Mate has discussed, innovation in the form of beer brewing offered some immigrants commercial opportunities in the early fifteenth century, although the numbers involved were seemingly small. By the later decades the numbers had not increased substantially, but the geographical spread had grown from Sandwich in the east to Appledore in the west of the county, and therefore the innovative role of overseas immigrants in Kent's late medieval economy more broadly. Nevertheless, in the last years of the century, even though Kent did not experience levels of anti-immigrant feeling seen at various times towards the Flemish and Hanse merchants, especially in London, the situation towards immigrants in some towns deteriorated. In Canterbury, for example, protectionist policies in the form of new craft guild regulations were initiated by the smiths, who were keen to ensure aliens and strangers could only trade in the liberty if they paid a set fee to the city chamberlains and similarly to the guild. A comparable relationship between the civic authorities and the senior masters of several crafts in Sandwich led, in 1482, to the creation of guild regulations for the barbers, surgeons and wax chandlers. Eight years later wardens were appointed for a further three crafts with a responsibility to protect their members' trade and regulate training.[40] Interestingly, the civic authorities in these towns undertook a further initiative to establish craft guilds in the later years of Henry VIII, and then again during Elizabeth's reign, with various corporations seemingly keen to oversee such regulation of their towns' artisans for the benefit of their towns as a whole.

Similarly, the desire to protect the towns' citizens from outsiders was especially valued concerning foodstuffs, and at Sandwich in 1490 the mayor and jurats decreed that all non-freemen beer brewers, who were resident in the town, must pay the authorities a penny annually for every *bonne* (42 gallons) of beer sold in their houses.[41] At Dover, too, restrictions were placed on immigrants. An ordinance from 1480 made it illegal for aliens to carry any weapons except a knife to cut their food. The curfew was also set at an earlier time for foreigners and if they were found outside their house after 8 pm they could be fined and imprisoned. Similarly, they were forbidden to sell bread, ale or beer after this same time, and could be fined on each occasion.[42]

Notwithstanding this growing hesitancy of some authorities towards those from mainland Europe in these later decades, broadly across the county there remained an openness to the movement of people, with opportunities for them to trade or undertake specific contracts. This characterisation may also apply to

40 KHLC, Sa/AC/1, fol. 284v; Sa/AC/2, fols 34v, 35r.

41 KHLC, Sa/AC/2, fol. 7v.

42 BL, Add. MS 29616, fol. 195v. Further regulations concerning the selling of beer and ale by aliens were enacted in 1505; BL, Egerton MS 2107, fol. 100r.

the spread of ideas, whether these related to matters of land drainage or early sailing directions (rutters).[43] Nor was this confined to technical innovations. Religious ideas concerning new feasts and devotional practices from elsewhere in England as well as parts of Europe seemingly gained traction in Kent. By 1466, the feast of the Name of Jesus was already being celebrated in Sandwich, a year later there was a reference to it by a testator from Lydd and only four years later the Jesus Mass was similarly being supported by Canterbury testators.[44] Thereafter its popularity in the diocese of Canterbury is attested by the twenty-five towns where the Jesus Mass was celebrated in at least one parish church, while at Faversham, where the church was dedicated to Our Lady, the high altar was referred to as the Jesus altar.[45] Even though the mass had gained favour among Londoners, this does not appear to have extended into the diocese of Rochester and only two churches received such bequests and they relate to the early sixteenth century. How historians should interpret such devotional innovations as part of debates about the regional significance or otherwise of heterodoxy in relation to orthodoxy within the late medieval laity remains open to debate. Nevertheless, Lutton's detailed analysis of the Wealden parish and Cinque Port of Tenterden in response to what appears to have been considerable support for the cult has suggested that, while the matter is complex, there seems to be a marked correlation between those who enthusiastically supported the mass and those he characterises as parsimonious.[46] These families showed little if any interest in the various saints' cults in the town's parish church, preferring instead to support their community and kin. Assuming Lutton is right that the prevalence of this Christocentric devotion in towns does have some link to higher levels of education and literacy, it is perhaps not surprising that it gained a hold in Kent. Such townspeople were 'the most likely beneficiaries of a humanist programme of moderate reform that aimed to disseminate the truth of Scripture, albeit through the safe mediation of the clergy'.[47]

In relation to such ideas, it is worth noting the prevalence of schooling available in fifteenth-century Kent. The numerous chantry priests were well

[43] Rose, 'Port of Sandwich', p. 372, n. 3, for reference to the earliest rutters in English, including the Hastings MS.

[44] In Sandwich the first reference is in Richard Bilton's will; KHLC, PRC 17/1, fol. 256r. At Lydd, Thomas Aylewyn bequeathed the considerable sum of 13s 4d to the Jesus Mass there; KHLC, PRC 32/2, fol. 172r. John Budde of Holy Cross parish in Canterbury remembered the fraternity of the Jesus Mass in his will in 1470; KHLC, PRC 17/1, fol. 303v.

[45] Edward Thomasson; KHLC, PRC 32/4, fol. 59r.

[46] Robert Lutton, *Lollardy and Orthodox Religion in Pre-Reformation England* (Woodbridge, 2006), pp. 70–8.

[47] *Ibid.*, pp. 76–7.

placed to provide education for local boys, such as one of the three priests at Elys' chantry at St Peter's church in Sandwich or the many chaplains in New Romney and at the wealthier churches on Romney Marsh.[48] To these can be added the parish clerk at St Clement's church in Sandwich who was expected to teach local boys pricksong, thereby extending services to include polyphonic choral music, a development that had been available through the almonry school and new Lady Chapel at Canterbury Cathedral from 1438.[49] Furthermore, although the evidence is more limited, it seems this may also reflect the situation at St Augustine's Abbey because there was an almonry school, and the boys are known to have performed plays, as at Sandwich in 1515. Dover Priory, too, had long had a school, but it was not solely the monastic houses that could offer this more advanced educational provision to able boys locally because there were scholars at some secular colleges, at certain hospitals and a few town grammar schools. This twin approach of elementary education from parish clerks and chaplains with a grammar education through a local school or one of the secular colleges is exemplified by the situation at Faversham following the establishment of a free grammar school there in 1526. This was in addition to the schooling offered by the schoolmaster at the Maison Dieu in neighbouring Ospringe and the basic schooling provided by the clerks at the town's parish church.[50] Even though the Dissolution produced some disjuncture between such provision before and after the Henrician Reformation, in many ways, the desire for and availability of education is a story of continuity rather than change. Kent has several King's Schools (refounded monastic schools) though Cole's school in Faversham was not re-established until Elizabeth's reign to become the Queen Elizabeth Grammar School.

The need for this provision was increasingly recognised by members of the laity and clergy by the late Middle Ages, and even though pre-mortem support was presumably significant, such ideas are exemplified in late fifteenth-century wills.[51] For example, John Darell of Canterbury (1496) intended that a good

48 Gillian Draper, '"There hath not bene any Grammar Scole kepte, Preacher maytened or Pore People releved, other then … by the same Chauntreye": Educational Provision and Piety in Kent, c.1400–1640', in Robert Lutton and Elisabeth Salter (eds), *Pieties in Transition: Religious Practices and Experiences, c.1400–1640* (Aldershot, 2007), pp. 77–9.

49 KHLC, PRC 17/6, fol. 291r. Roger Bowers, 'The Liturgy of the Cathedral and its Music, c.1075–1642', in Patrick Collinson, Nigel Ramsey and Margaret Sparks (eds), *A History of Canterbury Cathedral* (Oxford, 1995), pp. 419–24.

50 Duncan Harrington and Patricia Hyde (eds), *The Early Town Books of Faversham c.1251 to 1581*, part 1 (Faversham, 2008), p. 88; Nicholas Orme, 'John Cole (c.1467–1536) and the Origins of Education in Faversham', *Archaeologia Cantiana*, 137 (2016), 108, 113–18.

51 As Butcher discusses, the Cinque Ports' system of maletote taxation based on the household presumably involved the keeping of 'rough household accounts' from

boy should be found who would be sent to grammar school where he would be under the watchful eye of Darell's executors.[52] When he became a priest, he was to reimburse the executors until that spent on his education had been covered. This desire to ensure there was an educated priesthood was widely valued, but it was recognised that education was similarly important for those seeking to join the inns of court in London, those involved in civic and royal administration, some of whom were in minor holy orders, as well as laymen organising their businesses. Such bequests are also seen in mid-sixteenth-century wills from the town and countryside, almost always for boys. For example, in 1549, Agnes Kyrby of Canterbury intended that the residue of her goods should be used to keep Lionel Lambert in school. While at Hope All Saints on Romney Marsh two years earlier, Christopher Sharpe the elder intended his son and namesake would be guided by his godfather for four years and during that time he was to learn to read and write in English, and how 'to lay an account perfectly'.[53]

These ideas and opportunities were equally part of London society, and the relationship between the capital and communities in Kent fostered a shared awareness of these benefits. Robert Flete (1486), a vicar in Canterbury, intended that the master of St Bartholomew's Hospital in Smithfield should receive books selected by his executors as the best for the hospital's use. All Flete's other books were to pass to other 'well-disposed' priests who in turn were to bequeath the books to similarly appropriate clerical beneficiaries.[54] Even though it is impossible to gain an accurate idea of this movement of books, whether through purchase or as bequests or gifts linked to people and institutions in Kent, there is evidence of book ownership and use of a variety of texts beyond traditional theological, liturgical, moral and historical works.[55] This suggests that by the early sixteenth century or earlier, humanist

at least the fifteenth century and potentially earlier; Andrew Butcher, 'The Function of Script in the Speech Community of a Late Medieval Town, c.1300–1550', in Julia Crick and Alexandra Walsham (eds), *The Uses of Script and Print, 1300–1700* (Cambridge, 2004), p. 166.

52 KHLC, PRC 17/6, fol. 208r.

53 KHLC, PRC 17/26, fol. 286r; PRC 17/26, fol. 59r. Nevertheless, although exceedingly rare some did wish to ensure the education of a favoured daughter and the contemporary interlude *Nice Wanton* refers to three siblings as schoolchildren, including the daughter Dalila: John Farmer (ed.), *Nice Wanton 1560* (London and Edinburgh, 1909).

54 KHLC, PRC 17/4, fol. 139v.

55 Among those who had such texts was the monk Richard Stone who died in 1508; C. E. Woodruff, 'An Inventory of the Contents of the Bed-Chamber of Brother Richard Stone, Monk of Christ Church, Canterbury', *Archaeologia Cantiana*, 43 (1931), 105–7.

and other new works were present in Kent, potentially being discussed, even if only by a small number of people.[56]

Keeping with Canterbury, the socioeconomic and political challenges of the early Tudor decades markedly affected the city, and at the same time, the county's landed elite were experiencing profound difficulties, with first the fall of Sir Richard Guildford and then his rival George Neville, 3rd Lord Abergavenny. As a result, from the succession of Henry VIII the dominant force in political and other aspects of Kentish society had become the Tudor court. This was reflected in the heraldic decoration of large Tudor roses and other Tudor badges on the new Renaissance-style Christ Church Gate that led into the cathedral precincts at Canterbury and, as Mercer notes, the realisation by members of the gentry that royal service was the key to advancement.[57]

Additionally, just as the Becket Jubilee of 1420 had benefited from Henry V, for 1520 another young king who actively supported Canterbury's and Kent's international saint was viewed as exceedingly valuable, especially when coupled with his progresses and visits to the county that year. Furthermore, from early in the century, both the city and cathedral communities sought to enhance the experience for pilgrims and other visitors regarding the celebrations on the eve of the feast day of the Translation.[58] Such initiatives may have helped to keep pilgrim numbers from falling in Canterbury, and the Dover civic authorities, backed by the townspeople, continued to send the town's votive offering of a great candle to the shrine, every three years, until 1536.[59] Other late medieval cults such as the Holy Rood of Boxley may similarly have retained support, albeit St William of Rochester and St Robert of Newington were of modest significance.[60] Furthermore, the testamentary evidence from both the Rochester and Canterbury dioceses for this period indicates that orthodox religious devotion continued to dominate parish worship in the county.[61] Yet, there were pockets, such as Tenterden, where some families displayed heterodox views and in Archbishop Wareham's investigations of

56 Rundle, *Renaissance*, pp. 141, 278–9; Orme, 'John Cole', 112–13.

57 Mercer, 'Kent and National Politics', p. 271.

58 Sheila Sweetinburgh, 'Looking to the Past: The St Thomas Pageant in Early Tudor Canterbury', *Archaeologia Cantiana*, 137 (2016), 163–83.

59 Stuart Palmer, 'Politics, Corporation and Commonwealth: The Early Reformation in Canterbury, c.1450–1559' (unpublished Ph.D. thesis, University of Kent, 2016), p. 228; BL, Add. MS 29618B, fol. 304v.

60 Even though the shrine keeper's accounts at Boxley only survive until the early fifteenth century, wills from a century later mention the Holy Rood; Elizabeth Eastlake, 'Redressing the Balance: Boxley 1146–1538' (unpublished Ph.D. thesis, University of Winchester, 2014), p. 125; Arthur Hussey (ed.), *Testamenta Cantiana: East Kent* (London, 1907), p. 348.

61 Lee, 'Monastic', pp. 144–97; Lutton, 'Heresy and Heterodoxy', p. 179.

1511–12 just over fifty people were accused of heresy. Even though in terms of the population this is a relatively small number, it comprised a cluster in the Weald and another of parishes in the Medway valley in and around Maidstone, with five more individuals from Canterbury.[62] This may suggest, as Lutton has discussed, the significance of heterodoxy as a factor in 'the county's early positive response to evangelical reform and Protestant doctrine from the 1520s onwards'. Other factors are similarly relevant, including Cranmer's influence and his use of preaching and plays, as well as the permeable nature of Kent society whereby its trade networks could be used to import from continental Europe illegal texts such as Tyndale's *New Testaments*.[63] Indeed, there are examples in the 1520s and early 1530s of individuals from both dioceses who had embraced such new evangelical ideas.[64] In addition, at St Mary's church in Faversham the mayor and his colleagues oversaw the churchwardens and the parish clerks. At All Saints' church in Lydd the situation was similar and at St Peter's church in Sandwich the corporation held the advowson jointly with St Augustine's Abbey, which meant the civic authorities had a significant role in selecting the parish priest. At Sandwich, this would lead in 1532 to the imprisonment of several clerics from St Peter's church by the mayor and jurats as they sought to reassert their control over the annual St Bartholomew's Day procession from the church to the civic-controlled hospital.[65]

This same period also witnessed a reversal of the demographic downturn that had been in evidence since at least the mid-fourteenth century. Moreover, as population figures rose, the demographic profile changed, with growing numbers of young people. This had a range of consequences. One was greater use of the land market by people from across the social spectrum, and although individual transactions generally involved small plots, it was common for individual farmers to have dispersed landholdings, often on different manors.[66] Farmers were also able to take advantage of rising demand, fuelled by the population increase and the county's prosperity. Some of these rural landholders, depending on their location, might combine farming or renting land with other commercial activities, and for those in the Wealden parishes, this extended from the clothiers at the apex of the Wealden cloth industry to the

62 Lutton, 'Heresy and Heterodoxy', p. 172.

63 *Ibid.*, pp. 180, 181, 184–7; Palmer, 'Politics', p. 225.

64 Michael Zell, 'The Coming of Religious Reform', in Michael Zell (ed.), *Early Modern Kent, 1540–1640* (Woodbridge, 2000), pp. 180–1.

65 Sheila Sweetinburgh, 'Discord in the Public Arena: Processes and Meanings of the St Bartholomew's Day Festivities in Early Sixteenth-Century Sandwich', in Sheila Sweetinburgh (ed.), *Negotiating the Political in Northern European Urban Society, c.1400–c.1600* (Tempe, AZ and Turnhout, 2013), pp. 85–96.

66 Zell, 'Landholding', pp. 44–6, 53–4.

craftsmen such as weavers and shearmen.[67] Of the cloths produced, the narrow kerseys were principally for the home market, but the greater value broadcloths continued to be for export, being traded through Blackwell Hall in London as either finished or unfinished cloths that frequently involved merchants from the capital.[68] Moreover, clothmaking in the Weald would continue to flourish in the sixteenth century, although the arrival of religious immigrants into Sandwich and later Canterbury, Dover and Maidstone during Elizabeth's reign, with their 'new draperies', offered a challenge to the Wealden clothiers.[69]

The 1524–25 lay subsidy returns show Kent taxpayers were second only to Middlesex in terms of the tax paid per square mile, and the actual figure would have been higher were it not for the exemption of the Cinque Ports.[70] Yet a county-wide comparative assessment, while useful, masks the differentiation between towns. Furthermore, as Mate notes, because at Canterbury and Faversham several of those assessed were substantial rural landowners, in addition to their urban residence, the figures do 'not necessarily reflect the size and wealth of the *business* community'.[71] However, these figures do seemingly highlight the considerable prosperity of this community at Gravesend, which was reflected in the furnishings, clothes and other goods mentioned in wills and is presumably due in part to the presence of the royal palace at Greenwich and the port's proximity to London.[72]

Another of the factors that economically boosted Kentish urban communities was the presence of aliens, just as it had done in the previous century. These men and a few women were primarily designated as Dutch, Flemings, with some Frenchmen, but there were also some from Scotland, especially in Dover, and one Scot was a fisherman at Hythe.[73] Again, they were mostly in Canterbury, the east Kent ports of Sandwich and Dover, and in Greenwich and Gravesend.[74] In Canterbury, several were independent craftsmen, including several shoemakers, a currier, a fletcher and a glazier, while John Crouch was a wealthy mercer, but almost a third were listed in the 1524–25 returns as

67 Michael Zell, *Industry in the Countryside: Wealden Society in the Sixteenth Century* (Cambridge, 1994), pp. 153–9.

68 Zell, *Industry*, pp. 183, 217–21.

69 Mate, *Trade*, p. 119, n. 5.

70 Zell, 'Landholding', pp. 47–8.

71 Mate, *Trade*, pp. 110–11.

72 Elisabeth Salter, 'Some Differences in the Cultural Production of Household Consumption in Three North Kent Communities, c.1450–1550', in Cordelia Beattie, Anna Maslakovic and Sarah Rees Jones (eds), *The Medieval Household in Christian Europe, c.850–1550* (Turnhout, 2003), pp. 391–407.

73 Mate, *Trade*, p. 116.

74 *Ibid.*, pp. 117–18.

servants in English households or of other aliens.[75] For Sandwich, the national sources can be supplemented by those produced by the civic authorities and these highlight that it was not solely men who had come from overseas.[76] Of the men, several were beer brewers or worked for English beer brewers in the town, and at least two of the most successful aliens became long-term residents.[77] Those at Dover were listed by the town clerk in several years, including mariners, hackneymen, while others ran alehouses. The 1524 subsidy included Levyn Buskyn, a wealthy Flemish beer brewer, and another Fleming was fined for being out after curfew and insulting the watch and mayor.[78] Nevertheless, in Kent alien populations at this time were generally viewed without hostility. In contrast, at the national level, the introduction of further parliamentary legislation in the 1520s was intended to restrict their numbers and activities, just as it had under the 1483 legislation when it was claimed the employment of foreign workers was leading to the impoverishment of their native counterparts.[79]

Even though it is often difficult to disentangle contemporary perceptions from reality, the socioeconomic implications of increasing population, alongside other factors in the 1520s and 1530s, meant that 'there were numerous small property-owners in all parts of Kent'.[80] Consequently, at the level of the individual or household, both rural and urban, many people needed to find suitable waged employment. However, this was not always straightforward because contracts might relate to seasonal work, piecework or a specific task, and as prices rose, having sufficient income to buy food could become challenging, even more so in very poor harvest years such as 1520 and 1527 when dearth became an issue.[81] Additionally, for those completely dependent on waged labour, including the landless, potentially this was an even greater issue. It was for those whom John Henderson has categorised as the episodic (life-cycle poverty), epidemic (those suddenly forced below subsistence level by severe dearth or epidemic disease) and endemic (the elderly and chronically

75 *Ibid.*, p. 119.

76 BL, Add. MS 33511; KHLC, Sa/Fat/16, 17, especially 33.

77 Mate, *Trade*, p. 115.

78 BL, Egerton MS 2092, fols 137r, 248v, 253r–255v; Mate, *Trade*, p. 117.

79 Mate, *Trade*, p. 120.

80 For Kent, Zell highlights the importance of gavelkind and the land market, not enclosure which was a factor elsewhere in the country; Zell, 'Landholding', pp. 40–3. For other factors, see Nicholas Brodie, 'Beggary, Vagabondage and Poor Relief: English Statutes in the Urban Context, 1495–1572' (unpublished Ph.D. thesis, University of Tasmania, 2010), p. 60.

81 Mate, *Trade*, pp. 144, 146–9.

sick) poor.[82] Such people in the first instance presumably sought familial or communal support. Furthermore, testamentary evidence concerning bequests to the poor provided for specific categories within this group, to hospitals and very occasionally to named poor people, thereby offering a measure of the levels of such post-mortem charity locally and regionally, as well as ideas regarding any changes over time. For example, during the period 1500–30, at Canterbury about a third of testators aided the poor, for Dover over 17 per cent of testators included the poor among their beneficiaries, whereas only 14 per cent did so at Sandwich and Tenterden, a level comparable to that in the Rochester diocese more generally.[83] Canterbury testators during the same period were similarly more generous to the city's hospitals, although three were especially favoured, and in total about 15 per cent of these will-makers gave at least one hospital bequest, a level almost matched by those in Rochester.[84] At Hythe and Sandwich, whereas the presence of their early civic hospitals, a feature of these Kentish head ports, had seemingly been sufficient for them to receive post-mortem support in the period up to the first decade of the sixteenth century, thereafter and especially from the early 1520s this had declined significantly, and at New Romney such bequests were even more limited.[85] Although there continued to be some testamentary support for the early pilgrim hospitals at Dover, Strood near Rochester and to a lesser extent at Ospringe near Faversham, it was not for the poor pilgrims. At Dover, by 1500 the civic authorities had their almshouses, while at Faversham the provision of almshouses in the town and near the quay was undertaken by individuals.[86] Only at St Thomas' Hospital at Canterbury did testators occasionally remember the poor accommodated there.

The identity of the poor people aided through testamentary bequests and institutional provision can rarely if ever be recovered from the sources for the early sixteenth century, which means it is difficult to know if or to what degree a criterion such as local residence was applied by donors or the civic

82 John Henderson, *Piety and Charity in Late Medieval Florence* (Chicago and London, 1997), p. 246.

83 Sheila Sweetinburgh, *The Role of the Hospital in Medieval England: Gift-Giving and the Spiritual Economy* (Dublin, 2004), pp. 167, 211–13; Lutton, *Lollardy*, pp. 95–8; Lee, 'Monastic', 179–84.

84 Sheila Sweetinburgh, 'The Poor, Hospitals and Charity in Sixteenth Century Canterbury', in Lutton and Salter (eds), *Pieties in Transition*, pp. 66–7; Sweetinburgh, *Role of the Hospital*, p. 117.

85 Sheila Sweetinburgh, 'Community Care: Civic Charitable Institutions in the Kentish Cinque Ports, c. 1300–c. 1500', *Archaeologia Cantiana*, 141 (2020), 185–9; Sweetinburgh, *Role of the Hospital*, p. 117.

86 Sweetinburgh, *Role of the Hospital*, pp. 205–6, 209–10; Sheila Sweetinburgh, 'More Continuity than Change: Almshouses in Tudor Kent', *Southern History*, 42 (2020/21), 30–1.

authorities in these towns. Where the mayor and jurats sought to regulate the prices of essential commodities, as at Sandwich for example, it seems likely this was undertaken to aid the local community, especially poorer townspeople. However, it appears the pilgrim hospitals at Dover and Canterbury continued to aid the poor and those who came to their gates until at least the mid-1530s, including poor pilgrims and other travellers.[87] Yet the situation at St John's, one of Sandwich's civic hospitals, apparently changed in the early 1520s. The first of two new civic regulations stated that nobody was to accommodate any beggars and instead, while in Sandwich, those specifically permitted to beg in the town were required to stay at the harbinge, three rooms at the rear of the hospital previously allocated to the sick-poor.[88] One of these rooms was known as 'the chamber for strange women' which suggests it had been meant for poor itinerant women, including those in childbirth. Two months later it was decreed that the mayor would examine any person he suspected of being a vagabond, and any found to 'live evilly and will not fall to labour' were to be banished from the town.[89] Even though the first record of vagabonds in the Sandwich town books was in 1483 and at Dover the authorities had instituted a night watch to 'see good rule of vacabundes' from the mid-1510s, such ordinances a decade later indicate that local official attitudes were hardening against those seen as potential troublemakers.[90] Furthermore, these regulations remained in place into the following decade, the mayor and jurats seeing it as their civic responsibility to maintain order, both in terms of criminal and moral behaviour. For example, in 1535–36 there were a total of nine people who were banished for a range of petty offences including vagrancy.[91]

In part, the civic authorities were presumably also responding to parliamentary legislation, especially the 1531 Act which was intended to help magistrates to remedy the perceived widespread problem that 'Vacabundes & Beggers have of longe time increased & daily do increase in great & excessyve nombres', because such people were likely to engage in criminal activity, thereby damaging the commonweal.[92] This identification of the distinct categories of beggars and vagabonds – the poor were not mentioned – by the legislators was important to ensure that appropriate punitive measures

87 For Dover: John Caley and Joseph Hunter (eds), *Valor Ecclesiasticus*, 1 (London, 1810), pp. 56–7; for Canterbury: Arthur Hussey (ed.), *Kent Chantries* (1932), p. 65.

88 KHLC, Sa/AC/2, fol. 326r. Yet even before this regulation was introduced two people had been prosecuted for harbouring beggars: KHLC, Sa/AC/2, fol. 287v.

89 KHLC, Sa/AC/2, fol. 328r.

90 KHLC, Sa/AC/1, fols 292v–293r; BL, Egerton MS 2092, fols 145v, 170v.

91 KHLC, Sa/AC/2, fols 326, 328; Sa/AC/3, fol. 74r.

92 Brodie, 'Beggary', pp. 23–4. Nevertheless, at the local level the Sandwich mayor, in 1535, punished a man from Ludlow and another from Denby whom he called 'valianute beggers' by whipping; KHLC, Sa/AC/3, fol. 74r.

were enacted to safeguard the physical and moral wellbeing of the community, thereby avoiding God's displeasure.[93] Whipping as the official punishment for vagabonds had been added to the earlier use of the stocks, but as Mate notes, there were instances, as in Canterbury, where constables were presented for not punishing beggars and vagrants according to the statute.[94] The authorities at Sandwich viewed banishment from the town as a valuable final measure, as in the case of Elizabeth Webbes, a widow from Doncaster, who was convicted of 'certain offences and misdemeanors' committed in Sandwich and was sentenced to be banished from the town for a year and a day with the proviso that if she returned sooner she would be branded.[95]

For the civic authorities, idleness was similarly seen as reprehensible, as were prostitution and illicit games, which resulted in offenders being presented in the town courts.[96] However, there appear to have been plenty of people willing to provide premises for the playing of such games.[97] Yet, as Mate comments, national studies have suggested that 'contemporary fears were overdrawn', but in part, as Brodie has discussed, this should be seen in the context of the rhetoric of the early Tudor legislators.[98] Notwithstanding such comments, the recruitment and organisation of a large workforce could lead to problems locally, as occurred in Dover during the construction of the new harbour in the 1530s. Yet equally, such a scheme was envisaged by the Crown as suitable for central government intervention concerning the management of compulsory labour and how such a scheme should be funded for the common good.[99]

Before this exceedingly ambitious scheme, Sir John Clerke – as master of the Maison Dieu and warden of the harbour – had overseen a plan in the 1520s to improve the harbour which had been welcomed by the local authorities, having been relatively successful.[100] By 1533 Clerke was very ill, and an ambitious clergyman seemingly sought to take Clerke's place, first proposing a far grander scheme for the harbour that year to the king and then courting Cromwell's favour, thereby securing both the mastership of the Maison Dieu and control over the new harbour works in 1535. As master of the hospital, Sir John Thompson was a disaster, becoming embroiled in local

93 Brodie, 'Beggary', p. 25.

94 Mate, *Trade*, p. 167.

95 KHLC, Sa/AC/2, fol. 332r.

96 In the Dover records for 1523 there are four consecutive entries concerning six men fined for playing dice or allowing others to do so; BL, Egerton MS 2092, fol. 279v.

97 Mate, *Trade*, pp. 164–5.

98 *Ibid.*, p. 167.

99 Brodie, 'Beggary', p. 214.

100 BL, Egerton MS 2108, fols 25r, 26v, 28r, 44v, 55r, 61r, 70r, 75r.

issues, and he appears to have viewed the place as a useful storehouse for materials needed for the harbour works. Furthermore, his relationship with the royal paymaster was similarly fractious, due to his hiring and seeking to retain a much larger workforce than could be employed from the available funds.[101] Additionally, there were problems concerning the workers in both 1535 and the following year, including their desire to leave the harbour works during harvest time because they could earn more in the fields.[102] Such issues, as Brodie has noted, coincided with the draft parliamentary bill of 1535 that envisaged similar work schemes, administered and managed through central government, thereby building on the 1531 Act where conceptually the idea of making vagabonds undertake compulsory work as directed by magistrates was already on the statute books.[103] Thus, when the 1536 Act was passed, the clause whereby magistrates were empowered to compel 'sturdie vacabunds and valeant beggers' to work as directed was a predictable outcome and, if Brodie is right, was deployed at Dover at least to a degree.[104] Nevertheless, as he says, there is little evidence to indicate that other places followed suit, but the Elizabethan bridewells, including a number of early examples in Kent, can be seen as having their roots in the principles set out in the 1530s.

Turning to other important matters in the county during the 1530s and 1540s, the ongoing religious changes, as elsewhere in England, had far-reaching implications for the whole of society. Of the county's many religious houses, the early, small leper hospitals had been the most vulnerable and several had been granted to the new colleges at Oxford or Cambridge by the early sixteenth century, while others had become little more than chantry chapels. Cardinal Wolsey's 'Little Dissolution' of the mid-1520s witnessed further casualties: Tonbridge Priory, Lesnes Abbey and Bayham Abbey, as well as other 'moribund' houses, were used by him to endow Cardinal College in Oxford. However, the greatest losses occurred a decade later including the ancient monasteries of St Augustine's Abbey, Christ Church Priory and Rochester Priory, as well as Dover Priory, Boxley Abbey, Faversham Abbey, the priory at Folkestone, various nunneries, the county's friaries, the canons at Canterbury, Bilsington, Langdon and Bradsole, but only a few more of the hospitals: St John's at Sevenoaks, St Mary's at Strood, and St Bartholomew's at Dover. Additionally, shrines were destroyed, the greatest being St Thomas of Canterbury and the Holy Rood of Boxley, but across the county the number would have been considerable. The 1540s saw further casualties such as St John's Hospital at New Romney and the secular colleges at Maidstone, Wye, Bredgar, Wingham, Cobham and Ashford. Of the remaining hospitals,

[101] Sweetinburgh, *Role of the Hospital*, p. 181; Brodie, 'Beggary', pp. 210–14.
[102] Brodie, 'Beggary', pp. 208–10.
[103] *Ibid.*, pp. 216–17.
[104] *Ibid.*, pp. 206–16.

by 1550, most were either under episcopal or civic patronage. This meant almost all survived or were re-founded as almshouses, but the Poor Priests' Hospital in Canterbury would become the city's bridewell and the ancient leper hospitals of St James and St Lawrence, also in Canterbury, would become gentry residences. Unlike the reaction seen in northern England, there seems to have been little overt lay opposition in Kent, although whether this was a consequence of the fate that Elizabeth Barton and her followers had met in 1534 is a possibility. Among the religious, the level of opposition to the king displayed by the friar John Stone was exceptional.[105] Yet there were also new foundations; the cathedrals at Canterbury and Rochester were each established as a dean and chapter in 1541, and at the former in addition to the prebendaries there were clerics known as the 'Six Preachers'. The new emphasis on preaching, whether at the cathedral or across the dioceses, was intended by the central authorities to aid the establishment of the new religious orthodoxy, and potentially political conformity.[106]

Nevertheless, presumably the years around 1540 were a very difficult time for many of those coming to terms with the religious changes, and for the diocese of Canterbury the evidence from the Prebendaries' Plot is extremely valuable.[107] While avoiding the old debate regarding the impetus for the Reformation, the depositions collected by Archbishop Cranmer in response to those among his cathedral community, in particular, who were plotting against him in 1543, offer a snapshot of the religious state across the diocese of Canterbury.[108] Moreover, this is similarly visible at the level of the parish, involving groups of parishioners and the clergy on both sides of the religious divide.[109] From the depositions it seems religious conflict extended beyond the areas of those accused of heresy in 1511–12 to include Sandwich and

[105] Andrew Hope, 'Martyrs of the Marsh: Elizabeth Barton, Joan Bocher and Trajectories of Martyrdom in Reformation Kent', in Lutton and Salter (eds), *Pieties in Transition*, pp. 45–8.

[106] Palmer, 'Politics', pp. 235–7.

[107] For the depositions, see: James Gairdner and R. H. Brodie (eds), *Letters and Papers, Foreign and Domestic, of the Reign of Henry VIII*, 18 ii (London, 1902), pp. 291–378; CCCC MS 128.

[108] Michael Zell, 'The Prebendaries' Plot of 1543: A Reconsideration', *Journal of Ecclesiastical History*, 27 (1976), 241–53; Peter Clark, *English Provincial Society from the Reformation to the Revolution: Religion, Politics and Society in Kent, 1500–1640* (Hassocks, 1977), pp. 56–73; Brian Hogben, 'Preaching and the Reformation in Henrician Kent', *Archaeologia Cantiana*, 101 (1984), 169–85; Patrick Collinson, 'The Protestant Cathedral, 1541–1660', in Collinson, Ramsey and Sparks (eds), *Canterbury Cathedral*, pp. 159–61; Ethan Shagan, *Popular Politics and the English Reformation* (Cambridge, 2003), pp. 197–232.

[109] Sheila Sweetinburgh, 'Neighbours across the Religious Divide: Coping with Difference in Henrician Kent', in Bronach Kane and Simon Sandall (eds), *The*

surrounding parishes, the upper Stour valley near Ashford, Faversham and its hinterland, and a smaller cluster in the Romney Marshes. Moreover, some of those caught up in these disputes in 1543, whether in Canterbury, Sandwich, Tenterden and possibly other places, had held evangelical views for perhaps at least a decade. Stuart Palmer has discussed a network that was actively propagating continental reformist texts in Canterbury during the 1530s with the additional dimension that copies of such texts were being printed locally near the abbey.[110] Nor were such books only to be found in Canterbury, for Cranmer's investigators noted that a man in Frittenden in the eastern Weald had a copy of Tyndale's English translation of the Bible.[111]

Yet for all the religious uncertainties and changes of the Henrician Reformation, economically the dissolving of many of the county's religious houses meant that relatively quickly a large acreage of land came into the land market, as well as a considerable number of urban properties. Even though the dean and chapter at Canterbury Cathedral regained much of the priory's old landholdings, the corporation petitioned the king to secure from the Crown all of St Augustine's urban properties within the city's liberty and, aided by Cranmer, the price was reduced by half.[112] Furthermore, as Palmer indicated, the city authorities sought to increase the number of freemen, drawing in many of the former *intrantes* and charging higher entry fees.[113] As well as raising revenue through these fees and the increase in the city's rent roll, the corporation ensured that the number of craft guilds in the city increased substantially, thereby attempting to foster unity among the city's artisan population and as a way to strengthen the economy.[114] At the same time, Palmer sees little appetite among the corporation to prosecute those holding more extreme religious views, even though central government had changed the legislation to allow this to happen; rather pragmatism and a desire to safeguard the community was seemingly the priority.[115]

In addition to purchasing former monastic urban properties, certain members of the gentry were able to acquire monastic and friary buildings to form residences, and some of these were in or on the edge of towns, while others had been rural monastic granges. Similarly, the ability of individuals to benefit from the availability of monastic agricultural land was considerable in rural Kent. Buyers were primarily members of the gentry, many of whom

---

Experience of Neighbourhood in Medieval and Early Modern Europe (London and New York, 2022), pp. 63–77.

[110] Palmer, 'Politics', pp. 239, 241–4, 246–52, 254–6, 258.

[111] *Letters and Papers* 18 ii, 312, CCCC MS 128, 71.

[112] Zell, 'Landholding', p. 59; Bower, 'Kent Towns', p. 145.

[113] Palmer, 'Politics', pp. 269–73.

[114] *Ibid.*, pp. 267–9.

[115] *Ibid.*, pp. 260–6.

had a link to the court or royal government, although some were leading townsmen who were extending their holdings as they sought to capitalise on the expanding land market, such purchased land frequently rented out to tenants, which in turn benefited the successful yeoman farmers.[116] Nor were members of the gentry averse to acquiring urban properties, and Lord Cobham paid over £1,000 in 1549 for part of Maidstone College's lands. Equally, when Maidstone became an incorporated borough, the mayor and jurats bought the Corpus Christi Fraternity properties in the town, while the hall became the town's grammar school.[117] Furthermore, during the later years of Henry's reign, Zell sees the same pragmatic approach to religious matters from both the reformers and traditionalist members of the Kentish squirarchy, as Palmer does for Canterbury's civic governors.[118]

Many yeoman farmers were able to benefit from selling locally, but there were also considerable opportunities for those who chose to supply London and Calais, often through ports such as Faversham and Sandwich.[119] These prosperous farmers were in east and central Kent, including parts of the Weald, where they raised cattle and sheep as well as growing cereals, alongside more specialised crops such as hemp, saffron and fruit.[120] The leather industry similarly benefited from the continuing emphasis placed on mixed farming and although tanners were found in many parts of Kent, tanning was especially important in certain Wealden parishes because many of the cattle reared in the area were driven to London to supply the capital's meat trade. Thereafter Maidstone acted as the fulcrum for the trade, the Medway used by the butchers to transport the raw hides from London to the town for distribution to the tanners, the tanned leather shipped back to the capital.[121]

One side-effect of the Dissolution was that it released vast quantities of building materials, especially dressed stone, timber and lead, onto the market, and apart from some local use where stone could be purchased by the cartload, a large quantity of masonry was shipped to Calais to repair the fortifications there. Such materials were seen as equally valuable for the construction of a series of Device Forts that were built along the English and Welsh coasts between 1539 and 1545, including in Kent at Deal, Walmer, Sandown with associated works at Dover. These royal projects were extremely expensive; the three Kent forts cost £27,000 and required a large labour force, the Deal fort alone having 14,000 workers which meant craftsmen and labourers were drawn to the port, and the works also provided opportunities for local townspeople

116 Zell, 'Landholding', pp. 58–62.

117 *Ibid.*, p. 59.

118 Zell, 'Religious Reform', p. 204.

119 Mate, *Trade*, pp. 191–2.

120 *Ibid.*, pp. 188–9.

121 Andrewes, 'Industries in Kent', pp. 134–5.

in terms of supplying board and lodging.[122] Although costing the Crown far less, a series of blockhouses were also built along the Thames Estuary that similarly provided employment for construction workers at Gravesend, Milton-next-Gravesend and Higham. As well as guarding the approach to London, they gave protection to the major royal dockyards at Deptford and Woolwich in wartime, which was again important in the 1540s.[123]

For domestic and commercial premises both in the town and countryside, construction using timber-framing remained the norm. Even though there had been a few small brickworks in the fifteenth century, including one near Sandwich, brick was rarely used as a building material and some was shipped from the Low Countries.[124] By the 1540s things were changing, such as the greater use of clay tiles rather than thatch, while the use of brick was slowly increasing, both as brick nogging and for the construction of whole buildings, which offered opportunities to provide decorative features as a way of displaying wealth. The mid-sixteenth-century Roper gateway near Canterbury being a good example that highlights the value placed on conspicuous consumption by Kent's gentry families. For those of more modest wealth but within the higher levels of the middling sort, such display was achieved through household goods, as in the case of John Bryngborne, a merchant of Faversham who in 1545 bequeathed to his well-beloved wife a hundred pounds in money and his nest of gilt goblets with a cover, the only household item mentioned in his will, the remainder of his bequests being very sizeable sums of money.[125] Yet, as Richardson and Salter have demonstrated, such wealth among townspeople was not uniform across the county. Those in northwest Kent seemingly had a greater range of luxury goods far earlier than their peers in places such as Sandwich, probably largely due to the influence of Londoners and the Tudor court.[126]

Even though there were new commercial opportunities on the continent for east Kent merchants such as Bryngborne in the mid-1530s, the next decade was challenging, for not only were there attacks on shipping by Flemish privateers, but the introduction of a requirement for a licence from the government concerning goods for export further disrupted these merchants'

[122] Christopher Ware, 'To Defend the Coast', in Bligh, Edwards and Sweetinburgh (eds), *Maritime Kent*, pp. 134–5.

[123] *Ibid.*, p. 136; Andrewes, 'Trade and Industry', p. 236.

[124] Helen Clarke, Sarah Pearson, Mavis Mate and Keith Parfitt (with contributions from Sheila Sweetinburgh and B. Jones), *Sandwich: The 'Completest Medieval Town in England'. A Study of the Town and Port from its Origins to 1600* (Oxford, 2010), p. 135.

[125] TNA, PROB 11/30/401.

[126] Catherine Richardson, 'Household Objects and Domestic Ties', in Beattie, Maslakovic and Jones (eds), *Medieval Household*, p. 446.

trade.[127] Nevertheless, it seems an unknown number of merchants and shipmasters ignored the ban and illegally shipped grain to the Low Counties to take advantage of the high prices resulting from a growing population and lost crops due to sporadic flooding.[128] In the early 1540s, intermittent warfare compounded the merchants' problems because as well as royal seizures of grain and other foodstuffs, shipping was commandeered to ferry troops and supplies to France, and further taxation was introduced. Mate also considers that the debasement of the coinage would have had detrimental effects.[129] However, the situation was not wholly dire, as the war meant Calais was heavily dependent on supplies from Kent, especially livestock for the butchers, although Dover was no longer the primary port of departure, being replaced largely by Hythe and to a lesser extent by Folkestone.[130] Moreover, overseas trade was still attractive for some Kentish merchants while others seemingly concentrated on the coastal trade. Those from places like Faversham, Milton and Rochester on the north coast supplied considerable quantities of wheat, malt and firewood to London, as well as commodities such as fruit, especially apples and pears but potentially cherries from the orchard at Teynham, while Whitstable with its neighbouring coastal communities provided oysters.[131] For those at Sandwich, they had more choice, being able to ship grain north to Dartford, Maidstone or London, but equally to Calais, as well as to several Sussex ports. Furthermore, for the shallow draught ships from Low Country ports such as Ostend and Rotterdam, Sandwich remained the destination of choice, bringing hops and salt fish and taking away grain and beer.[132]

In contrast, Dover's recurrent problems concerning the silting of its harbour had only gained a short respite following the work undertaken in the 1530s, and it was not until Elizabeth's reign that such issues concerning the harbour were tackled more successfully. As Mary Dixon has discussed, this had serious implications for maritime trade in the later years of Henry's reign and those of his son Edward VI because only shallow draught boats could use Dover safely. Such vessels had been used by local fishermen for catching a range of fish in the waters around Dover, but the number of fishermen had declined over the first half of the century, although this may relate to depleted fish stocks in these coastal waters.[133] However, such men were able to deploy their boats to carry both goods and passengers across the Channel, including beer to Flemish ports, corn and firewood to various ports, and returning with hops and other

127 Mate, *Trade*, pp. 90–1.
128 *Ibid.*, pp. 92–3.
129 *Ibid.*, pp. 93–4.
130 *Ibid.*, pp. 94–5.
131 *Ibid.*, pp. 40–1, 44–5, 47, 48–9.
132 *Ibid.*, pp. 41, 95.
133 Dixon, 'Economy', pp. 230–1.

commodities. Additionally, they engaged in coastal trade as far as Devon to the west and north to Newcastle. Yet, as at all the ports engaged in overseas trade, piracy and war seriously disrupted these activities. For example, in John Halyday's will (1545), he wanted any compensation if it came following the burning of his crayer by the French while it was being used in the king's service – the ship having been chased and run aground – to be used to repair highways in and around Dover.[134] Much of the overseas trade was in the hands of London and Calais merchants, although some Dover mariners were able to develop longstanding arrangements that benefited both parties.[135] As noted above, Dover had first sought to hold a monopoly on the carrying of passengers across the Channel in 1226, but was yet again facing competition in the 1540s, this time from Calais mariners. Nonetheless, such undertakings still aided other sectors of the local economy, especially innkeepers and hackney men, as well as those who supplied victuals.[136]

Yet, the desire of certain merchants to capitalise on the grain trade to London and overseas at times caused serious hardship for the poorer townspeople and, as noted above, the exceedingly large workforce employed on the new harbour at Dover in the previous decade accentuated the problem. This came to a crisis point more generally across the county in 1549 when there was a revolt in Kent and East Anglia. Rebels were active at Canterbury, the Isle of Sheppey and near Maidstone at Boxley, while the following year, which saw the second of three failed harvests, it was reported that at Sittingbourne around 10,000 peasants had congregated. They complained that, amongst other issues, the gentry's activities in the property market had doubled the price of land, thereby taking it beyond the reach of their poorer neighbours. In the towns as in the countryside, there was considerable disparity in terms of wealth and as Mate notes: 'The gap was widening between those who were able to benefit from rising prices and those like smallholders and wage-earners who suffered from them.'[137]

Nevertheless, looking across the period under study, it had begun in the depth of the mid-fifteenth-century depression and even though it ended with a minor on the throne, with the country experiencing religious and political uncertainty as well as issues such as inflation and unemployment, for many this would have seemed a far better time than that experienced by their forebears in 1450. To illustrate what this may have meant in 1550, it is helpful to look at a couple of examples, one from west Kent and another from east Kent.

Starting in the west, while activities in the county's land market by London merchants and senior royal servants were not new, circa 1540 the large number

[134] KHLC, PRC 32/22, fol. 58r.
[135] Dixon, 'Economy', pp. 236–8.
[136] *Ibid.*, pp. 233–4.
[137] Mate, *Trade*, p. 189.

of monastic estates and other assets such as church advowsons and tithes which had been surrendered to the Crown provided major opportunities for such men from the capital. One of these was John Gresham, who had served Henry VIII loyally and, like his brother, shared the king's religious views. Consequently, he was rewarded with the manor of Westerham and its church, in addition to other Kent property, for just under £1,500. During the next decade, he seems to have had a special interest in Westerham's parish church, which would be shared by his nephew Thomas Gresham. However, in the later 1540s, the older man did not approve of his nephew's enthusiasm for the young king's reforming stance, which David Boston believes meant that it was Thomas, a friend of John Foxe, who commissioned in about 1550/1 the painting of Edward VI's royal arms to be displayed where the rood had recently stood in Westerham church.[138] The design and execution of the painting, Boston believes, owes much to earlier paintings of royal arms in Bruges Cathedral and 'indicates the influence of the Northern Renaissance and the employment of a Netherlandish … artist as responsible for the early Renaissance touches detected in Westerham's Arms'. Moreover, as well as such links, the oak boards on which the arms are painted had originated in the eastern Baltic, and having arrived in Antwerp, had been treated as required by the panel and frame makers' guild. Thomas Gresham was based in the city from the later 1540s and headed the family's commercial operations there, including exporting woollen cloths and importing luxury items for the king and Londoners more generally. Therefore, commissioning such a work for his family's church was presumably wholly appropriate. Yet, his uncle retained more conservative religious views and at Mary's accession Boston believes it was the older Gresham who had a pediment added with the religious inscription 'ihs' when it was moved to a different part of the church. This case highlights that in 1550, one family – through commercial and social interrelationships at London, Kent and Antwerp – influenced religiously, politically, artistically, and therefore culturally at least one community and potentially others in Kent.

Edward Mylwarde of Dover was not among the gentry. Nevertheless, as a prosperous local beer brewer, he benefited from the growth in this trade and when he made his will in 1547, he ensured that both his eldest son and his widow could continue in the same industry.[139] John was to receive the principal messuage, brewhouse, barn, stable and garden in Dover with all the implements belonging there. This meant all the stuff for the brewhouse, grain, wood, horses, carts, hay, and most importantly hops, as well as other

138 For his new assessment of this work, see David Boston, 'England's Earliest Painted and Framed Royal Coat of Arms (Edward VI, 1547–53) in St Mary's Church, Westerham: The Work of a Low Countries' Artist Commissioned by the Gresham Family', *Archaeologia Cantiana*, 141 (2020), 84–97.

139 KHLC, PRC 32/21, fol. 68r.

commodities due to arrive except for ten quarters of wheat and a similar quantity of malt that Edward had bought from Giles Sutton. These were to go to Margaret, Edward's wife. She was also to receive a tenement, a brewhouse, two closes in Hythe and the stores there which comprised thirty-seven quarters of malt, a hundred loads of wood, five quarters of oats, three loads of hay, three cart horses and all the implements belonging to the brewhouse. After her death, all of this would be inherited by Edward's second son Thomas. Partly as a means of keeping these enterprises working together, she was to have for herself the parlour and chamber in the family home during her widowhood with twenty loads of wood, also purchased from Giles Sutton, and the little yard between the brewhouse and the gate at the Dover house to store her firewood. Moreover, she was to have Edward's 'book of remembrance' in which were itemised all the debts owed to him and the rest of his goods. His wealth can also be measured in the number of silver items bequeathed to both sons and his wife, while each of his four unmarried daughters was to receive a broad range of household goods and £5 in cash at marriage. As an indicator, presumably, of the number of poor people in Dover, as well as his affluence, Edward left 6s 8d to the poor men's chest in the town's main parish church. This statement of intent at the end of his life suggests that he had confidence in the future of his large family and that of the whole town, where such businesses as beer brewing would thrive, serving Dover's community, those passing through the town to and from mainland Europe and potentially more widely still. Thus, at both Westerham and Dover in 1550, while there was a recognition that poverty was a serious issue, the commercial and other networks that successful families could and did employ continued to demonstrate how Kent as a whole was a maritime county.

2

Maritime Trade and Kent's Ports, *c*.1540–*c*.1640

ROBERT BLACKMORE

Trade connects people and places through the exchange of goods. This chapter concerns that which linked the ports of Kent, in the southeast of England, with – to a degree – the rest of the kingdom, but above all across the so-called 'Narrow Seas', to the European continent and beyond. It describes the socioeconomic connections generated and sustained by merchants and mariners. Though it will – at times – refer back to the mid-fifteenth century and before, this chapter will concentrate on the mid-sixteenth to mid-seventeenth century: the so-called 'Tawney's century' (commonly described as 1540–1640).[1] In a period about which much scholarly attention has been on market integration and the rise of entrepôts, and large distributive commercial hubs, it explores the role of provincial maritime communities in the English and wider European economy in this period and how this changed.[2]

In this respect, C. W. Chalklin argued, in his seminal work on seventeenth-century Kent, for the overwhelming importance of London to the county's development, but that 'the commercial significance of Kent's position as the nearest county to the Continent was comparatively small'.[3] This chapter will re-examine this view and reconsider how Kent's ports engaged in local, translocal, regional or transregional markets. It will evaluate their interactions within broader socioeconomic trends and how they were impacted by England's shifting relationships with other European polities. The precise contribution this period's economic actors made towards the development of modern capitalism and industrialisation may be debatable.[4] Nonetheless, it is

1 Michael Zell, 'Introduction', in Zell (ed.), *Early Modern Kent* (Woodbridge, 2000), pp. 1–6.

2 Eric Kerridge, *Trade and Banking in Early Modern England* (Manchester, 1988), pp. 5–32.

3 Chalklin, *Seventeenth-Century Kent*, pp. 1–4, 161–88, quotation at p. 4.

4 For these debates, see John H. Munro, 'Tawney's Century (1540–1640): The Roots of Modern Capitalist Entrepreneurship in England', in David S. Landes, Joel

a time frequently presented as transformative for the economy and society of England, and Europe more generally: not least for commerce, which saw expansion amid intermittent crises.[5]

First, a description of those merchants and mariners involved is presented, then an account of the trading relationships through which they operated, and how these altered. Subsequently, it offers a summary of the commodities traded, followed by a discussion of the association between migration and commerce, as well as the varieties of capital that accumulated. Evidence is presented here from a variety of, mostly, English national sources, alongside others: some local county, and some European. The core derives from the analysis of customs records in the form of the port books, introduced in 1565.[6] These have been long understood as flawed records in many ways, not least for what they omit and oversimplify.[7] Yet, when used judiciously with other documents, these can still offer a detailed and vivid picture of a lost maritime world.

Merchants and Masters

For the merchants and mariners who operated from Kent's ports into the Narrow Seas during this period – Sandwich and Dover principally, but also places like Faversham, Milton Regis, Rochester and also Margate, Ramsgate, Broadstairs, Hythe and Gravesend – their trading environment saw much continuity alongside some dramatic change. As Jane Andrewes opened and closed her excellent outline: 'during the sixteenth and seventeenth centuries, maritime Kent experienced increasing economic activity and expansion in waterborne commerce and industry along the coast', and 'despite fluctuations in fortunes and some areas of decline, this period can be characterised as one of enterprise by individuals and communities'.[8]

Mokyr and William J. Baumol (eds), *The Invention of Enterprise: Entrepreneurship from Ancient Mesopotamia to Modern Times* (Princeton, 2010), pp. 107–55.

5 See, for example, C. G. A. Clay, *Economic Expansion and Social Change: England 1500–1700* (Cambridge, 1984), pp. 103–202.

6 Port books analysed for this chapter include: TNA, E 190/635/13–19; E 190/640/1–6, 9–12; E 190/641/1–2, 7–8; E 190/641/10–11, 13; E 190/642/1–15; E 190/643/1–8, 10–20; E 190/644/1, 3–14; E 190/645/1–8, 10–15; E 190/646/1–7, 9–13; E 190/647/1–10, 12; E 190/648/1–6; E 190/648/9–12, 14–18; E 190/649/1, 3, 5–8, 11–12, 16, 18–20; E 190/650/1–10, 13, 16, 18, E 190/651/1–3, 6–11, 13, 15; E 190/652/2, 5, 8–9, 11–12; E 190/653/4–6; E 190/655/1; E 190/736/7.

7 J. H. Andrews, 'Two Problems in the Interpretation of the Port Books', *Economic History Review*, 2nd series, 9:1 (1956), 119–22.

8 Andrewes, 'Trade and Industry', pp. 235–52, at pp. 235, 252.

Such people are a challenge to characterise. As Keith Wrightson indicated, those who traded from provincial ports could range from modest to great merchants.[9] They could likewise be native or foreign-born, denizens or aliens, or some intermediate status in between. Some were masters and owners (or part-owners) of small hoys of perhaps 5–25 tons in burden, who might journey in person, to specific locations, to buy and sell, while also engaged in other occupations. Jacob Skellworth (also Scelewaert, Scellewaert, etc. in Dutch sources), for example, the master of the *Pelican* of Vlissingen – known to the English as Flushing – a 6-ton vessel, made voyages between Vlissingen and Faversham during the late sixteenth and early seventeenth centuries. Ostensibly a Dutchman, but occasionally appearing as a native in English records, he carried largely humble goods, primarily trading fish, salt, Dutch cheese and hops. Others, by contrast, might own a good number of larger ships as well as shore infrastructure, such as warehouses, and trade with a far larger variety of places. Such traders handled luxury goods, spices or quality cloth or shipped necessities or raw materials in bulk. An example: James Hugessen the younger (1575–1646), a merchant adventurer of Dover, son of James Hugessen the elder (1557–1638) who, with his brother Cornelius (1568–), were immigrants from Dunkirk in Flanders.

The number and categories of such merchants could vary considerably, both place-to-place and over time. A larger port such as Dover averaged about 220 merchants operating to and from overseas destinations, rising to about 250 if you include those who traded coastal only. A more modest port, like Faversham, had perhaps around 120 involved in both, though most trafficked domestically. Some were more visited or settled by merchants deemed foreign than others. In Dover, from Michaelmas 1579 to Michaelmas 1580, there were 69 merchants designated as 'indigenous' (36.3 per cent) and 121 as 'alien' (63.7 per cent). By Christmas 1615 to Christmas 1616, this had shifted to 93 natives (52.3 per cent) and 85 foreign (47.8 per cent). In Faversham, from Michaelmas 1603 to Michaelmas 1604, by contrast, just a dozen of 107 (11.2 per cent) were not considered native. Oftentimes overseas or domestic trade was markedly dominated by one group. The overseas trade of Sandwich in 1610–11, for example, involved 66 merchants, of which 44 (66.7 per cent) were foreign. By contrast, coastal trade was almost entirely controlled by English interests. Not all merchants were equally active. The median number of cargo shipments for each trader per year was always one, and the mean usually 2–3.5. This skew suggests a considerable, if changeable, proportion of trade was handled by a few prominent merchants, with the rest only intermittently active.

Commercial careers were shaped by a subtle blend of broad contemporary socioeconomic trends, past and present conflicts, idiosyncrasies in local conditions and geographical chance. Much of Europe experienced

[9] Wrightson, *Earthly Necessities*, pp. 190–2.

considerable economic growth during this time, together with a substantial rise in population. Even as established markets expanded to meet the demand this generated, prices rose, and real wages fell, a condition in which inventive merchants were well placed to profit.[10]

Extent and Intensity of Trade

Kent's ports had access to extremely busy and prosperous sea lanes. The Narrow Seas lay at the intersection of two very old trade routes, a place described in the fourteenth century as the 'rich sea frontier'.[11] One ran from the Atlantic Ocean to the North Sea and the Baltic, linking western France, Spain, Portugal and the Mediterranean with the Low Countries, Germany, Poland and Scandinavia. Another connected England – centred on London – with the European continent, particularly through Flanders and northern France. During the Middle Ages, the first brought foreign merchant ships to Kent's ports, Sandwich especially. These included carracks from Genoa and galleys from Venice carrying luxury goods like spices and ornate cloth, as well as some ships of the Hanseatic League, the 'Hanse' – the confederation of North Sea and Baltic ports.[12] The second route bisected the first, partly because, as Thomas Willan argued, 'east-coast ports' would have also been 'well placed for trade with north-west Europe'.[13] England had long enjoyed strong commercial links with the continent via Flanders thanks to the considerable English wool trade, which Flemish merchants dominated in the thirteenth century before being replaced by Italian, and then eventually English merchants.[14]

A great legacy, in this respect, of the Hundred Years' War (1337–1453) was the English control of Calais and the surrounding territory, its Pale, captured from the French by Edward III (r. 1327–77) in 1347.[15] In 1363, Calais was established as the staple town for the export of wool under the authority of the Merchants of the Staple: a company with a monopoly over the trade. Politically mandated staple ports helped a nascent state impose taxation on the movement

[10] Kamen, *European Society*; also see Wrightson, *Earthly Necessities*, more generally.

[11] Jean Froissart, *Chronicles*, MS Besançon 865, fol. 144v, in P. Ainsworth and G. Croenen (eds), *The Online Froissart* (Sheffield, 2013), http://www.hrionline.ac.uk/onlinefroissart: 'Ou pouons nous mieulx faire nostre prouf fit que de entrer en celle riche frontiere de mer de Bourbourc, de Dunequer que, de Neufport et en la chastelle rie de Berghes, de Cassel, de Yppre et de Propringhe?'

[12] Kowaleski, 'Maritime Trade', pp. 215–33, at pp. 216–17; T. H. Lloyd, *England and the German Hanse, 1157–1611: A Study of Their Trade and Commercial Diplomacy* (Cambridge, 1991), pp. 220–1.

[13] T. S. Willan, *Studies in Elizabethan Foreign Trade* (Manchester, 1959), p. 67.

[14] See T. H. Lloyd, *The English Wool Trade in the Middle Ages* (Cambridge, 1977).

[15] See Susan Rose, *Calais: An English Town in France* (Woodbridge, 2008).

of goods, but such places also functioned as entrepôts, transshipment centres that tied together multiple trade routes. For merchants, having goods and counterparties accumulate in such locations helped lower transaction costs. For a time, Calais became the hub of England's continental trade that connected the kingdom with the then richest cities of Flanders, such as Ghent, Bruges and Ypres. Kent's ports, Sandwich especially, played a noteworthy role in this trade system, while providing Calais with food and fuel.[16] Indeed, Dover had an important role ferrying people to and from the town, a function the town gained a confirmed monopoly over in 1440.[17]

Typically, it has been assumed that by the time Calais was retaken by France at the beginning of 1558 the town had lost much of its commercial value. Geoffrey Elton famously wrote that, at its fall, 'probably Calais – expensive and useless – was better lost than kept'.[18] This was largely because wool had begun to lose its place as England's main export to cloth from the mid-fourteenth century, and by the mid-sixteenth the role of the Merchants of the Staple at Calais had been similarly outshone by the Company of Merchant Adventurers of London, trading cloth through Antwerp in Brabant.[19] Yet, the loss of Calais was strongly felt at the nearest English ports across the Channel. After the event, Dover was reported to have been in a terrible state. One appeal in 1562 describes its 'great decay and poverty'.[20] In 1566, nineteen houses in the town were described in the royal survey of that year as being 'voyde for Lacke of inhabitantes', just over 5 per cent of the total.[21] This decrepitude and its twin causes were later remembered in 1674:

> Thus, the decay of the haven at Dover, and the loss of Calais, hapning both about one time, made such an utter desolation there, that of [a] brave rich and populous town, it became presently a poor and desolate village.[22]

Nonetheless, the cross-channel connections that had existed for more than two centuries were restored. For, as the merchant and diarist Peter Mundy wrote pointedly, in September 1620, the route from Calais to Dover 'cannot

16 Mate, *Trade*, pp. 88, 92, 94, 98–100.

17 *Ibid.*, pp. 98–9.

18 G. R. Elton, *England Under the Tudors* (1955, repr. Abingdon, 1991), p. 222.

19 For a characteristic summary of the shifting trends in England's trade, see Ralph Davis, *English Overseas Trade 1500–1700* (London, 1973).

20 Dixon, 'Economy', pp. 85–6.

21 J. M. Gibson, 'The 1566 Survey of the Kent Coast', *Archaeologia Cantiana*, 112 (1993), 341–53, at p. 346.

22 'A Brief memorial of what hath been done in former times, concerning the making and repairing of Dover harbour, and the present state thereof', *Early English Books Online*, https://name.umdl.umich.edu/A29459.0001.001. University of Michigan Library Digital Collections (accessed 4 July 2024).

bee avoyded, no more then the crossinge of rivers'.[23] In the twelve months from Michaelmas (29 September) 1576 to 1577, English and foreign ships made 190 trips back and forth between Dover and Calais, a crossing that took Mundy just three and a half hours. Not only had links via Dover returned, the year before, 1575–76, there had been 76 crossings back and forth between Sandwich and Calais. There were also important connections with other ports of Flanders, particularly Dunkirk, Nieuwpoort and Ostend. There were 168 crossings between Sandwich and Nieuwpoort in 1575–76 and 93 with Ostend. For Dover, Dunkirk was especially important with 87 crossings in 1576–77.[24]

Kent's ports had some links with the great sixteenth-century entrepôt at Antwerp too, though not to the degree that London, much less wider Europe, had. The water-bailiffs' anchorage accounts of Arnemuiden show that, in the 1530s and 1540s, only one or two ships from Kent's ports arrived in Antwerp each year. This gradually increased during the 1560s, hitting a peak in the year 1566–67 when 13 of the 50 Kentish ships charged anchorage by the water-bailiff ventured that far up the Scheldt. Visits seem to have dropped off precipitously over the following years as English ships were embargoed in 1568, around the time of the first phase of the Dutch Revolt.[25] This, with the ensuing Eighty Years' War (1568–1648), was the central event for the Narrow Seas between the mid-sixteenth and mid-seventeenth centuries, around which all things political, military and economic turned. It pitted rebels in the Habsburg Netherlands against the Spanish Crown and resulted in the creation of the Protestant-led Republic of the Seven United Netherlands (the United Provinces) in the north following the Union of Utrecht (1579).

After the 1576 sack of Antwerp by Spanish mutineers, and final capture by Hapsburg forces in 1585, the centre of commerce moved to the new republic, especially Amsterdam. Indeed, of the 741 voyages that left from or arrived at Sandwich harbour in 1575–76 not one single ship sailed to or from Antwerp.[26] Yet, neither were there any crossings to or from Holland. Rather, Kent's links were with nearby Zeeland, with its key ports of Middelburg and Vlissingen. These had been long established and would have far greater resilience. The attraction, a petition of the Merchant Adventurers in the 1580s explained, was that it was the 'shortest and most safest' route to the Low Countries,

[23] Richard Carnac Temple (ed.), *The Travels of Peter Mundy, in Europe and Asia, 1608–1667: Volume I: Travels in Europe, 1608–1628* (Cambridge, 1907), pp. 134, 136.

[24] TNA, E 190/639/13; E 190/640/1.

[25] H. J. Smit (ed.), *Bronnen tot de geschiedenis van den handel met Engeland, Schotland en Ierland 1150–1585*, vol. 2 (The Hague, 1950), pp. 459–61, 463, 476, 495–6, 515–21, 538, 684, 702–4, 715, 829–37, 851, 870, 922–6, 963–4, 975, 993–4, 1010–11, 1020, 1028–31; Jason Eldred, '"The Just will pay for the Sinners": English Merchants, the Trade with Spain, and Elizabethan Foreign Policy, 1563–1585', *Journal for Early Modern Cultural Studies*, 10:1 (2010), 5–28.

[26] TNA, E 190/639/13.

blessed with propitious natural features for navigation.[27] The county's ships were extremely regular visitors to Middelburg and were particularly numerous during 1538–41 and 1565–67. There was a noteworthy peak in 1539–40 when no fewer than 43 Kentish ships visited in one year, of which 15 were from Faversham, 14 from Ramsgate and eight from Sandwich. They began to visit Vlissingen in larger numbers from the mid-1560s, peaking at 25 ships arriving there in 1567–68, of the 66 from Kent recorded that year – of which nine were from Faversham and seven from Whitstable. Indeed, between 1536 and 1569, visits to Vlissingen by ships of Kent far outnumbered those of London almost every year for which records survive, by a multiple of 4.75 on average.[28] By 1575–76, Sandwich's ties were especially strong. Its port book for that year shows 105 crossings between the two.[29] This connection with Zeeland in general – 'the island' which a 1585 report to the Crown about the United Provinces identified as 'the principal key of the country' – only solidified further that year as England gained control of Vlissingen as one of the Cautionary Towns (along with Brielle and Fort Rammekens) under the Treaty of Nonsuch.[30] From then, the kingdom openly joined the Dutch rebels in their war with Spain, despite Sir Walter Mildmay's warning the previous year that such a conflict would lead to 'an interuption of the whole traffique of this realme by sea'.[31]

Given this threat, it is pertinent to consider how the scale and structure of trade changed during the first Anglo-Spanish War (1585–1604). Experiences varied considerably. Some suffered, some saw stability and some even prospered. The total number of payments of the Zeeland toll by ships rose almost every year, from 6,332 in 1585 to 8,728 in 1592. Where the places of departure are cited the most frequently mentioned was London with 15.5 per cent, followed by Fort Lillo, at the approach to Antwerp, with 10.3 per cent, but third was Sandwich, with 7.5 per cent.[32] Yet, the contemporary Sandwich water-bailiff's accounts indicate considerable volatility in the various revenues from trade (anchorage, profits of the fair, tolls for cross-binding packs of cloth, for buying and selling of ships, horses, etc.). A possible recession from the late 1580s to mid-1590s, and subsequent recovery, seems evident, but it is difficult to distinguish the hardship of war from that associated with the London plague outbreak of 1592–93, which likely hit Kent's ports sometime

27 BL, Add. MSS 48009, fols 554–555b.

28 Smit (ed.), *Den handel*, pp. 459–61, 463, 476, 495–6, 515–21, 538, 684, 702–4, 715, 829–37, 851, 870, 922–6, 963–4, 975, 993–4, 1010–11, 1020, 1028–31.

29 TNA, E 190/639/13.

30 TNA, SP 84/5, fols 169–176, quotation on 173v: 'Prenant regard que ceste isle est la clef principalle du pays.'

31 TNA, SP 83/23, fols 55–58.

32 Zeeuwsarchief, GIDS103: *Tol van Zeeland, 1584–1805*, 2.02–2.07, 2.10, 2.12, 2.14–6.

earlier.[33] Commercial activity through Dover remained steady. In the year from Michaelmas (29 September) 1576 to Michaelmas 1577, there were 301 overseas voyages in and out of Dover harbour, constituting 4,916 tons of shipping. Levels subsequently remained at 250–300 voyages and 4,000–4,500 tons per year for most of the rest of the sixteenth century, aside from the year from Michaelmas 1597 to Michaelmas 1598, when trade briefly declined. This is reflected in the decennial averages of Dover's income from harbour dues which fell only slightly between 1579–88 and 1589–98.[34]

Remarkably, by the 1620s, Dover had been transformed from a 'a poor and desolate village' into a great international entrepôt.[35] Its population surged from 1,200–1,900 in 1562, to perhaps 4,000–6,000 towards the end of the 1630s.[36] The spectacular recovery of Dover's fortunes was firmly in step with a transformation of the port's trade, which grew precipitously (see Table 2.1). Average harbour dues more than doubled between 1589–98 and 1599–1608, and then continued to rise in the subsequent two decades.[37] By the year from Christmas 1621 to Christmas 1622 there were 563 overseas voyages, and the tonnage had dramatically increased. Of those ships where their burden was noted in the port books, there were 17,171 tons, but this detail was missing from 196 voyages. If those voyages involved ships of around the average burden, one can estimate the quantity of shipping that passed through the harbour at over 25,000 tons.

In other words, the productivity of the port of Dover, regarding the volume of overseas trade, had increased five-fold compared with the mid-1570s.[38] There was likewise some significant growth in coastal trade. During Michaelmas 1579 to 1580, there were just 41 voyages in and out of Dover, to or from other domestic ports: shipping of just 1,004 tons. By the year from Christmas 1615, there were 145. If we account for missing tonnages by the same method, the latter would have comprised well over 3,000 further tons of shipping, a three-fold increase.[39]

33 TNA, E 122/230/16; E 122/133/23; E 122/215/29.

34 Dixon, 'Economy', p. 24.

35 See Kepler, *The Exchange*.

36 Dixon, 'Economy', pp. 359–75.

37 *Ibid.*, p. 24.

38 TNA, E 190/640/1; E 190/641/2; E 190/641/7; E 190/645/5; E 190/645/13; E 190/646/4; E 190/647/3; E 190/653/6. There were 563 voyages during Christmas 1621–22, but only 17,171 tons noted. If we add the 196 voyages missing tonnage, at the mean of 46.787 tons per ship, you arrive at a total of 26,341.25.

39 TNA, E 190/641/8; E 190/651/7. There were 145 coastal voyages in X1615–X16 but only 1,789 tons noted. If we add 61 voyages missing tonnage at the mean of 21.3 tons per ship, you get a total of 3,088.3.

Table 2.1 Overseas commercial activity, port of Dover, 1576–1622.

Year	Voyages			Tonnage		
	Export	Import	Total	Export	Import	Total
M1576–M77	143	158	301	2049	2867	4916
M1579–M80	149	134	283	2456	2220	4676
M1594–M95	181	103	284	3406	1393	4799
M1597–M98	139	46	185	2664	866	3530
M1598–M99	226	91	317	3446	1344	4790
X1604–X05	160	172	332	4592	3611	8203
X1615–X16	103	135	238	2773	3260	6033
X1621–X22	257	306	563	6953	10218	17171*

Source: TNA, E 190/640/1; E 190/641/2; E 190/641/7; E 190/645/5; E 190/645/13; E 190/646/4; E 190/647/3; E 190/653/6. NB. M = Michaelmas; X = Christmas.

* 196 voyages were missing tonnage. At an average of 46.8 tons per voyage a total of around 26,341.3 tons is realistic.

Table 2.2 Distribution of overseas connections, port of Dover, 1576–1622.

Year	Origins and destinations			
	No. of trading ports	Voyages per port	Voyages top five ports (per cent)	Tons per port
M1576–M77	8	37.6	99.0	614.5
M1579–M80	13	21.8	94.3	359.7
M1594–M95	27	10.5	62.0	177.7
M1597–M98	29	6.4	61.6	121.7
M1598–M99	21	15.1	78.2	228.1
X1604–X05	39	8.5	64.2	210.3
X1615–X16	36	6.6	68.9	167.6
X1621–X22	32	17.6	56.5	536.6*

Source: see Table 2.1.

* If above assumption for the 196 voyages missing tonnage is followed, the tons per port would reach 823.2 tons.

These figures account for the intensity but not the extent of trade. The expansion in Dover's coastal trade principally comprised more shipping to and from London (from six voyages in 1579–80 to 56 in 1615–16) and Newcastle or Sunderland (from 17 voyages in 1579–80 to 49 in 1615–16). These destinations alone accounted for 72.4 per cent of all the town's domestic commercial activity in 1615–16, so an evident intensification of trade. For overseas the picture is far more complex (see Table 2.2). In 1576–77, Dover traded with just eight overseas destinations, of which 63.1 per cent of voyages and 57.6 per cent of tonnage were with Calais alone. The only other significant port was Dunkirk, 28.9 per cent of voyages and 37.1 per cent of tonnage. Therefore, at that time, well over 90 per cent of Dover's overseas trade was with just two continental ports. In subsequent decades, there was a major, albeit erratic, diversification of Dover's overseas trade links. The town went from trading with fewer than ten ports in the mid-1570s, to 30–40 in the first decades of the seventeenth century. The distribution of voyages to these ports also broadened: before, 99 per cent of trade was with the top five ports but just 56 per cent after. Even while the overall number of voyages or tonnage remained flat in the 1580s and 1590s, such extensive growth increased economic output, which is calculated by multiplying shipping volume by the distance carried. By such a measure, Dover's port was already more productive by the end of the sixteenth century.

As well as fitting with a broader pattern of economic growth, this also embodied adaptation to sudden changes in local conditions generated by political and military events. There was a break in some longstanding trade links with the parts of the Low Countries under Spanish rule, principally Dunkirk – retaken from rebels in 1583 – whilst those with the new United Provinces matured – especially the ports of Zeeland – and grew elsewhere, like with Dieppe in Normandy. We must bear in mind that, as Pauline Croft explained, just as the Dutch continued to trade with the Spanish Empire during the Eighty Years' War, so too did English merchants sustain commercial connections with the enemy illicitly. Voyages left unrecorded in official records or trade via intermediaries and neutral ports were common and impossible to quantify.[40] Yet, in many respects, Spanish territory in the Low Countries was already an unattractive place to do business, even before the emergence of open conflict in 1585. The revolt had left the southern Netherlands devastated. It has been suggested that the population of almost everywhere in Flanders and Brabant declined to between half and a third of its former level between 1572 and 1609.[41] In May 1585, even before Antwerp's final fall to Hapsburg

40 Pauline Croft, 'Trading with the Enemy 1585–1604', *The Historical Journal*, 32:2 (1989), 281–302.

41 Geoffrey Parker, 'War and Economic Change: The Economic Costs of the Dutch Revolt', in J. M. Winter (ed.), *War and Economic Development: Essays in Memory of David Joslin* (Cambridge, 1975), pp. 49–72, at pp. 50–5.

forces that August, Thomas Robinson, a merchant from Sandwich, conveyed from Dunkirk to Sir Francis Walsingham that the 'sea townes are left so weke [...] by reason the men of warr have of late restrayned the trade hither'.[42]

So, some consequences of conflict were unavoidable, and by the end of the 1590s, even Dover's trade with Calais was displaced while the town was occupied by Spain for two years from April 1596 to May 1598. The primacy of this route briefly returned with peace in 1604 but then lost out again to Middelburg. By then, legal voyages to Portugal and Spain appear in the port books, to places such as Lisbon, San Sebastián, Santoña, Sanlúcar de Barrameda, Cadiz and Malaga. In short, this period saw some continuity – Calais, Dunkirk and Dieppe remained important into the seventeenth century – but also a great deal of adaptation and evolution, as Dover's trade expanded from its locality. The experience of Kent's other ports mirrored Dover's to some degree. The revenues of Sandwich's water-bailiff indicate that by the early seventeenth century the value of trade was at a low ebb but subsequently enjoyed a moderate peacetime recovery. The town's interests overseas, which included Calais, Nieuwpoort and Ostend before 1585, shifted decisively towards Vlissingen in successive decades. At the same time, its domestic links with London intensified.[43]

Other, smaller, ports followed suit. For Faversham, in the years 1576–1625, 65.4 per cent of overseas voyages were to or from Vlissingen alone. Including other ports of the Dutch Republic, like Middelburg, Brouwershaven, Enkhuizen, Rotterdam, Veere and Zierikzee, increases that figure to 74.8 per cent. Interestingly, Amsterdam is almost completely absent. Milton Regis and Rochester, likewise, had an overseas focus almost entirely on Vlissingen and stronger links around the coast with London. The exception to this trend was a brief period after the first Anglo-Spanish War ended with the 1604 Treaty of London. Peace brought a sudden brief surge of traffic towards Spain, Portugal and the Mediterranean.[44] There was a similarly noteworthy shift in the merchants involved. In 1575–84, the proportion of shipments carried by native or foreign merchants in Kent's trade had been roughly equal, but during the war, foreigners dropped to around a fifth, likely due to Spanish and Flemish merchants being unable to trade openly. This trend reversed by 1615–24, with foreigners, mainly the Dutch, comprising most merchants handling Kent's overseas trade.

42 TNA, SP 77/1, fol. 40.

43 TNA, E 122/133/25; E 101/522/13; E 101/526/9; E 101/526/16; E 101/526/36; E 101/527/4.

44 TNA, E 190/640/2; E 190/640/10; E 190/643/10; E 190/643/7; E 190/645/14; E 190/646/6; E 190/647/8; E 190/648/4; E 190/648/8; E 190/648/7; E 190/648/17; E 190/649/5; E 190/650/17; E 190/650/17; E 190/650/4; E 190/650/8; E 190/651/6; E 190/651/11; E 190/652/2; E 190/652/9; E 190/653/5; E 190/655/1.

A complicating factor is that ships did not always use regulated ports, either because they could not – due to the deterioration of harbours – or they did not need to. Indeed, the intricacy of coastal economies belies any simple explanation of trade as just a set of neatly interconnected entrepôts. Traders often found it convenient to operate in a creek or minor harbour. Passing vessels could load and unload cargo to and from smaller vessels at sea at places like the Dover Road, or the Downs. Indeed, for Dover, this was a rapidly growing preference. For the year Michaelmas 1594 to Michaelmas 1595, there were just 20 such merchant shipments, in 1598–99, 46. In the year Christmas 1604 to Christmas 1605, there were 44. Just over a decade later, in 1615–16, there were 148, and by 1621–22 there were 236 in one year. Where the cargo's ports of origin or destination are mentioned, the most common are Calais, Dieppe, Caen, or France more generally, and San Sebastián, Seville, Sanlúcar de Barrameda, Malaga, or Spain with the port unspecified.[45] Yet, goods were frequently transhipped at sea and never reached a port or creek. In March 1622, the royal council informed Lord Zouche, Warden of the Cinque Ports, that this was taking place to and from the Spanish Empire and Calais, Flanders, and the United Provinces, in 'the Downes, Gore-end, Dover Roade' and elsewhere. In May 1635, a similar concern was expressed by the Lords of the Admiralty. Their main worry was customs revenues, but it hints at trade beyond the view of historians.[46]

Nevertheless, in the first half of the seventeenth century, Dover's overseas traffic still swamped that of all other Kentish harbours. To Kepler, the main causes were 'its geographical position', alongside English neutrality in the Eighty Years' War after the Twelve Years Truce between the Spanish and Dutch ended in April 1621, as well as in the Thirty Years' War (1618–48). One might add that Dover had feasibly long acted as an informal information nexus. In 1580, the crew and passengers of one Spanish ship testified that while their destination was ultimately London or Zeeland, they planned to pause at the Dover Road to ascertain the prices in each.[47] All these factors favoured Dover as a hub between belligerents, principally the Spanish, Flemish and Dutch, without which, Kepler said, 'the great artery of sea trade between northern and southern Europe was in danger of being cut'.[48] Aside from the brief hiatus during the Anglo-Spanish War of 1625–30, trade grew continuously for two decades. The number of ships carrying re-exports went from 66 between Christmas 1621 and 1622, to 129 one decade later. Through the 1630s the number rose, to peak at 408 ships in 1637–38. Most ships involved were English. Usually between a third and a half were from Dover. Other

45 TNA, E 190/645/5; E 190/646/4; E 190/650/5; E 190/651/8; E 190/653/6.

46 TNA, SP 14/128, fol. 71; SP 16/264, fol. 130.

47 TNA, SP 94/1, fol. 46.

48 Kepler, *The Exchange*, pp. 11–35, quotations from pp. 12, 17, 21.

Kent ports were also involved, especially Sandwich vessels in the mid- to late 1630s.[49] The value of cargo transhipped, excluding wine and silver, was £44,749 in 1621–22, but £193,427 a decade later and rose through the 1630s to a peak of £598,451 in 1637–38.[50] The onward destinations were predominately in Spanish Hapsburg territories; 36.5 per cent of the cargo by value (again excluding wines and silver) went to Spain or Portugal, mainly Sanlúcar de Barrameda, and 20 per cent to Spanish Flanders, principally Dunkirk. Of the remainder, 15.5 per cent went to France, mainly Rouen, 10.5 per cent to Italy, principally Genoa, 5.6 per cent to Germany – almost always Hamburg – and, remarkably, just 5.4 per cent to the Dutch Republic, mostly Amsterdam.[51] Yet, much of the considerable and valuable wine cargoes, which peaked in 1637–38 with an estimated value of £135,552, ended up in Amsterdam.[52]

The Hugessen family were major participants, especially James Hugessen the elder, his brother Cornelius and his son James the younger. In the year from Christmas 1621 to Christmas 1622, these three merchants alone had 123 cargo shipments (68 import and 55 export). The two largest destinations for the goods they handled were – by far – Middelburg, at 21.8 per cent, and Sanlúcar de Barrameda, at 17.3 per cent, but other ports of note were Hamburg and San Sebastián, both at 8.2 per cent, Dunkirk, at 7.3 per cent, and Amsterdam, at 6.4 per cent. In keeping with the general trend, the Hugessens mainly contracted English ships (63.3 per cent of shipments), of which most were from Dover (40.4 per cent of the total) and London (18.4 per cent). Nonetheless, a significant minority of shippers were Dutch (17.5 per cent).[53] Such prodigious commerce would prove temporary, however, and the entrepôt declined precipitously in the 1640s with the onset of the Civil Wars (1642–51), and Peace of Westphalia (1648), which ended the boon of neutrality. Between 15 February 1643 and Christmas 1643, just 110 ships carried re-exported goods from Dover.[54]

In short, Kent's links with Europe were generally through adjacent ports, but some merchants and mariners were remarkably adaptable to local and regional conditions and could rapidly establish or dismantle networks with other, sometimes farther, destinations. They were, however, late to engage in much trade beyond the continent. On 10 January 1606, the 50-ton *Pericles* of London left Milton Regis bound for 'Nova Terra'. It was carrying grain for the merchant Edward Beale and company, probably to supply the fishing fleet

49 *Ibid.*, pp. 168–70 (Kepler's appendix F).

50 *Ibid.*, pp. 162–3 (his appendix C).

51 Percentages are the author's own calculations from *ibid.*, pp. 162–3 (his appendix C).

52 *Ibid.*, p. 164 (his appendix D).

53 TNA, E 190/653/6.

54 Kepler, *The Exchange*, pp. 168–70 (his appendix F).

off the Grand Banks of Newfoundland.[55] This was very much the exception that proved the rule.

Outbound and Inbound Goods

In his summary of Elizabethan trade, Willan asserted, with regard to Kent, that the exports of Sandwich were 'almost entirely', and, in the case of Dover, 'chiefly', cloth and beer, while Kent's imports were primarily 'cloth, woolen yarn, hops and wine from Calais and Dunkirk'.[56] This was certainly an oversimplification. There were some significant and growing complexities in exchange, especially from the turn of the seventeenth century. Kent's ports were part of a greater regional and transregional economy, and the commodities they traded reflected this. Yet certainly, the county, like England more broadly, manufactured and exported textiles. A great deal has been written on the waning of the 'old draperies', typically thick broadcloth, and the rise of the finer and more elaborate 'new draperies'.[57] Much of Kent's production of either would have been exported via London. As with much of the country, the influence of an increasingly centralised 'metropolitan market' was keenly felt in this respect, as Kerridge and Chalklin emphasised.[58] By the 1540s, exports of broadcloth from Sandwich were reduced to just 18 cloths in 1542–43 and 19 in 1543–44, compared with 71,268 and 119,441 cloths respectively from the capital.[59] This was largely because of the Merchant Adventurers' hold over the broadcloth trade into, for a time, Antwerp, then later Middelburg, and finally Hamburg. By 1605, Sandwich exported 18 times more new draperies than old draperies by value. In 1610, 1,970 double bays were shipped, by 1618, the equivalent of 4,495 left the port. The trend for Dover was markedly different, for as Stephens put it, the 'cloth trade of Dover follows a more erratic course than that of any of the other provincial ports' in England. Until the end of the 1620s, the town shipped slightly more old draperies than new, but thereafter this reversed. Both left in large quantities during the period of the Dover entrepôt, with peak years in 1626 and 1633.[60]

55 TNA, E 190/649/3, fol. 1r.

56 Willan, *Elizabethan Foreign Trade*, pp. 75–6.

57 For example, see D. C. Coleman, 'An Innovation and Its Diffusion: The "New Draperies"', *Economic History Review*, 2nd series, 22:3 (1969), 417–29.

58 Kerridge, *Trade and Banking*, pp. 5–32; Chalklin, *Seventeenth-Century Kent*, pp. 1–4, 161–88.

59 E. M. Carus-Wilson and O. Coleman, *England's Export Trade, 1275–1547* (Oxford, 1963), p. 119.

60 Figures calculated from W. B. Stephens, 'The Cloth Exports of the Provincial Ports, 1600–1640', *Economic History Review*, 2nd series, 22:2 (1969), 228–48, at p. 245 (his appendix A), quotation is from p. 240.

Alongside fardels and trusses of cloth, barrels of beer were undoubtedly an important export. The brewing industry had been growing apace since the late Middle Ages and Mavis Mate observed exports from Kent's ports doubled from the 1480s to the 1540s, although she noted this was probably dwarfed by the domestic trade. In the second half of the sixteenth and into the seventeenth century exports were impressive. Mate highlighted a report from 1590 that the 'twenty or more great brew-houses situated on the side of the Thames sent 39,700 barrels of beer to the Low Countries, Calais, Dieppe, and thereabouts'.[61] Sandwich alone exported just under 200 tuns per year on average, but 871 tuns in the year from Michaelmas 1576, and 758 tuns from Christmas to Christmas 1604–05.[62] Most of this was destined for Vlissingen and other ports of the Netherlands.

Beyond beer, successive scholars have stressed the role of Kent as a breadbasket. F. J. Fisher and later Stephen Hipkin described the county's role in supplying London in the sixteenth and seventeenth centuries.[63] Hipkin highlighted 'the anciently enclosed landscape of east Kent, a region farmed predominantly in severalty by tenants holding on short commercial leases, was home to a great many grain producers, large and small, who practised individualistic agricultural capitalism' and also the 'impressively organized, large-scale middlemen living in the north-east Kent ports'. The quantities involved could be staggering, and therefore generated resentment among consumers in the county. From the 1560s through to the 1580s, a time of rising food prices, Kent's ports were shipping between 15,000 and 30,000 quarters of cereals to the capital each year, along with a few thousand more to other domestic regions. Around the turn of the century, this trade gathered speed, and by the early 1630s, surpassed 60,000 quarters, worth at least £120,000 each year at prevailing prices.[64] For most of the sixteenth century, the greatest proportion was wheat, as grains or as meal, with some smaller quantities of barley, rye, oats and malted grain. However, from the late 1590s and into the first decades of the seventeenth century, most of the cereal products shipped were malt, principally for beer production in London.[65]

Prices across England and Wales, surveyed in 1563, indicate Kent's position in the market. Wheat traded in the county at 15s per quarter, below the 15.72s average. Barley was at 10s per quarter, also below the 11.77s average, rye at

61 Mate, *Trade*, pp. 60–80, especially pp. 67–9.

62 Calculated from Hipkin 'Kent Grain Trade', pp. 99–139, at p. 105.

63 F. J. Fisher, 'The Development of the London Food Market, 1540–1640', in E. M. Carus-Wilson (ed.), *Essays in Economic History*, vol. 1 (1954), pp. 135–51; Hipkin, 'Kent Grain Trade', 99–139.

64 Calculated by the author using prices in Gregory Clark, *English Prices and Wages, 1209–1914* (2003), https://gpih.ucdavis.edu/files/England_1209-1914_(Clark).xls.

65 Hipkin, 'Kent Grain Trade', 99–139, at pp. 107–8, 116, 124–31, 133.

12s, below the average of 13.28s. Yet, Kent's cereals were not the cheapest that year. Prices were the same in Essex and lower in Sussex, Suffolk, Norfolk, Lincolnshire and Yorkshire, where wheat was 13s 4d per quarter. Only in other more central and western counties was grain more expensive.[66] So, while other surplus-producing counties had lower prices, the role of Kent and Essex as the key suppliers to the capital raised their prices marginally. This allowed a profitable flow of grain into London from anywhere, via Kent and Essex's coastal trade systems.

Kent's overseas grain trade during this period was more enigmatic. It has been observed that, in the sixteenth century, grain prices rose consistently higher on the western European continent than in England.[67] However, it could only be shipped abroad legally when domestic market prices were below a fixed low ceiling. This had been the case since the Middle Ages and would largely continue until 1670.[68] One could often purchase a licence to export, but, as Evan Jones has explained, this could be costly and introduce risk.[69] Nevertheless, when permitted, the quantities exported were considerable. From Christmas 1604 to Christmas 1605 some 25,514 quarters went abroad legitimately: from Sandwich (27.3 per cent), Faversham (27.4 per cent) and Milton Regis (26 per cent), with some smaller contributions from Dover (11.1 per cent) and Rochester (8.3 per cent).[70] This was principally carried by larger ships from outside the county, often London, to destinations in southern Europe: Seville and Sanlúcar de Barrameda in Spain, Marseille in France, Genoa and Livorno in Italy, Larache and Agadir in Morocco and Zakynthos in Greece.[71] Meanwhile, Kent's ports were well placed to supply English and allied forces in Europe during the first Anglo-Spanish War, particularly those in Vlissingen, Brielle and Fort Rammekens, between 1585 and 1616. Indeed, in December 1588, the authorities in Vlissingen wrote directly to William Cecil, Lord Burghley, the Lord High Treasurer, to request one Robert Scott,

66 TNA, SP 12/28, fol. 66.

67 Evan T. Jones, 'Illicit Business: Accounting for Smuggling in Mid Sixteenth-Century Bristol', *Economic History Review*, 2nd series, 54:1 (2001), 17–38, at p. 34.

68 Hipkin 'Kent Grain Trade', 99–139, at pp. 102–6; for an overview of grain market regulation see Buchanan Sharp, *Famine and Scarcity in Late Medieval and Early Modern England: The Regulation of Grain Marketing, 1256–1631* (Cambridge, 2016); also R. B. Outhwaite, 'Dearth and Government Intervention in English Grain Markets, 1590–1700', *Economic History Review*, 2nd series, 34:3 (1981), 389–406.

69 Evan T. Jones, *Inside the Illicit Economy: Reconstructing the Smugglers' Trade of Sixteenth Century Bristol* (London, 2012, repr. 2016), pp. 27–32.

70 Hipkin 'Kent Grain Trade', 99–139, at pp. 103–4.

71 For examples of these southern European shipments around this time, see TNA, E 190/648/10, fol. 2r; E 190/648/9, fol. 3r; E 190/648/17, fols 1v, 2v; E 190/649/3, fol. 1v; E 190/649/5, fol. 2r.

a Sandwich-based merchant, be permitted to ship grain to sustain the townspeople and garrison.[72]

Beyond the legal trade, there is substantial evidence for smuggling. In 1576 William Cromer (*c.*1531–98) wrote to William Cecil to inform him that grain and other victuals were leaving Faversham, Sandwich and Dover for Vlissingen, Dunkirk and elsewhere.[73] There were similar reports of their arrival. In 1582 Thomas Stokes described to Walsingham from Flanders how wheat and malt would arrive every day from Sandwich.[74] This trade would continue after open war began in 1585; when, Pauline Croft highlighted, 'grain and other foodstuffs went from Dover, Sandwich and Margate to Dunkirk, Sluys, Dieppe and Calais, where they were sold to the enemies of the realm, both Spaniards and French Leaguers'. Indeed, one report from March 1588, for example, states that grain, beer and meat, shipped under licence, were diverted to Alexander Farnese, duke of Parma, the governor of the Spanish Netherlands. It was even claimed that illicit English food supplied the Spanish Armada later that year.[75]

Other strategic goods Kent exported included cannon. These were cast in the Weald from locally-produced iron and then transported, alongside the raw metal, down the Medway and past Rochester.[76] Whilst most of both went to London, some guns were exported under licence, mainly on foreign ships, by a mixture of native and alien merchants. Between November 1598 and August 1599, nine shipments of demi-culverins, sakers and minions left, with a weight of over 288 tons in iron. One was destined for Emden via Tilbury, but the rest went to Amsterdam. The merchant for most was Robert Sackville, son of the earl of Dorset, who held the patent for ordnance exports, and he engaged five Dutch ships from Amsterdam for the purpose.[77] In 1605, 117 demi-culverins and minions left Rochester, of which one shipment was for Friesland and all the others were for Copenhagen. The merchants were an Englishman, John Fearne, and Ludolph Englested, a non-native though based in London, utilising

72 TNA, SP 84/29, fol. 11.

73 TNA, SP 12/108, fol. 160; N. M. Fuidge, 'CROMER, William (c.1531–98), of Tunstall, nr. Sittingbourne, Kent', in P. W. Hasler (ed.) *The History of Parliament: The House of Commons 1558–1603* (Woodbridge, 1981).

74 TNA, SP 83/16, fol. 37.

75 TNA, SP 78/18, fol. 110; Croft, 'Trading with the Enemy', 281–302, at 292–3.

76 J. S. Hodgkinson, 'Ironworks in Late-16th Century Kent', *Bulletin of the Wealden Iron Research Group*, 2nd series, 24 (2004), 6–15. For details on Kent's role in ordnance manufacture, see also Ruth R. Brown, 'The Ordnance Records: Thomas Browne', *ibid.*, 16–25.

77 TNA, E 190/646/2, fols 1r–v; Michael A. R. Graves, 'Sackville, Robert, second earl of Dorset', *Oxford Dictionary of National Biography*, https://doi.org/10.1093/ref:odnb/24449 (accessed 14 March 2025).

again only foreign vessels: Dutch, Danish or from Gdańsk (Danzig).[78] In the years that followed, shipments continued to Amsterdam and Copenhagen but also significant numbers of larger culverins to Dordrecht and Emden, usually by the respective political authorities there.[79]

Another crucial export was lime, used in the production of mortar for construction, and in agriculture for the deacidification of the soil. A little was shipped from Margate, as in 1616, but almost all left from Dover.[80] With its plentiful chalk from the White Cliffs, lime production became vital to the local economy. As noted in 1674, it was 'the only support of the poor people thereabouts'.[81] In the 1570s, lime was shipped to Flanders, notably Dunkirk, Nieuwpoort and Bruges, and subsequently in the 1580s to Middelburg, Vlissingen, Emden and elsewhere, but this only then comprised a couple of hundred chaldrons (*c.*284 metric tonnes) each year. Then, from the 1590s, far larger quantities of lime were shipped, with no fewer than 2,640 chaldrons (3,696 metric tonnes) leaving Dover harbour in the year from Michaelmas 1594–95. Exports averaged well over 1,500 chaldrons (2,100 metric tonnes) per year in subsequent decades. Over half went to Middelburg and Vlissingen, mostly the former. Other noteworthy destinations included Zierikzee, Rotterdam, Veere, Goes, Dordrecht, Brielle, Schiedam, Emden, Arnemuiden, Brouwershaven and Amsterdam.[82] Almost all was handled by Dutch ships and merchants. On the rare occasions it was shipped by English ships it was traded by immigrant or immigrant-descended residents of Dover. Examples include James Hugessen the elder, who exported 30 chaldrons, valued at £5, to Middelburg on the 50-ton *Jonas* of Dover in February 1622.[83] Charles Brames shipped 60 chaldrons to Sluys in April 1605 on the 120-ton *Thomas* of Aldeburgh.[84]

While essential, lime was a bulky and cheap export. There were several other export goods of similarly low value deserving of brief mention. Fresh fruit was one, especially common apples and pippins, traded from smaller ports like Milton Regis and Faversham to destinations in Zeeland and Holland. Sometimes these could leave in large quantities on small ships, like the 200 bushels of apples taken by one Gideon Johnsone (Janssen), master of the

78 TNA, E 190/648/9, fols 2v, 3r, 4v.

79 TNA, E 190/649/16, fols 1r–v; E 190/651/3, fols 1v, 2r–v; E 190/651/9, fols 1v–2r.

80 TNA, E 190/651/13, fols 12r, 13r–v, 14r–v.

81 'Entry Book: May 1674', in William A Shaw (ed.), *Calendar of Treasury Books*, vol. 4, 1672–1675 (London, 1909), pp. 514–33. *British History Online*, http://www.british-history.ac.uk/cal-treasury-books/vol4/pp514-533 (accessed 10 December 2022).

82 TNA, E 190/641/2; E 190/643/8; E 190/645/5; E 190/645/13; E 190/646/4; E 190/650/5; E 190/651/8; E 190/653/6.

83 TNA, E 190/653/6, fol. 14r.

84 TNA, E 190/650/5, fol. 15v.

4/6-ton *Peeter* of Vlissingen in February 1604, or 200 bushels shipped to Rotterdam by William Newland aboard the 18-ton *Edward* of Sittingbourne that May.[85] Oysters, especially from Faversham, also passed by this route. These only appear in port books when pickled, like the 58 barrels shipped to Vlissingen by Henry Bess aboard the *Greihownde* of that town in February 1612.[86] The short crossing meant a far greater quantity could be shipped fresh and these appear in the records of the Zeeland toll. Between 1584 and 1592, Jacob Skellworth carried oysters on practically every voyage from Faversham to Vlissingen, alongside barrels of beer and pork products.[87]

Nonetheless, it should be emphasised that a far wider variety of goods were imported than exported. Inbound cloth tended to be high quality and diverse, which, Willan observed for the sixteenth century, 'must surely have been destined for the London market'.[88] In this sense, coastal trade also constituted part of Kent's overseas trade system via the metropole. Luxuries and manufactured goods from abroad would concurrently flow into the county via London. At the same time, England saw a rapid rise in the scale and variety of domestic manufacture that substituted imports: glass, starch, soap, paper or metal tools, for example.[89] Such products, from or via London, would make their way into Kent. Yet, some direct imports of manufactures persisted. In 1603, for instance, one Henry Bland imported 'one hundred & tenne dozen thousand of pins' from Vlissingen to Faversham aboard the *Susan* of Margate.[90] In 1608, John Young, the master of the *Gift of God* of Rainham, shipped eight cases of Normandy glass, worth £8, from Boulogne to Rochester.[91]

Certain luxuries were likewise imported directly, silks and spices among them. For instance, on 3 November 1576 – one day before the sack of Antwerp – the *Christ* of Sandwich arrived in the town from Vlissingen on which Peter More and Dominic Paraviro, the two foreign merchants, imported undyed silk and bone lace respectively, while William Topkins, a native trader, shipped in 80 lb of pepper.[92] In June 1610, John Duffeild, another native, imported 20 lb of black 'Naples silk' and 5 lb of black silk lace from Calais on the *Gift of God* of Sandwich.[93] A wide assortment of spices arrived, even into the more minor

85 TNA, E 190/648/3, fols 1v, 2r; for an example of apples and pippins from Faversham, see E 190/647/8, fol. 2r.

86 TNA, E 190/650/1, fol. 1r.

87 Zeeuwsarchief, GIDS103: *Tol van Zeeland*, 1584–1805, 505-4931, 505-4941, 505-5041, 505-5051, 505-5061, 505-5081, 505-5091 (Acquittals 1584–92).

88 Willan, *Elizabethan Foreign Trade*, p. 76.

89 Wrightson, *Earthly Necessities*, pp. 167–9.

90 TNA, E 190/648/4, fol. 1r.

91 TNA, E 190/649/6, fol. 2v.

92 TNA, E 190/640/4, fol. 10v.

93 TNA, E 190/649/11, fol. 5r.

ports, usually from Vlissingen on Dutch ships. For example, in October 1613, Thomas Johnson had 273 lb of cloves, and a comparatively large quantity of nutmeg, on the *Seahorse* of Vlissingen as it came into Faversham.[94] In June 1612, Thomas Highwood imported from Vlissingen into Rochester, 30 lb of mace alongside 1 cwt of São Tomé sugar aboard the *Fortune* of Vlissingen.[95] In 1605, Charles Hawkins shipped 350 lb of tobacco from Dieppe to Dover on the *Cygnet* (*Signot*) of Dieppe.[96]

Citrous fruits, particularly oranges, and dried fruits – raisins and figs from Iberia or currants from the eastern Mediterranean – were similarly imported via the Low Countries by native and foreign merchants. For example, in January 1595, Jan Verbeake imported 500 lb of figs and 4,000 oranges into Faversham from Vlissingen aboard the *Abraham* of Vlissingen. Meanwhile, that March, Denis Stunotte, a native, brought 1,600 lb figs and a barrel of lemons in the *Roger* of Queenborough by the same route.[97] However, these increasingly came straight from the source, such as the raisins shipped from Alicante to Sandwich in March 1616 aboard the *Concord* of Fowey, or those that arrived in Ramsgate from Malaga aboard the *Dove* of Topsham that November.[98] In Rochester in August 1602, John Beere even unloaded 10 cwt of currants off the *Anne Bonaventure* of London, which had come from Zakynthos (Zante) in Greece.[99]

The most abundant luxury import – certainly in terms of volume – was wine. The most common types were French, usually Gascon, and Spanish, often sherris sack from southern Iberia. Again, for much of the period, this tended to arrive in Kent's ports via intermediary ports, like Calais or Vlissingen. For example, in 1605, eight shipments of Gascon wine arrived in Faversham totalling 8.5 tuns (*c*.7,650 litres), all from Vlissingen, all but one shipped by the aforesaid Gideon Johnsone (Janssen).[100] There are some examples of direct imports. In March 1588, for instance, John Philpot of Faversham imported 100 tuns (*c*.90,000 litres) of Gascon wine from Bordeaux to his hometown aboard the *Toby* of Aldeburgh.[101] On 30 October and 2 November 1605, two Dover ships, the *Rose*, commanded by Francis Moren, and James Flinder's *Elizabeth Constance*, returned from Bordeaux. James Hugessen the younger, in one of his first commercial forays, imported 28 tuns (*c*.25,200 litres) of wine in the former, Samual Moore and company shipped 28 tuns from the

94 TNA, E 190/650/4, fol. 2v.
95 TNA, E 190/650/3, fol. 1v.
96 TNA, E 190/650/5, fol. 5r.
97 TNA, E 190/645/3, fol. 1r.
98 TNA, E 190/651/13, fols 2r, 8r.
99 TNA, E 190/647/9, fol. 1r.
100 TNA, E 190/648/10, fol. 3r.
101 TNA, E 190/643/10, fol. 1v.

latter.[102] In November 1616, James Hugessen the elder and his partners imported 91 pipes (45.5 tuns, *c*.40,950 litres) of Spanish wine to Dover from Malaga aboard the 45-ton *Welcome* of Dover.[103] Wine also constituted a significant proportion of the goods unloaded from ships at sea. From Christmas 1621 to Christmas 1622, 40 of 92 shipments of French and Spanish wine discharged in the Dover road (42.6 per cent), constituting 75.3 tuns (*c*.67,797 litres).[104]

There were circumstances when cereals were imported. In times of poor harvests and shortages, such as in the 1590s and 1630–31, Hipkin observed merchants continued to supply London from Kent despite efforts to prevent them.[105] Instead, localised dearth motivated merchants to import grain from northern Europe. For example, in September 1630, Daniel Skinner, a London merchant then based in Calais, recounted that he heard news of high prices in England and bought 200 quarters of wheat and maslin (mixed grain) in France 'at a high rate', purportedly £500, and shipped it to Dover. Having sold only a fraction, he alleged that prices collapsed such that he could not sell the remaining 1,500 bushels (187.5 quarters), without a loss, and requested he be allowed to sell it elsewhere.[106] On such occasions, cheap rye – usually originating in the Baltic – was most frequently brought in, a practice that had its roots in the Middle Ages and continued into the sixteenth century. For instance, in March 1546 – a year of very high wheat prices – one contract between an agent of Henry VIII and a group of burgesses of Gdańsk (Danzig) stipulated around 4,000 quarters of rye and wheat be shipped from the Baltic city, half to London and half to Dover.[107] This also persisted into the seventeenth century, but often with Dutch involvement. In August 1612, for example, Cornelis Verduce, merchant and master of the *Hope* of Vlissingen, brought 30 quarters of 'Dansk rye' into Rochester via his home port.[108] From Christmas 1621–22 no fewer than 13,368 quarters were imported through Dover, often in huge shipments.[109] The *Hope* of Hoorn arrived from Amsterdam in October 1622, on which Robert Mulabeck (Mulabeque), a foreign merchant, had 1,000 quarters of rye, valued at £200.[110] The Hugessens were especially involved. In 1622, James the elder, Cornelius and James the younger imported at least

[102] TNA, E 190/650/5, fol. 24r.

[103] TNA, E 190/651/8, fol. 8r.

[104] TNA, E 190/653/6, fols 5v, 11v, 12r–v.

[105] Hipkin 'Kent Grain Trade', 99–139.

[106] TNA, PC 2/40, fol. 121; SP 16/180, fol. 130.

[107] TNA, SP 1/215, fol. 7; also, for grain markets during the reign of Henry VIII, see Sharp, *Famine and Scarcity*, pp. 153–86.

[108] TNA, E 190/650/3, fol. 1v.

[109] Hipkin 'Kent Grain Trade', 99–139, at p. 104.

[110] TNA, E 190/653/6, fol. 9r.

3,670 quarters of rye, 750 of wheat and 180 of barley, valued officially at £1,212 15s. Theirs was a truly expansive network. The grain arrived in Dover from Middelburg, Vlissingen, Amsterdam, Schiedam, Hamburg, Bremen, Königsberg (now Kaliningrad), Gdańsk and St Malo in Dutch, French, Norwegian and Scottish vessels, as well as on English ships from London, Dover and Portsmouth.[111]

Such inbound grain most likely never equalled, let alone surpassed, the volume outbound. Yet, this was probably more than made up for – in calorie terms – by the quantity of cheese, butter and fish that arrived. In this respect, Kent exchanged carbohydrates for proteins and fats. Much of the cheese and butter arrived in the county via coastal trade with East Anglia, mainly Suffolk and Essex, usually from Maldon and Burnham-on-Crouch and in through the ports of Rochester and Faversham. This flow was remarkably stable. In 1598–99, at least 1,233 Suffolk weys (315,648 lb or 143,175.5 kg) of cheese arrived in Kent's ports. Fifteen years later, in 1613–14, 1,360 weys were shipped in (348,160 lb or 157,923 kg). In 1633–34, 4,143 firkins of butter arrived, and in 1662–63, there were 3,353.[112] Kent also imported a considerable amount. Some was Flemish, like the 20 cwt William Michell, a native merchant, imported in the *William* of Sandwich from Dunkirk to Sandwich in October 1616, or the 90 cwt that was brought from Ostend to Margate by Joas Steevens, master of the *Hope* of Ostend the same month. Other times French cheese might arrive, like the 20 cwt that Alexander Lambe imported to Faversham from Calais in February 1613, aboard the *Violet* of that town.[113] Yet primarily this was Holland cheese, shipped via the ports of Zeeland. Indeed, in 1590–91, 3,500 lb arrived at Faversham, mostly from Vlissingen.[114] Sometimes this would arrive via Flanders. For example, in August 1610, Thomas Nearing, master of the *Shallop* of Nieuwpoort, imported 20 cwt of Holland cheese from Nieuwpoort to Margate.[115] One noteworthy aspect of the cheese trade is the degree to which foreign merchants involved themselves in transhipping their wares via domestic coastal shipping. To illustrate, in October 1603, one Cornelis Walshe had 8 cwt of Holland cheese aboard the *Hinde* of Faversham when it sailed from there to London, and in September 1612 Cornelis Verduce had 8 cwt on the *Cross* of Rochester, also going to London from its home

[111] *Ibid.*, fols 3v, 4v, 5r, 6r–v, 9r–10r.

[112] Calculated by the author from figures in Paul Wilkinson, *The Historical Development of the Port of Faversham 1580–1780*, British Archaeological Reports British Series 413 (2006), p. 122.

[113] TNA, E 190/651/13, fol. 7r.

[114] TNA, E 190/643/19, fols 1r–v.

[115] TNA, E 190/649/11, fol. 7r.

port.[116] Alongside the latter merchant's cargo of cheese was a shipment of 40 barrels of onions. These and other vegetables were common features in cargoes from Flanders, Zeeland and Holland. In December 1606, for example, Adrian Clayson (Adriaan Claassen), master of the *Ice Fowle* of Rotterdam, transported from that city to Faversham no fewer than 24 barrels of onions and 400 cabbages together with one cwt of Holland cheese.[117] Meanwhile, in December 1616, Cornelis Huybertson (Huybertzoon), master of the *Lion* of Ostend, shipped 2,000 bunches of onions and ten barrels of carrots from there to Milton Regis.[118]

Hops had long been brought in from the Low Countries for Kent's brewing industry. Mate observed how 'between the 1480s and the 1520s, the amount [...] increased sixfold – from 5,600 lb imported in 1486/7 to 35,700 lb imported in 1519/20'.[119] Hops began to be grown domestically, with plentiful English hops recorded as shipped from Kent to London by the 1590s.[120] In 1580, there was one outward shipment of hops from Faversham, by 1650 just over one hundred were leaving each year.[121] Yet, imports continued, and there were some impressive single shipments. For example, the Flemish merchant Symon Sysson had 25 cwt, valued at £25, on the *Degest* of Dunkirk, coming from there to Margate in November 1610.[122]

Fish were caught by native fishermen in nearby or distant fishing grounds but were also imported. In the year from Michaelmas 1590 to 1591, some 1,450 ling, 1,975 cod, 775 coalfish (pollock), 200 Newland fish, as well as 17 barrels of cod or cod heads and five barrels of white herring, were shipped into Faversham alone. All came from Zeeland and were mostly carried by Dutch vessels and traders, especially Jacob Skellworth.[123] Sometimes single shipments could be substantial. In July 1598, for example, the *Cocke* of Veere arrived from its home port into Faversham and the master, Jan Mounse, himself a native of Veere, imported 400 ling and 600 cod, worth £25, whilst a London fishmonger, Richard Harris, brought in 600 ling, 1,000 cod and 700 coalfish, with a total value of £46.[124] A commodity commensurate with fish was salt. Usually 'bay salt', made through evaporation, it was an important preservative. Handled by both native and foreign merchants, the most common

116 TNA, E 190/648/1, fol. 1r; E 190/650/2, fol. 5v.

117 TNA, E 190/649/5, fol. 4r.

118 TNA, E 190/651/15, fol. 3r.

119 Mate, *Trade*, p. 70.

120 For example, George Spier shipped 40 cwt of 'Englyshe hoppes' from Faversham to London in October 1598: TNA, E 190/646/10, fol. 1r.

121 Wilkinson, *Faversham*, p. 84.

122 TNA, E 190/649/11, fol. 8r.

123 TNA, E 190/643/19, fols 1r–v.

124 TNA, E 190/646/6, fol. 1r.

origin was the Bay of Biscay, from where it was either shipped direct or via intermediaries from La Rochelle and the ports of Brittany and, increasingly in the seventeenth century, from Santoña in northern Spain, and Sanlúcar de Barrameda in the south.[125]

Kent supplied locally-sourced firewood, charcoal, timber and stone to London through much of the sixteenth century, but, like most of England, coal was increasingly shipped in.[126] Coastal shipments from Newcastle and Sunderland to Dover rose from 500 tons per year in the 1580s to around 1,500 tons in the first decades of the seventeenth century.[127] Whilst some of this may have been used as domestic fuel, it is probable much powered industrial production around the town: mainly brewing and lime-making. This was a trend largely followed by other ports. Sandwich had already surpassed 1,500 tons by 1598–99, and by 1633–34 was nearing 5,000 tons. If all the county's main ports were taken as a whole, the quantity of coal that arrived rose 158 per cent to over 10,000 tons between these two dates.[128] The addition of hydrocarbons may have contributed energy inputs into local industrial production that could then enter maritime trade. However, there was no domestic substitute for all woodland products. Timber, sourced from Norway or the Baltic, was shipped into Kent via Zeeland, principally Vlissingen and Middelburg. Balks and deals were most common, alongside ship timber, planks and barrel boards, even masts and oars. Along with these arrived naval stores, such as pitch and tar. A considerable proportion arrived at Rochester, near the growing royal dockyards at Chatham. Indeed, one order of imported shipbuilding material for the dockyards, in October 1590, included no fewer than 173 Norway masts of between 6 and 14 hands in width, along with some spars, capraves and deals.[129] Even when, into the seventeenth century, these products arrived directly they still tended to be handled by Dutch or Norwegian shipping.[130] Besides timber products, considerable quantities of building materials were also imported. For example, along with many deals and spars, the *Cocke* of Middelburg

[125] For examples of such French and Spanish salt imports, see TNA, E 190/646/4, fols 1v, 9v; E 190/653/6, fols 1r–10r.

[126] Mate, *Trade*, pp. 48–50; for an overview of the growth in the use of coal, see John Hatcher, *The History of the British Coal Industry: Volume 1: Before 1700: Towards the Age of Coal* (Oxford, 1993).

[127] TNA, E 190/642/14; E 190/643/2; E 190/644/14; E 190/645/6; E 190/646/3; E 190/649/8; E 190/649/19; E 190/651/7.

[128] Totals include Rochester, Milton, Faversham, Sandwich and Dover. Calculated by the author from Chalklin, *Seventeenth-Century Kent*, p. 180.

[129] TNA, SP 12/233, fol. 144.

[130] TNA, E 190/647/9, fol. 1r; E 190/648/9, fol. 3v; E 190/649/11, fols 3v, 4v, 6r 8r; E 190/649/6, fol. 2r; E 190/650/3, fol. 2r; E 190/651/13, fols 3r, 4r, 5v, 13r; E 190/651/3, fols 1v, 2r; E 190/651/6, fol. 1v; E 190/652/11, fol. 1v; E 190/652/12, fol. 1v; E 190/652/2, fol. 1v; E 190/652/9, fol. 2v; E 190/653/6, fols 7r, 9r, 10r; E 190/655/1, fol. 1r.

arrived from that town into Sandwich in July 1610 with 12,000 bricks and 2,000 pan tiles.[131]

The products re-exported from Dover during its entrepôt period reflected contemporary trade patterns more broadly. In the year from Christmas 1632, almost 20 per cent involved new draperies and 16.3 per cent Flemish linen. The largest proportion, 33.9 per cent, valued at £65,504, constituted what Kepler referred to as colonial produce: 'Spanish and Brazilian tobacco and unidentified sugars, probably Portuguese, accounted for most of this. Others include pepper, cloves, cinnamon, indigo, cochineal' as well as 'West India hides, West India ginger and logwood'. At its height, in 1637–38, Dover still handled £87,526 worth of such colonial wares, but these now comprised just 12.1 per cent of re-exports, surpassed by £186,761 (25.9 per cent) of new draperies and £123,648 worth of French wine (17.1 per cent). Even as the entrepôt began to decline in the 1640s, the new draperies remained central, which, at £59,890, constituted 28.8 per cent of a much-diminished exchange.[132]

While customs duties on these goods generated income for the Crown that peaked at £22,550 in 1637–38, as Kepler highlighted, the transmission of precious metals from the Spanish Empire, gold and especially silver, was also of political interest.[133] Rules required incoming coin and bullion be delivered to the royal mint to be coined, but there was considerable evasion.[134] In 1625, James Hugessen the younger confessed to having received Spanish cash and bars in Dover, which he sent on by wagon to merchants in London. One shipment alone comprised six chests, containing 120,000 Spanish silver reales (worth £3,000), and there were multiple further incoming shipments due on three ships from London, Hamburg and Leith, in Scotland. Hugessen had kept five bars of silver worth £500, presumably his fee. Another merchant of Dover, one 'Mr Burley', likely Michael, was also implicated.[135]

Finally, increasingly common items of trade during this period were books. In the sixteenth century, these principally arrived via coastal trade from London, such as the two hampers of books that arrived in Faversham among the goods of William Pennyngton, a London grocer, aboard the *Marie Anvild* of London in May 1580.[136] Yet, increasingly books arrived directly from the continent, usually unbound. For instance, in August 1613 the master of the *Hopewell* of Rochester, Edmund Holmwood, imported a vat of unbound books into Rochester from Middelburg.[137] This legitimate business sat alongside a

131 TNA, E 190/649/11, fol. 6r.
132 Kepler, *The Exchange*, p. 106.
133 *Ibid.*, p. 167 (Kepler's appendix E).
134 *Ibid.*, pp. 28–9.
135 TNA, SP 16/3, fols 125–6.
136 TNA, E 190/646/10, fol. 4r.
137 TNA, E 190/650/6, fol. 2r.

thriving illicit trade in material that encouraged Catholic recusants. One case is particularly revealing. In May 1598, Martin Audins was hired in Dover by William Gelke, an Englishman with connections in Kent but who lived in Calais, for £40 per annum for an unspecified job across the Channel, well above the prevailing skilled and unskilled yearly wage in Dover, which then stood at an estimated £12 19s and £10 16s per annum respectively.[138] When Audins arrived in Calais, he found it entailed taking 'sartaine bookes' back to England and circulating them. Then, on a return visit to Flanders that July, Audins was introduced into the network of Jesuits in Calais, Gravelines and Dunkirk.[139] This same trade was still flourishing into the next century. In November 1616, John Prettyman, a Dover customs official, handed 84 books seized as contraband over to the mayor, Thomas Foord, which were subsequently itemised. The resultant list reveals multiple copies of thirteen different pro-Catholic texts, many written by prominent Jesuits.[140]

Migration along Trade Routes

Ideas also travelled with people, whether merchants and mariners or others. Indeed, strong commercial connections encouraged an increased flow of people. This was heightened by the Wars of Religion, which triggered waves of Protestant refugees who constituted an injection of skills into the workforce of Kent's ports. In 1571, there were almost 300 Flemish men, women, and children living in Dover. Many were skilled in each stage of cloth production: wool combers, spinsters, twiners, weavers, and fullers. There were also tailors, cobblers, bakers, ropemakers, even three schoolmasters.[141] A similar 1622 survey recorded 148 strangers or children of strangers, with a similarly rich spread of occupations.[142] Much has been written about the stranger community in Sandwich, its role in the textile industry, as well as the local resentment generated.[143] Backhouse calculated that the native population remained fairly

[138] Calculated by the author from Jan Luiten van Zanden, 'Wages and the cost of living in Southern England (London) 1450–1700', https://hdl.handle.net/10622/VY7UY3, IISH Data Collection (accessed 14 March 2025), V2; annualised based on the estimated days worked, as per Stephen Broadberry, Bruce M. S. Campbell, Alexander Klein, Mark Overton and Bas van Leeuwen, *British Economic Growth, 1270–1870* (Cambridge, 2015), p. 264.

[139] TNA, SP 12/273, fol. 52.

[140] TNA, SP 14/89, fols 29–30.

[141] TNA, SP 12/78, fols 61–3.

[142] TNA, SP 14/131, fols 143–5.

[143] See, for example, Marcel F. Backhouse, 'The Strangers at Work in Sandwich: Native Envy of an Industrious Minority 1561–1603', *Immigrants & Minorities*, 10:3 (1991), 70–99.

stable from the 1560s to 1580s, while the Flemish and Walloon populations fluctuated rapidly. They made up about 35 per cent of the population in the 1560s, before rising to become the majority in the 1570s before declining in the 1580s. For this was not a one-way flow, there was also a great deal of migration out of Kent. In fact, after 1585, more than 300 Flemish strangers left Sandwich for the United Provinces.[144] There was internal outward migration also, with a constant pull towards London and elsewhere.[145] This and outward, overseas, migration make the resident or semi-resident foreign-born or descended population of Kent impossible to calculate precisely.[146] Moreover, even though the Crown tried to regulate travel via Commissioners of Passage, much migration was illicit and unrecorded. In 1616–17, many shipmasters and shipowners in Faversham contracted bonds not to covertly carry or lodge strangers.[147]

One later list of migrants that arrived in Dover from mid-July 1635 to the end of September does suggest the routes they took: 93 men, women and children of 121 (76.9 per cent) left the continent through Calais, the remainder, 15 (12.4 per cent) from Dunkirk, 7 (5.8 per cent) from Boulogne and 6 (5 per cent) from Ostend. These correspond with Dover's nearest and longest established European trading partners. Of the same sample, 72 (59.5 per cent) planned to live in Canterbury, 29 (24 per cent) in Yorkshire and 20 (16.5 per cent) in London.[148] Migrants also remained, and many worked directly in commerce. Nine resident Flemish merchants lived in Dover in 1571. In 1622, 13 individuals were specifically named as merchants of some kind and 15 as mariners. The former included the Hugessens: James Hugessen the elder and Cornelius, from Dunkirk, who had been resident for at least 24 years, and the former's sons, James the younger, Peter and Abraham. The latter included Cornelius and Joseph Looper, who became successful and wealthy shipmasters.[149] Generation after generation were absorbed into the local population. In 1636, a further report on strangers in the town reveals 61 individuals were involved in trade. Of these merchants, factors, shipmasters, pilots and sailors, all apart from 21, who were described as bachelors and sojourners, would likely have had

144 Marcel F. Backhouse, 'The Flemish and Walloon Communities at Sandwich during the Reign of Elizabeth I (1561–1603)' (unpublished Ph.D. thesis, University of Southampton, 1991), I, pp. 57–9, 287, III, p. 30.

145 Lien Bich Luu, *Immigrants and the Industries of London, 1500–1700* (London, 2005).

146 Elizabeth Edwards, 'Interpretations of the Influence of the Immigrant Population in Kent in the Sixteenth and Seventeenth Centuries', *Archaeologia Cantiana*, 122 (2002), 281–6.

147 TNA, SP 14/93, fols 54–5, 72–4, 96–7, 101–3; SP 14/94, fol. 1.

148 TNA, SP 16/298, fol. 177.

149 Dixon, 'Economy', p. 257.

their own households, so the population would have numbered perhaps 200. The preponderance of Catholics (82 per cent) in this group reflects Dover's commercial connections with Spanish Hapsburg lands during the entrepôt period. Their length of residence also reveals much about migration patterns. Merchants had been in Dover for an average of 10.9 months, though this rose to 12.1 months if they held property in the town. By comparison, mariners as a group had been based there for just 7.4 months on average, and this fell to 4.7 months for pilots and sailors.[150] This suggests a relatively continuous turnover, especially of foreign mariner labour. Also, given each port's core group of merchants or merchant-mariners could number perhaps only one hundred or so, even a small group of migrants could contribute significantly to the county's economy.

Capital Accumulation

Trade, like all forms of economic activity, required the input of factors of production, of land, labour or capital, in various combinations and proportions. Kent's ports dramatically increased their aggregated fixed capital stock during the period under discussion. First, there was investment in the port facilities and the distributive infrastructure. In 1555 in Faversham, for example, a wharf that belonged to the town was repaired for £9 13s 10d. In 1581, two wharves and the surrounding property, including two storerooms and a capstan and crane, were bought for £124, and repairing a wharf to support a crane cost more than £40.[151] The building and maintenance of whole harbours required a vast outlay of resources which explains the Crown's role in the development of Dover harbour across the period – which varied in ambition and success.[152] Upwards of £51,045 was expended on the harbour between July 1535 and June 1551, for work that was ultimately unsuccessful, as the haven continued to fill with shingle.[153] A more fruitful attempt was made in the 1580s and 1590s, for which enormous quantities of labour and materials were needed. The grant of a licence to Dover to export grain, intended to raise £3,000, was deemed insufficient, and in 1581 a special tonnage duty was imposed on all ships greater than 20 tons in burden passing through English ports.[154] This tax, originally planned for just seven years – but frequently renewed – provided a sustained stream of outside capital. In the first half of the 1580s,

150 TNA, SP 16/314, fols 15–20.

151 Wilkinson, *Faversham*, p. 11.

152 For overviews of the development of Dover harbour in this period, see Dixon, 'Economy', pp. 3–21; and H. M. Colvin (ed.), *The History of the King's Works*, vol. iv (London, 1982), pp. 729–64; also, see Margetts et al., 'Dover Harbour', 1–22.

153 Dixon, 'Economy', pp. 8–9; Colvin, *King's Works*, p. 736.

154 Dixon, 'Economy', pp. 10–13.

an average of £1,166 11s 10d per year in revenues was transferred from the exchequer for the Dover works.[155]

The benefits of these investments compounded over time. Dixon credited them with enabling Dover to exploit England's neutrality and become an important entrepôt in the second decade of the seventeenth century.[156] They also drew in spillover investment of private capital into Dover's mercantile assets, particularly its ships and sailors, but also its on-shore facilities. Dixon herself analysed the striking rise in the purchase, by merchants and mariners, of leases of plots beside the new harbour developments, on which they constructed sizeable buildings and light industrial equipment, such as herring hangers. There is evidence that the value of these leases inflated considerably into the seventeenth century, justifying such investment. For example, the wealthy merchant Charles Brames developed buildings on a plot he leased for just 30s per annum that were worth £300 in 1611, a rent of just 0.5 per cent, which implied the value had grown considerably. Similarly, in the decade from 1626, two houses of a mariner, Henry Stone, increased in value from £20 to £30. He paid 14s per annum for the lease so its relative cost fell from 3.5 to 2.3 per cent.[157]

As Jane Andrewes pointed out, 'by the second half of the seventeenth century, Kent's shipping tonnage had increased in size commensurate with increasing trade', yet this change was not consistent across all locations.[158] Ship surveys, undertaken by central government in an often-haphazard fashion, offer a vital if imperfect view of this. The two main ports with commercial connections overseas, Dover and Sandwich, gained the most. Between the 1560s and 1570s Dover had probably between 500 and 700 tons of shipping, and this rose to around 1,000 tons by the 1590s, surpassing 3,000 tons in the 1620s. Over the same periods, Sandwich went from below 700 tons, to over 1,000 towards the end of the sixteenth century and reached closer to 3,000 tons three decades later. Other, smaller, harbours would likewise see impressive rises in their stock of shipping. Ramsgate and Margate, for example, went from just over 100 tons in the 1560s to perhaps nearly 500 tons in the mid-1620s. Some, meanwhile, experienced a stagnation, like Faversham, which remained at between 300 and 400 tons through most of the period, and Milton Regis, at 200–300. Others declined, like Hythe, whose fleet shrank from over 500 tons in the mid-sixteenth century to between 65 and 150 in the early to mid-seventeenth.[159] This account excludes capital invested in non-local ships whether

155 TNA, SP 12/178, fol. 59; this was the average paid 26 March 1581–19 April 1584.

156 Dixon, 'Economy', pp. 13–14.

157 *Ibid.*, pp. 265–9.

158 Andrewes, 'Trade and Industry', pp. 235–52, at pp. 236–7.

159 Gibson, '1566 Survey', 341–53; KHLC, FA/CPM/24; FA/CPM/33; TNA, SP 15/22; SP 12/156, fols 88–90, 135; SP 12/198, fols 14, 18, 50, 53–4, 120; SP 12/204,

from London or, most critically, foreign. While some of the latter were simply visitors, foreign shipmasters would also reside in Kent's ports. By 1636, there were 12 ships with foreign masters based in Dover, eight were Catholic, mainly Flemish, and four Protestant, likely Dutch. Theirs were large vessels, averaging 156.7 tons, and all together added a further 1,880 tons of shipping in total.[160]

Such seemingly straightforward narratives belie the great complexity of the structural changes taking place. First, in many places, the mean size of the units of transportation, the vessels themselves, was shifting. There certainly remained some force to the late medieval trend towards modestly-sized craft, memorably described by Scammell as the 'ascendancy of the small ship'.[161] For the merchants of Kent, operating principally on coastal or short-to-medium cross-Channel trade routes, Scammell's noted efficiencies still held true, that ships below 100 tons that were 'comparatively cheap, easy to lade and man, quickly turned round, and usually able to reach even the most awkward ports and coasts, had obvious merits in an age of exploration and commercial expansion'.[162] However, even within these bounds, they were beginning to grow. The mean size of a Dover ship was probably 25–35 tons for most of the sixteenth century, but approximately 40 tons in the 1620s. Moreover, as Chapter 3 demonstrates, in Dover there was also a significant expansion in the number of ships 100 tons and over. Likewise, Sandwich, despite any practical problems with its haven, saw its vessels grow from below 20 tons, on average, in the 1560s and 1570s, to over 80 tons in 1622–26.[163] Dixon calculated the average value of a vessel in Dover probate inventories and showed how this changed from 'just over £6 between 1580–89, to over £9 in 1590–99, £25 in 1600–09, £43 in 1610–19, £126 in 1620–29 and £288 in 1630–39'. Such growth was practically exponential and far in excess of inflation.[164]

Larger vessels naturally tend towards labour efficiency because of economies of scale. Sure enough, despite short-term fluctuations, the number of mariners remained largely flat. Capital-labour ratios (conventionally represented as a number of tons per man) rose, indicating capital deepening, an increase in capital intensity and labour productivity. For Dover and Sandwich, the main overseas ports, this went from 5.26:1 and 4.97:1 respectively in 1566 to 11.53:1

fols 38–49; SP 16/34, fols 179–83; SP 16/39, fols 56–8, 60–1; SP 16/155, fols 82r–123v; Dixon, 'Economy', pp. 609–13 (her appendix A).

160 TNA, SP 16/314, fol. 18.

161 G. V. Scammell, 'English Merchant Shipping at the End of the Middle Ages: Some East Coast Evidence', *Economic History Review*, 2nd series, 13:3 (1961), 327–41, quotation at p. 333.

162 *Ibid.*, 327–41, at p. 334.

163 See Chapter 3, this volume, for a more comprehensive discussion of Kent's merchant fleets and ship sizes.

164 Dixon, 'Economy', p. 254.

and 21.59:1 in 1628–29. Such gains were not seen everywhere; for smaller ports the figures are largely stagnant. From 1566 to 1628–29, capital-labour ratios in harbours dominated by in-shore fishing, like Hythe and Lydd, remained very low, at about 2–3:1 or close to 1:1 respectively. Faversham's made some gains from 5.50:1 in 1566 but fell back to 4.85:1 by 1628–29. Milton Regis' ratio declined from 8.25:1 to 3.15:1. Such variations notwithstanding, Kent's aggregate capital-labour ratio in the maritime sector overall rose from 2.6:1 back in the fourteenth century to 3.27:1 in 1566 and from there increased steadily to 5.97:1 in 1628–29.

Because some of these changes can be explained by shifts in capital investment in ship sizes, they do not quite explain labour efficiency: the ratio of output produced to the labour input. Any marginal increase in this would come from other gains: from technological advances, such as in ship design or navigation equipment; or from a rise in the technical competence of the crew, their skills and knowledge, in short, their human capital. An inexhaustive list of this would include sailing and navigational skills, knowledge of sea routes and coastal topography, of the winds and tides, their experience in managing voyages. If one calculates the changing skill wage premium for Dover (see Table 2.3), taken as the pay for carpenters relative to that of unskilled labourers, one finds long periods after 1560 where the town had far lower ratios than nearby Canterbury, inland towns like Oxford or Cambridge, and even London. In 1600–09, the ratio was 1:1. These metrics suggest a highly skilled workforce and shortage of unskilled labour at precisely the time Dover's overseas trade expanded.

Imperfect measures of a key element of human capital, literacy, suggest the level was comparatively high among the population of Dover, especially those involved in maritime trade. On a certificate dated 1618 sent to Lord Zouche by twelve masters of Dover vessels, seven (James Cook, Nicholas Pett, John Mace, Jeffery Baceter, Christopher Bulger, Joseph Kitch and Gylles Parke) signed their names while five (James Harman, John Danyell, John Stanton, James Clarke and James Flinder) did not, which implies a crude literacy rate of 58.3 per cent.[165] Fortuitously, a petition survives from 1635 from the mayor, jurats and a subset of the Dover's population that includes signatures and marks. Because its subject was the petitioners' opposition to the imposition of a boom and tax in the town's harbour – on the basis that it would discourage shipping – it is appropriate to consider the list as somewhat representative of Dover's maritime community, with many prominent merchants and mariners. Of 256 petitioners, all men, just 64 made their mark rather than sign, which suggests a rough literacy rate of 75 per cent.[166] This compares very favourably

[165] TNA, SP 14/99, fol. 40.
[166] TNA, SP 16/288, fol. 126.

Table 2.3 Average wage skill premium (ratios of carpenter/labourer day wages) by decade across five urban areas, 1490–1649.

Decade	Dover	Canterbury	Oxford	Cambridge	London	Average
1490–99	1.50	1.55	1.50	2.40	1.60	1.65
1500–09	1.50	1.55	1.50	1.50	1.60	1.53
1510–19	1.37	1.48	1.50	1.50	1.60	1.49
1520–29	1.33	1.50	1.50	1.48	1.60	1.48
1530–39	1.47	1.65	1.63	1.58	1.60	1.57
1540–49	1.33	1.56	1.44	1.78	1.57	1.51
1550–59	1.51	1.33	1.59	1.74	1.49	1.50
1560–69	1.25	1.44	1.23	1.30	1.39	1.31
1570–79	1.35	1.55	1.50	1.47	1.49	1.47
1580–89	1.38	1.54	1.50	1.47	1.59	1.49
1590–99	1.20	1.63	1.50	1.50	1.47	1.45
1600–09	1.00	1.44	1.50	1.53	1.55	1.38
1610–19	1.60	1.59	1.44	1.44	1.70	1.56
1620–29	1.67	1.57	1.44	1.75	1.72	1.63
1630–39	1.67	1.47	1.50	1.85	1.65	1.63
1640–49	1.87	1.37	1.47	1.74	1.67	1.60

Source: Calculated by the author from Jan Luiten van Zanden, 'Wages and the cost of living in Southern England (London) 1450–1700', stored in Bram van den Hout, 'Historical Prices and Wages Dataset' (2023), https://hdl.handle.net/10622/VY7UY3, IISH Data Collection, V2.

with the average of 30 per cent (70 per cent illiteracy) that David Cressy calculated for men across England in 1641–44.[167]

Geoffrey Scammell asserted that capital 'flowed into the [shipping] industry from all directions – from land, trade, the professions, from home and abroad'.[168] Yet there is some question as to the source of the private capital invested in Kent's ports and maritime trade. Capital is just unconsumed output, productively applied. As such, it can come from a variety of places, surplus wages or profits not expended on consumption or taxed. Dixon noted that, in Dover, consumption of luxury goods was extremely limited throughout the

167 David Cressy, *Literacy and the Social Order: Reading and Writing in Tudor and Stuart England* (Cambridge, 1980), p. 176.

168 G. V. Scammell, 'Shipowning in the Economy and Politics of Early Modern England', *The Historical Journal*, 15:3 (1972), 385–407, at p. 390.

period, and confined to 'a very small elite', which may have been significant for investment.[169] It is unclear if the tax privileges of the Cinque Ports, enjoyed by the likes of Sandwich and Dover, had any positive impact in this respect. That these were gradually eroded across the period, and did not cover customs charges, suggests possibly not.[170] Most mercantile capital is conventionally thought to have been accumulated through inheritance within kinship groups and the gradual reinvestment of retained surplus profits of merchants.[171] The rise of formal companies was slow to impact provincial ports in Kent, so more established forms of partnerships remained necessary to pool capital more rapidly. One example, from February 1625, demonstrates the risks of a 'commenda'-style contract. John Berry and Thomas Fulnetby had made an agreement with Jacob Brames of Dover, whereby the latter was 'merchant and cheife adventurer' and they were 'adventurers with him', i.e. investors 'for a voyage made in shipp from Dovor'. Yet, Brames refused to disclose his account books that might show 'the profitts of the voyage by the shipps retorne'.[172]

Liquid capital might increasingly be raised through debt. This was only practical if the rate of return on capital was higher than the cost of capital, the latter fixed by a legal usury rate, which was permitted at 10 per cent interest during 1545–52 and 1571–1624, at which point it was lowered to 8 per cent.[173] Using debt pleas recorded in the Dover Hundred Court, Dixon noted that 'credit relationships were mostly made within the town itself', but that the wealthy 'were likely to extend such relationships throughout a region that included the nearest coastal towns and their hinterland, and that could extend to Canterbury and London and to certain Continental ports'. Most foreign lenders came from the nearest ports – specifically Boulogne, Calais, Dieppe and Vlissingen – though later there are several Flemish and Spanish litigants, probably factors living in the town during the entrepôt period.[174]

There is, in fact, one noteworthy source which can allow us to understand contemporary financial practices and how they were changing. The 'Sandwich

169 Dixon, 'Economy', pp. 320–36.

170 Brindle, 'Cinque Ports', pp. 354, 389. A negative correlation between taxation and investment has been suggested for the mid-sixteenth century: R. W. Hoyle, 'Taxation and the Mid-Tudor Crisis', *Economic History Review*, 2nd series, 51:4 (1998), 649–75.

171 Richard Grassby, *The Business Community of Seventeenth-Century England* (Cambridge, 1995), pp. 82–91.

172 TNA, SP 14/184, fol. 104.

173 John H. Munro, 'Usury, Calvinism, and Credit in Protestant England: From the Sixteenth Century to the Industrial Revolution', University of Toronto Working Paper no. 439 (2011), pp. 15–19.

174 Dixon, 'Economy', pp. 307–19.

Book of Orphans' is the accounts of the wardens who oversaw the guardianship of the town's orphans. They record how the assets for their upkeep were managed between 1586 and 1649, the revenues gained, and the sums of money issued for their sustenance. At the start of the period, income was almost entirely generated from the rents from real estate, typically urban property in Sandwich itself: various houses and gardens. While such payments persist through the accounts, increasingly over time they record capital being lent to several notable merchants and mariners, clearly at interest. For example, the entry for 6 March 1629 records the interest paid on two loans of £50 to Andrew Gosfright, a jurat, and the former mayor of Sandwich in 1636–37. They had been lent by Henry Forstall, the warden tasked with managing the assets of the orphans of Robert Wilds. Interest at £4 13s 4d on £50 for ten months and £2 10s for seven and a half months implies an interest rate of 11.2 per cent for one bond and 8 per cent for the other. This puts the first loan well above the permitted maximum interest rate.[175]

As discussed, a ship was an increasingly large investment. The need to achieve these sums and a desire to diversify capital fostered a propensity to co-own vessels. Consequently, the capital stock rested upon interconnected groups of owners who shared risk and pooled capital. Through such networks, merchants also pooled their human capital, their accumulated stock of commercial knowledge and skills. This was not just their financial acumen, their ability to manage their business shrewdly, invest capital profitably, understand logistics and supply chain management, but also their comprehension of trade laws and regulations in the ports and polities along the sea lanes, even their ability to speak multiple languages could be useful for trade negotiations.

These networks are particularly observable for the year 1626, when officials chose to include almost complete details of ownership in a ship survey of Dover, Sandwich, Hythe, Ramsgate, Walmer, St Peters and Broadstairs.[176] At that time, the certificates for Dover and Sandwich, the two main ports, recorded similar tonnages, 3,146 and 2,959 tons respectively, and a similar number of unique owners (where known), 81 and 77, but the structure of capital ownership was subtly different. While the size of each share was similar, at 17.7 and 18.5 tons per share, Dover averaged 2.4 shares per ship and Sandwich 4.4. Moreover, the average individual investor owned 1.7 shares in the former and 2.1 in the latter. This suggests that Sandwich's investor network had greater diversification, with investors distributing their capital across a wider spread of investments than Dover – where there was a greater appetite for risk or a

[175] T. Dorman, 'The Sandwich Book of Orphans', *Archaeologia Cantiana*, 16 (1886), 179–206.

[176] TNA, SP 16/34, fols 179–83; SP 16/39, fols 56–8, 60–1; Dixon, 'Economy', pp. 609–13 (her appendix A).

larger overall supply of capital. With the smaller ports these metrics are more idiosyncratic. Ramsgate, which had a much smaller fleet but still some overseas shipping activity, had 34 unique owners, averaged two shares per ship, each representing an average of 11.5 tons – significantly less than the larger ports. The average investor had just 1.2 shares in ships. Walmer's maritime activity was dominated by fishing and had just two vessels, but nine unique owners, giving an average of 5.5 shares per boat, while Hythe had similar fleets to St Peters/Broadstairs, and a comparable average number of shares per investor, at 1.4 and 1.2 respectively, but the former had smaller shares per ship at 1.7 compared with 2.5 for the latter. If we measure the distribution of ownership by family name, we see that Dover had the largest number of families owning capital, at 71, ahead of Sandwich with 66, both far more than the others. It was in Sandwich, however, that the average family owned the most tonnage, with 44.8 tons per family, compared with 33.7 in Dover, and 22.0, 25.7 and 10.5 for Ramsgate, Hythe and St Peters/Broadstairs respectively.

Like most of the debt relationships observed by Dixon, capital networks in 1626 were primarily local, though there were exceptions. Dover and Sandwich drew in outside investors, with six of the former's larger ships co-owned with 'merchants' or 'others of London'. The individual most closely connected with these investors was the once and future mayor, Nicholas Eaton, who himself held shares in seven of the bigger ships. One vessel, the 120-ton *John*, was co-owned by 'others of Calais', a certain 'Mr Williams' of Sandwich, and a local, Walter Taylor, from Dover. There were also some noteworthy foreign-born residents of Dover, or their descendants, among shipowners. Indeed, as Dixon noted, their careers illustrate 'the greater availability of capital to men with connections in Bruges, Rotterdam and Hamburg'.[177] That year, the Hugessens held ten shares across eight ships, including the 240-ton *Assurance*. The successful mariner Joseph Looper owned the ship he mastered, the *Willing Mind*, outright, but also held shares in seven other ships. By his death in 1644, he owned shares in seventeen ships worth £500.[178] In Sandwich, the London merchant Marmaduke Roydon (1583–1646) had a one-fifth share in the 160-ton *Vintage*, whose master was John Woolters. Alongside Woolters himself, the other owners included one Robert Bauck of Newcastle, as well as Robert Constable and Nicholas Hurlstone, who were local to the town. Meanwhile, Sir Thomas Love (*c*.1571–1627), then captain of Sandown Castle, had shares in two Sandwich ships, the eponymous 180-ton *Love* and the 160-ton *Hester*. In both cases these were co-owned with William Crosse, a prominent London merchant (*c*.1579–*c*.1679). In the case of the *Hester*, Isaac Rucasies was the only other shareholder, who also co-owned the *Love*, alongside several other Sandwich merchants, including Andrew Gosfright and Hopestill Tilden.

177 Dixon, 'Economy', p. 588.
178 *Ibid.*, p. 257.

Finally, of commensurate importance to the capital investment by interconnected investor networks, was the stock of social capital in Kent's maritime trade. This constituted the networks of relationships between mariners and merchants, the accumulated interpersonal connections with other traders, other sailors and local authorities in the ports along the route, their agreed norms or codes of behaviour and stock of trust. While such a concept is notoriously difficult to measure, we have one possible metric for the trust and cooperation the county's merchants and masters had with their overseas partners: the frequency with which native merchants carried goods on foreign ships and vice versa, and how this changed over time (see Table 2.4).

Table 2.4 Percentages of collaboration between foreign or native shipmasters and merchants in the overseas trade of the port of Dover, 1576–1622.

Year	Native master/ native merchant*	Foreign master/ foreign merchant*	Native master/ foreign merchant	Foreign master/ native merchant	Total collaboration
M1576–M77	29.5	16.3	49.7	3.3	52.9
M1579–M80	20.0	12.9	64.1	3.1	67.2
M1594–M95	18.5	53.1	21.2	6.5	27.7
M1597–M98	10.0	67.0	9.6	12.4	22.0
M1598–M99	19.7	56.5	11.3	11.8	23.1
X1604–X05	36.3	27.9	17.1	18.5	35.6
X1615–X16	20.0	62.6	10.7	6.3	17.0
X1621–X22	26.0	23.1	28.3	7.4	35.7

Source: TNA, E 190/640/1; E 190/641/2; E 190/641/7; E 190/645/5; E 190/645/13; E 190/646/4; E 190/650/5; E 190/651/8; E 190/653/6.

*It is important to note that masters and merchants could be the same person.

In the Dover overseas port book for Michaelmas 1576 to Michaelmas 1577, just over half of merchant entries involving goods carried into or out of the harbour involved collaboration, of which almost all saw a foreign merchant contracted to an English shipmaster. By the end of the decade the collaboration rate reached two-thirds. Fast forward to the 1590s, midway through the first Anglo-Spanish War, and the frequency of such arrangements had collapsed. Peacetime brought a brief revival in collaboration, again with the orientation of masters and merchants roughly equal. Into the seventeenth century the trend is more ambiguous, with a fall to the lowest recorded rate of collaboration in 1615–16 and then a recovery by 1621–22. Yet, in both years, the pre-war arrangement of the foreign merchant contracted to an English shipper had returned to its previous predominance. So, for this example of Dover, at least, the explanation for these trends must include conflict. During 1585–1604 merchants and shippers operating through the port restructured their businesses to work with their compatriots rather than foreigners, indicative of a temporary loss of social capital. In this case, the benefits of peace are manifest.

Conclusion

As might be considered typical, the principal consequence of trade was to foster economic specialisation – evident in the greater diversity of inbound than outbound commodities – and so promote economic growth. While Kent's commercial connections may have stimulated some industrial output, especially of cloth, vigorous agricultural production was the primary effect. The county's justices of the peace aptly reported to the privy council in 1620 that 'tillage […] is the generall wealth'.[179] The trade in its surplus – principally as grain and beer – to London, other English regions and Europe, was the engine of Kent's economy. This generated the earnings that paid for the other goods that poured into its towns and villages, whether from adjacent English regions or abroad – or very often from overseas but via London.

This assertion, however valid, undersells the broader complexity of commercial life in sixteenth- and seventeenth-century provincial maritime communities. Kent's ports bridged two trade systems, one a metropolitan market – centred on the capital – and the other a transregional market, that stretched across the Channel and North Sea. These were very much interlinked and overlapping, but still essentially separate. Within both, many native or foreign merchants and mariners inherited and perpetuated centuries-old trading activities and relationships. Typically translocal, their transactions formed the basic substructure of provincial commerce. Yet, at the same time, there was the superstructure: those more enterprising actors who systematically adjusted the extent and intensity of their trading networks in response to changing

[179] TNA, SP 14/112, fol. 15.

local and regional conditions. They would likewise pursue trade further afield, but this tended to be transitory at this time, often a consequence of external geopolitical pressures. The commercial significance of Europe was somewhat greater than Chalklin claimed.[180]

Despite many challenges, in the ports themselves individual merchants did well from a growing stream of profits from their trade and investments. Capital accumulated in a variety of forms. In keeping with age-old merchant aspirations, James Hugessen the elder and younger became considerable landowners across Kent. In 1640, the latter became High Sheriff of Kent.[181] Mariners too could flourish if they also managed to invest in capital assets, such as ships, though these would only constitute a small minority.[182] The county's agricultural producers gained from flows of victuals but middlemen traders in the ports predictably profited most and were justly termed 'oligarchs' by Hipkin.[183] Luxury imports, like high-quality cloth, wine, sugars, spices, or new manufactures, once the preserve of the elites across the county – the aristocracy or gentry – were increasingly consumed by the 'middling sort of people'. These were, Wrightson termed, 'people of intermediate wealth' and could include 'commercial farmers, prosperous manufacturers, independent tradesmen', merchants or those in professions, such as the law.[184] Grain shipped out was widely begrudged by the less well off, but trade also offered a diversity of more nutritious comestibles in return, not least plentiful vegetables, dairy products and fish. The benefits of these, as well as imported raw materials and building supplies, have been largely underemphasised. To some extent, trade fed and housed the growing population, even as social stratification increased.

Equally transformative were concomitant movements of capital and labour. Kent enjoyed precisely directed outside investment and had sizeable resident minorities from its nearest continental neighbours. These added further to the stock of physical and human capital. Beyond long discussed industries such as clothmaking, foreign-born or descended persons added their skills and resources to Kent's mercantile communities in ports like Dover and Sandwich. They became mariners, shipmasters, shipowners and merchants and formed part of the social and economic networks of their home ports, even while they retained links to their places of origin. Where people moved, trade would have also fostered cultural exchange and the movement of ideas. In an age of religious conflict, smuggling networks in the county's ports connected diaspora communities in the Low Countries and England, bringing flows of written propaganda. Such things give provincial maritime commercial connections a real sense of having been part of the wider history of early modern Europe.

180 Chalklin, *Seventeenth-Century Kent*, p. 4.

181 TNA, PROB 11/167/138; PROB 11/198/184; Hasted, *Survey*, p. 206.

182 See, for example, Cobham Doves, a Dover mariner: TNA, PROB 11/112/214.

183 Hipkin 'Kent Grain Trade', 99–139, throughout, but especially pp. 130–4.

184 Wrightson, *Earthly Necessities*, pp. 200–1.

3

The Merchant Fleet and Maritime Community of Kent, 1580–1630

CRAIG LAMBERT

From 1724 to 1727, Daniel Defoe travelled across England and one of the counties he visited was Kent.[1] Defoe was impressed by the naval foundations at Deptford and Woolwich and provided details on the hospitals erected to care for seafarers. He said Greenwich was the 'pleasantest' town in England. In Woolwich, he said, the 'biggest cables' were made for ships of war and the town had a 'prodigious quantity of cannon of all sorts', stating there could be as many as 8,000 pieces of ordnance. After discussing the naval centres, Defoe described the towns of Erith, Greenhithe and Northfleet. Here deposits from the nearby hills provided large quantities of chalk, which was used to make lime before it was shipped to the Low Countries. He describes how Kentish folk would use lighters and hoys to remove the chalk deposits and transfer these to local forts and the counties of Essex, Suffolk and Norfolk for the farmers to 'lay upon their land which they do in prodigious quantities and are glad to give 2s 6d to 4s per load'. He marvelled at how many people were ferried from Gravesend to London, stating that 'all the people of East Kent, when they go to London, go no farther by land than this town'. He added that Gravesend was an important staging post for ships leaving London, not least because it was here where the searcher of customs would make one final check of the goods aboard each ship. Rochester, Faversham, Broadstairs, Margate and Ramsgate he notes were important places for oyster dredging and fishing, saying their activities at sea were 'exceedingly industrious'. Chatham docks he described as bristling with all manner of stores for building and equipping the largest ships. Dover, he says, was an important town that traded with the Low Countries and welcomed ships from New York and Virginia.

[1] Daniel Defoe, *A Tour Through the island of Great Britain. Divided into Circuits or Journeys*, 8th edition, vol. 1 (London, 1778). Kent is covered over pp. 106–55.

Reading Defoe's tour of Kent there is no mistaking that what he described was a 'maritime county'. Easy access to the wealthy cities of the Low Countries provided trading opportunities. The River Thames connected Kent's towns with an expanding London. Maritime activity, whether fishing, ferrying, or trading, linked Kent with the counties of Essex, Suffolk, Norfolk, Sussex and Hampshire. Put simply, central to Kent's social and economic life were its ships and maritime community. This chapter aims to reconstruct Kent's merchant fleet from 1580 to 1630 by focusing on a series of well-documented years. It will also analyse Kent's maritime community paying close attention to its size and occupational structure.

The sources that underpin most of this chapter are customs accounts which record the taxation of maritime trade. Customs charges in England had been collected locally since at least the early thirteenth century.[2] In the late thirteenth century, Edward I implemented a countrywide customs service: charges on exported wool (later expanded to cover other goods) were to be levied at a series of head ports.[3] By the fifteenth century, there were fifteen head ports, and all imported and exported commodities were taxed.[4] In 1565 Elizabeth and her ministers improved the system by introducing the port books, and from Easter that year blank port books were sent to each head port. Stationed at each was a controller, a customer, and a searcher. The customer was responsible for recording the levied customs. To reduce fraudulent practices the controller would check the accuracy of the customer's records, while the searcher examined the cargo. The resultant port books recorded the name of each ship, its tonnage, the name of the master, the date each vessel left or entered port and its journey details. Although coastal trade was untaxed, the officials recorded this aspect of the maritime economy to enforce taxation

2 Nicholas Karn, 'England's Trade with the Continent in the Early Thirteenth Century: Customs and the Port of Dover', *Journal of Medieval History*, 46 (2020), 306–34.

3 See Stuart Jenks, 'A Guide to the Perplexed', which is the introduction to his volumes of the London customs accounts, such as Stuart Jenks (ed.), *The London Custom Accounts Part II: The Dynasty of Lancaster (1400–1461) Number 1: 2 Henry IV (1400/01) – 8 Henry V (1420/21)* (Cologne, 2016). These can be found here: https://www.hansischergeschichtsverein.de/london-customs-accounts (accessed 2 September 2024).

4 There were different duties such as the great customs, the petty custom, and tunnage and poundage, but by the late fifteenth century the payable rates were standardised and all merchants, denizen and foreign, were expected to pay, excepting groups (or individuals) with exemptions such as the Hansards: Wendy R. Childs (ed.), *The Customs Accounts of Hull, 1453–1490*, Yorkshire Archaeological Society Record Series, vol. 144 (1986), see introduction.

and rules governing overseas trade. This is important because at least three-quarters of English ship-voyages sailed coastwise.[5]

The government would occasionally undertake surveys of shipping. These could be taken locally or regionally, or – in some circumstances – a countrywide survey might be undertaken. While these are useful, they often omit information. The large survey of 1571–72, for example, does not record information relating to sixty-four ports.[6] Sometimes surveys also included the number of mariners living within each port. Such information can be misleading because it is not clear whether the whole maritime community is captured in these censuses; for example, fisherfolk might not be included. Nonetheless, the information contained in surveys can be used with the port books to enrich our understanding of the shipping capacity and the maritime community of Kent.

To investigate the size and geographical distribution of Kent's merchant fleet requires us to link together the evidence from port books and government surveys and apply a series of methodological approaches. These methodologies need to accommodate the fact that the same ships will appear in several records; thus, we need to develop methods that reduce the instances of double counting (failure to link references to the same ship) and 'conflation' (erroneous linkage of references to separate ships). There are three principal ways of doing this. These methods have been explained in detail elsewhere, so we only need to briefly discuss them here.[7] The first method is called the three-identifier. For this method, we link the ship's name with its master and its home port. Within a specified timeframe, records of ships that are identical according to these three 'identifiers' are deemed to be referring to the same vessel. The second method is to use the ship's name and home port but discount the master. Therefore, all ships with the same name from the same port within a specified time are counted only once. The third way of measuring the English merchant fleet is to combine the best attributes of the above methods and apply a more nuanced approach to the data. This involves scrutiny of the numbers of ships and their tonnages produced by the methods

5 On the Elizabethan port books, see Neville J. Williams, *The Maritime Trade of the East Anglian Ports, 1550–1590* (Oxford, 1988), chapter 1; Gary P. Baker, 'Domestic Maritime Trade in Late Tudor England c.1565–85: A Case Study of King's Lynn and Plymouth', in Claire Jowitt, Craig Lambert and Steve Mentz (eds), *The Routledge Companion to Marine and Maritime Worlds, 1400–1800* (London, 2020), pp. 95–124.

6 Craig Lambert and Gary P. Baker, 'An Investigation of the Size and Geographical Distribution of the English, Welsh, and Channel Islands Merchant Fleet: A Case Study of 1571–72', in Richard J. Blakemore and James Davey (eds), *The Maritime World of Early Modern Britain* (Amsterdam, 2020), pp. 79–102.

7 Craig Lambert and Gary P. Baker, 'The Merchant Fleet and Shipboard Community of Kent, *c*.1565–*c*.1580', *Archaeologia Cantiana*, 140 (2019), 89–110; Lambert and Baker, 'An Investigation'.

above and eliminating any ship from the inquiry that is double counted or conflated.

Each of these methods has certain limitations. Tonnages, for example, are not precisely recorded. In 1580, the *Grace of God* of Faversham, commanded by Thomas Chartham, was recorded at 30 tons (July) and 16 tons (September).[8] In 1594, the *Martin* of Dover, commanded by Robert Garret, was recorded at 20 tons (July) and 16 tons (August).[9] In 1609 the *Philip* of Milton Regis, commanded by Arthur Kneland, was registered at both 18 tons (June) and 10 tons (September).[10] These are undoubtedly the same vessels as they are commanded by the same masters within a few months. The difference between the tonnages could be small, as in the case of the *Martin*. However, over a few months, the *Grace of God* and the *Philip* almost doubled in size. The ship-name method also creates problems. A ship survey of 1587, for example, reveals that there were two ships in Sandwich called the *Grace of God*, one was 40 tons, the other 100 tons. A survey of Faversham's ships in 1580 reveals three vessels called the *Anne*, and two of these had the same tonnage (4 tons).[11] Given some ship names could be common if we applied the ship-name method across dozens of ports we would significantly reduce the size of Kent's merchant fleet. Linking the master's name with a ship and a port (the three-identifier method) can also produce unreliable figures. This is especially so if a vessel is in family ownership. In 1593, the 8-ton *John* of Broadstairs was commanded by Thomas, Jerome and Stephen Sampson.[12] In 1599, the 12-ton *Richard* of Margate was commanded by three different masters.[13] Applying the three-identifier method to both examples would count two ships six times. In short, the three-identifier overestimates and the ship-name method underestimates the number of ships.

Masters might also work out of different ports using the same ship. In 1612–14, Morgan Hall sailed out of New Hythe in command of the 30-ton *Anne*, but in 1614 he also operated this vessel out of Millhall (Milhale).[14] In 1594, John Winter skippered the 12-ton *Helen* out of Faversham, but in 1595 and 1598 he also commanded this vessel from Whitstable.[15] This kind of pattern is more prevalent in places like Kent which had numerous ports and creeks. Thus, when using the port as one of the identifiers some ships might be double counted. Of course, many masters commanded separate ships from

8 TNA, E 190/6/8, fol. 73r; E 190/6/8, fol. 74v.

9 TNA, E 190/185/6, fols 26r, 31v.

10 TNA, E 190/649/7, fols 1v, 2r.

11 KHLC, Fa/CPm/24.

12 TNA, E 190/644/1, fol. 2r; E 190/644/2, fol. 2r; E 190/644/3, fol. 1r.

13 Gilbert Shouck, John Russell and William Chappelle: TNA, E 190/646/7, fol. 2v; E 190/646/14; E 190/646/7, fol. 2v; E 190/646/14; E 190/647/1, fol. 1v.

14 TNA, E 190/650/2, fol. 4r; E 190/650/9, fols 4v, 6v, 8v.

15 TNA, E 190/645/2, fol. 3r; E 190/645/10, fols 1v, 2r.

different ports. In 1622, John Swanton commanded the 15-ton *Anne* out of Whitstable but in a ship survey of 1630, he appears as the master of the 8-ton *Rebecca* of Seasalter.[16] The nuanced method allows you to compensate for such service patterns. The key problem of the nuanced method is scalability. Applying this method to a nationwide study of the merchant fleet is extremely time-consuming. In 1572–73, for example, the port books record shipping from 324 ports.[17] The nuanced method, however, is possible when undertaking a county-based study of shipping, especially when using short well-documented sample years.

A recent study of Kent's merchant fleet argued that over a long period (1565–80) there were at least 419 separate ships in Kent, measuring just under 10,000 tons.[18] Of course, these figures do not show how many ships were based in the county in any one year. The earlier work took 1580 as a convenient stopping point. This chapter pushes the analysis further by examining Kent's merchant fleet in the period *c*.1582–*c*.1630. These dates are chosen because in 1582 the government undertook a nationwide survey of shipping, and it ends before the beginning of the English Civil War. The Civil War's impact on Kent's shipping, trade, and maritime communities would require a separate study.

The 1582 survey is organised by county and port. It provides two lists: one records ships 100 tons or over; the other only those under 100 tons.[19] For the former, the survey begins with London before detailing the shipping of Essex, Norfolk, Suffolk, Cornwall, Devon, Dorset, Bristol, Southampton/Hampshire, Yorkshire and Northumberland. From folio 93 the survey lists the counties that contained ships under 100 tons, which in addition to those just mentioned included Sussex, Kent, Somerset, Lincolnshire, Cumberland, Gloucestershire and Chester. That Kent contained no ships over 100 tons in 1582 is surprising. The 1572 ship survey, for example, tells us that the *Luke Evangelist* of Erith commanded by William Ferrers measured 100 tons.[20] On 1 October 1575, the 180-ton *Hunter* of Queenborough commanded by Thomas Potter left Southampton for Portsmouth carrying 2,000 lb of hemp and 400 lb of wax.[21] In January 1576, the 250-ton *Bull* of Queenborough commanded by Andrew Tyse came into Southampton from Gdańsk before heading to Lisbon.[22] Of course, these ships may have ceased to operate by 1582 but it

16 TNA, E 190/653/5, fol. 5v; SP 12/198, fol. 121r.

17 Lambert and Baker, 'An Investigation'.

18 Lambert and Baker, 'The Merchant Fleet and Shipboard Community of Kent'.

19 TNA, SP 156/45, fols 88–105 provides information on the numbers and tonnages of ships.

20 TNA, SP 15/22, fol. 12r.

21 TNA, E 190/814/10, fol. 19r.

22 *Ibid.*, fol. 22r. The tonnage is slightly difficult to read, and it could be 150 tons. Either way, it was above 100 tons. The vessel was carrying 70 quarters of rye.

is still surprising to find no vessels of over 100 tons in Kent. In addition to the survey, several port books can be incorporated into the analysis. Table 3.1 reconstructs Kent's merchant fleet using three methods, thus demonstrating the differences between them.

Table 3.1 Number of ships in Kent, 1581–82.

Port	Numbers of ships (three-identifier)	Numbers of ships (ship-name)	Numbers of Ships (nuanced)	Tonnage (nuanced)	Average tonnage
Aylesford	3	2	3	93	31
Broadstairs	5	5	5	74	15
Dartford	8	5	8	70	9
Deal	5	5	5	19	4
Dover	55	33	37	868	23
Erith	1	1	1	20	20
Faversham	78	33	43	774	18
Folkestone	12	8	8	79	10
Fordwich	1	1	1	40	40
Gillingham	10	9	10	145	15
Gravesend	4	3	3	85	28
Halling	2	2	2	75	38
Halstow (Low. & High.)	11	11	11	141	13
Hoo	1	1	1	7	7
Hythe	48	22	24	368	15
Kingsdown	1	1	1	4	4
Lydd	11	10	11	59	5
Maidstone	22	9	10	304	34
Margate	7	4	4	49	12
Millhall	15	7	8	232	29
Milton Regis	46	24	29	464	16
Minster on Sea	1	1	1	10	10
New Hythe	7	5	5	155	31
Northfleet	1	1	1	25	25
Queenborough, Minster & Leysdown	14	13	14	114	10

Table 3.1 Number of ships in Kent, 1581–82. (*continued*)

Port	Numbers of ships (three-identifier)	Numbers of ships (ship-name)	Numbers of Ships (nuanced)	Tonnage (nuanced)	Average tonnage
Rainham	17	11	13	248	19
Ramsgate	19	15	17	213	13
Reculver	1	1	1	8	8
Ringwould	2	2	2	25	13
Rochester	8	8	8	272	34
Sandwich	55	36	40	955	24
Sittingbourne	3	3	3	27	9
St Johns	3	3	3	7	2
St Peter's	6	5	6	71	12
Strood	3	2	2	23	12
Tonge	1	1	1	6	6
Upchurch	5	5	5	34	7
Walmer	3	3	3	9	3
Whitstable	22	21	22	155	7
Total	517	332	372	6327	17

Source: TNA, SP 12/156, fols 88v–120r; E 190/6/6; E 190/6/7; E 190/6/8; E 190/7/4; E 190/307/19; E 190/429/1; E 190/592/7; E 190/592/10; E 190/641/1; E 190/641/7; E 190/641/8; E 190/641/10; E 190/641/11; E 190/741/13; E 190/741/17; E 190/741/21; E 190/741/25; E 190/741/26; E 190/742/10; E 190/742/22; E 190/934/7.

If we follow the nuanced method in 1581–82 Kent's merchant fleet consisted of 372 separate ships measuring 6,327 tons. Following the same method, and linking the ship survey of 1572 with the port books from 1572–73, shows that Kent's fleet numbered 256 ships at 5,868 tons.[23] From 1573 to 1582, the number of ships in Kent increased by 45 per cent and the tonnage grew by 8 per cent. There was, therefore, a significant increase in the number of ships but only a minor change in tonnage. Indeed, on average, ships in 1573 were larger (23 tons) than they were in 1582 (17 tons). As Kent was close to the Spanish-held Low Countries it is no surprise the government was keen to know how many ships the county possessed. In 1587, as the threat from Spain

[23] TNA, E 190/5/3, 4, 5; E 190/6/1; E 190/306/1, 9–12, 16; E 190/306/7; E 190/388/4, 7; E 190/427/1, 3, 4; E 190/473/3, 7; E 190/589/4, 6, 10; E 190/591/8, 13; E 190/639/1–4, 6, 10; E 190/736/5, 6; E 190/739/8, 9, 13, 24, 25; E 190/739/10; E 190/814/8; E 190/865/1; E 190/928/4; SP 12/55.

increased, Elizabeth's ministers surveyed several of Kent's ports.[24] Table 3.2 presents the results of that survey. The survey of 1587 is unusual. Many of the ports from the 1582 survey are not included. By linking the port books which cover 1586–88 with the survey of 1587 we get a better picture of the potential size of Kent's merchant fleet during the period of the Spanish Armada.

Table 3.2 Ship survey of 1587.

Port	Number of ships	Tonnage	Average tonnage
Dover	31	1075	35
Faversham	20	340	17
Folkestone	3	54	18
Hythe	10	183	18
Lydd	7	29	4
Ramsgate	13	167	13
Sandwich	49	1242	25
Walmer	5	11	2
Total	138	3101	22

Source: TNA, SP 12/198, fols 5r, 14r, 19r, 22r, 53r–54r, 121r.

Table 3.3 Kent's ships in 1586–88, according to the port books and the ship survey.

Port	Number of ships	Tonnage	Average tonnage
Birling	1	10	10
Broadstairs	1	24	24
Dartford	3	40	13
Dover	47	1317	28
Faversham	30	497	17
Gillingham	1	10	10
Halling	3	75	25
Halstow (Low. & High.)	3	48	16
Herne Bay	1	12	12
Hythe	14	208	15

24 TNA, SP 12/198, fols 5r–121r.

Table 3.3 Kent's ships in 1586–88, according to the port books and the ship survey. *(continued)*

Port	Number of ships	Tonnage	Average tonnage
Lydd	8	33	4
Maidstone	7	240	34
Margate	10	123	12
Millhall	2	86	43
Milton Regis	10	169	17
New Hythe	2	70	35
Queenborough	1	9	9
Rainham	6	196	33
Ramsgate	13	174	13
Rochester	5	152	30
Sandwich	61	1508	25
Snodland	1	7	7
Stoke/Hoo	1	10	10
Strood	1	18	18
Tonge	2	17	9
Walmer	5	11	2
Whitstable	4	54	14
Total	243	5118	21

Source: TNA, SP 12/198, fols 5r, 14r, 19r, 22r, 53r–54r, 121r; E 190/639/12; E 190/639/13; E 190/639/14; E 190/640/1; E 190/640/4; E 190/642/11; E 190/642/12; E 190/642/13; E 190/642/14; E 190/643/1; E 190/643/2; E 190/643/3; E 190/643/4; E 190/643/5; E 190/643/6; E 190/643/8; E 190/643/11; E 190/643/12; E 190/643/13; E 190/643/14; E 190/643/15; E 190/643/17; E 190/744/4; E 190/745/3; E 190/744/4; E 190/745/9; E 190/745/12; E 190/745/13; E 190/745/16; E 190/745/20.

Table 3.3 shows a decline in Kent's merchant fleet from over 350 ships in 1581–82 to 243 in 1586–88. Likewise, there is a reduction in the tonnage from 6,327 to 5,118 tons. There are fewer ports recorded during 1586–88 but those missing are mostly small places such as Ringwould and Reculver. Indeed, the sixteen ports which are in the 1581–82 sample, but missing from the sources linked with 1586–88, amounted to sixty-six ships and 702 tons. Even if these vessels were added to the above table there would still be a reduction in Kent's shipping capacity. The key reason for the decline in the merchant fleet and tonnage from 1582 to 1588 was the reduction in shipping within some ports. From 1582 to 1588 Gillingham's fleet decreased from ten ships to one, and Faversham's reduced by thirteen vessels. In 1582, Milton Regis had twenty-nine ships but in 1588 only ten. Some ports bucked the trend. From 1582 to 1588 Dover's fleet increased from thirty-seven (868 tons) to forty-seven vessels measuring a total of 1,317 tons; a 52 per cent increase in tonnage. Sandwich also increased its shipping and tonnage. In 1582 Sandwich had forty ships totalling 955 tons, by 1588 this had increased to sixty-one ships measuring 1,508 tons.

In the seventeenth century, there were some interesting developments to Kent's merchant fleet. Table 3.4 examines the period after the first Anglo-Spanish War. For Kent's maritime community peace was probably welcome. While clandestine trade could be undertaken with the Spanish Netherlands, lawful trade was more secure from seizures by eagle-eyed customs officials on both sides of the Channel. Peace also brought security. True, the Channel was not an entirely safe-haven and small-scale piracy was part of the warp and weft of maritime commerce, but the ability to now access more freely the Spanish Netherlands and the breakaway United Provinces, especially Holland and Zeeland, must have presented opportunities for Kent's shippers.

Table 3.4 Kent's ships in 1604–05.

Port	Number of ships	Tonnage	Average tonnage
Broadstairs	1	8	8
Dover	56	1456	26
Faversham*	24	323	17
Folkestone	1	16	16
Gillingham	7	241	34
Hythe	5	65	13
Maidstone	6	142	24
Margate	4	32	8
Millhall	2	70	35
Milton Regis	14	200	14
New Hythe	1	20	20
Rainham	7	98	14
Rochester	13	408	31
Sandwich	52	981	19
Sittingbourne	2	35	18
Snodland	1	20	20

Table 3.4 Kent's ships in 1604–05. (*continued*)

Port	Number of ships	Tonnage	Average tonnage
Strood	1	10	10
Teynham	1	16	16
Whitstable	4	51	13
Total	202	4192	21

Source: TNA, E 190/648/1; E 190/648/2; E 190/648/3; E 190/648/4; E 190/648/5; E 190/648/6; E 190/648/9; E 190/648/11; E 190/648/12; E 190/648/14; E 190/648/15; E 190/648/16; E 190/648/17; E 190/648/18; E 190/649/1; E 190/650/5.

* Five ships of Faversham have no tonnage data.

While it appears there might have been a decline in Kent's fleet from 1581–82 to 1604–05 it is worth bearing in mind that twenty-two ports from 1581–82 do not appear in the sources used for the 1604–05 table – Ramsgate and Queenborough, for example. In 1581–2, the ports missing from the 1604–05 table had 100 ships measuring 1,235 tons. If we were to include these 'missing ships' from the above table, the tonnage of Kent's fleet in 1604–05 was broadly similar to that of 1586–88.

More important, however, is the rise of Dover. In 1581–82 Dover's fleet was thirty-seven ships measuring 868 tons. By 1586–88 Dover's fleet had increased to forty-seven ships measuring 1,317 tons: a 27 per cent increase in the number of ships and a 52 per cent increase in tonnage. In 1604–05 Dover's fleet increased to fifty-six ships (a 51 per cent increase from 1581–82) and 1,456 tons (a 68 per cent increase from 1581–82). The size of Dover's ships remained relatively stable (24–28 tons), meaning the increase in tonnage was due to investment in new ships. The story of Sandwich seems more complex. From 1581–82 to 1586–88 the port increased its shipping considerably, but by 1604–05 its fleet had decreased by nine ships and 527 tons.

The next period of investigation covers the 1620s. Examining this period is not easy because, by the 1620s, many of the Sandwich port books ceased to record the tonnage data, making the nuanced method difficult. Fortunately, there is a ship survey from 1626 that names the ships and provides tonnages for Sandwich and information on the shipping of Broadstairs.[25] We can draw on evidence from the 1622 port books for Dover and Faversham.[26] Additional information relating to Dover's merchant fleet can be found in a series of letters

25 TNA, SP 16/34, fols 179r–182r.

26 TNA, E 190/653/4; E 190/653/45; E 190/653/6.

to Lord Zouche, Warden of the Cinque Ports.[27] Moreover, another survey in 1630 provides us with tonnage information for Northfleet/Gravesend, Strood, Chatham, Gillingham, Halstow, Rainham, Upchurch, Queenborough, Milton Regis, Sittingbourne, Oare, Tenyham and Whitstable/Seasalter.[28]

Table 3.5 Evidence from ship surveys and port books for some of Kent's ports, 1622–30.

Port	Number of ships	Tonnage	Average tonnage
1622/26 port books/survey			
Broadstairs	11	178	16
Dover	76	3166	42
Faversham	9	110	16
Sandwich	35	2959	84
1630 survey			
Chatham	2	60	30
Gillingham	3	30	10
Halstow	8	109	14
Milton Regis	20	318	16
Northfleet/Gravesend	3	48	16
Oare	1	24	24
Queenborough	7	147	21
Rainham	4	68	17
Sittingbourne	3	58	19
Strood	6	158	26
Upchurch	3	36	12
Whitstable/Seasalter	9	117	13
Total	200	7586	38

Source: see footnotes 26–8; and Dixon, 'Economy' (at pp. 609–13).

27 The survey is dated 1626 and can be found in BL Egerton MS 2584. Dixon, 'Economy', 609–13 provides a transcription of the 1626 Dover ship survey.

28 TNA, SP 16/155, fols 90r–91v.

Table 3.5 shows Kent's ports had a propensity for growth. In 1581, Broadstairs had five ships measuring 74 tons. From 1587–88 to 1604–05, the shipping capacity of Broadstairs was reduced to one 8-ton ship. By 1626, Broadstairs had eleven ships (a 1,000 per cent increase from 1604–05) measuring 178 tons (a 2,125 per cent increase from 1604–05). Over the same period, Dover and Sandwich increased their fleets. In 1581–82, Dover had thirty-seven ships totalling 868 tons. By 1605, its fleet consisted of fifty-six ships measuring 1,456 tons. In 1626, Dover's fleet had increased to seventy-six ships measuring 3,166 tons. In 1581–82, Sandwich had forty ships totalling 955 tons; over 1586–88 this increased to sixty-one ships measuring 1,508 tons. In 1604–05, there was a reduction in Sandwich's fleet to fifty-two ships measuring 981 tons. By the mid- to late 1620s, however, there is evidence of significant growth in the shipping capacity of Sandwich. True, the number of ships dropped from fifty-two in 1605 to thirty-five in the 1620s, but the size of the ships increased dramatically. Indeed, from 1586–88 to 1626 the tonnage of Sandwich's merchant fleet increased by 96 per cent. This trend is visible in other ports. The average size of Strood's ships increased from 10 tons in 1604/5 to 26 tons in 1630. In 1586–88, Queenborough had one 9-ton ship, by 1630 this port's ships averaged 21 tons. From 1588 to 1630, the average size of Kent's ships grew from 21 tons to 38 tons – an increase of over 80 per cent. From the late sixteenth century to the early decades of the seventeenth century there was a gradual move towards investment in bigger ships. Table 3.6 uses the examples of Dover and Sandwich to show how the number of bigger ships increased.

There are a few key points about the tables above which need noting. First, from the 1580s to the early seventeenth century shipping and tonnage remained relatively stable. There are some peaks and troughs, but this might be due to some sample years being better documented than others. We can demonstrate the stability of Kent's fleet by looking at county totals of ships and tonnage over a series of snapshot years.

Table 3.7 shows the 1620s were an important decade for Kent's merchant fleet. From 1622–30, fifteen ports had more tonnage than the thirty-nine places surveyed in 1581–82. During 1622–30, the three ports of Broadstairs, Dover and Sandwich had more tonnage than the ships from the twenty-seven ports examined in 1586–88. There are thirty ports included in the 1581–88 statistics for which we have no evidence in the sources used for the 1622–30 period.[29] If we assume these thirty ports still had ships by 1630, Kent's merchant fleet might have numbered approximately 350 ships measuring *c*.9,000 tons. Evidence suggests that the proportion of ships over 100 tons also increased. In the 1570s there were only three ships in Kent measuring 100 tons and over. This had not changed by the mid-1580s, with just three ships of this size, and one of these, the *Francis* of Rochester, appears several times in the records

29 Notable absences are Hythe, Ramsgate, Rochester, Margate, Isle of Thanet, New Hythe, Maidstone and Gravesend.

Table 3.6 Tonnage ranges of Dover and Sandwich ships in the 1580s and 1620s.

Port	Date	Under 10 tons	10–19 tons	20–29 tons	30–39 tons	40–49 tons	50–99 tons	100+ tons
Dover	1581–82	4	13	8	7	3	2	0
	1587–88	8	13	8	8	3	6	1
	1604–05	4	18	19	4	4	7	0
	1622*	0	8	20	6	4	12	5
	1626**	0	10	5	12	8	11	10
Sandwich	1581–82	3	12	8	11	5	1	0
	1587–88	19	10	6	10	10	5	1
	1604–05	20	5	14	6	6	1	0
	1626	0	1	2	2	4	14	12

Source: see above tables.

* There are six ships with no tonnages

** The 1626 information is taken from the ship survey transcribed in Dixon, 'Economy', pp. 609–13 which records fifty-six ships. Most of the ships in the survey also appear in the 1622 port books, although many have different tonnages associated with them. For example, in the port books, the *Assurance* is recorded at 160 tons, but in the survey 240 tons. As noted above, tonnages are not recorded accurately in this period.

Table 3.7 Ships and tonnage of Kent's merchant fleet over five periods.

Period	Number of ports	Numbers of ships	Total tonnage	Average tonnage
1572–73	35	256	5868	21
1581–82	39	372	6327	17
1586–88	27	243	5118	21
1604	19	202	4192	21
1622–30	15	200	7586	38

Source: see the above tables.

as being under 100 tons.[30] By the mid-1620s, over 34 per cent of Sandwich's ships and approximately 13 per cent of Dover's ships were 100 tons or more.

Investment in bigger ships might have been linked to government policy. Owners of large vessels (those over 100 tons) might be eligible for the bounty payments granted by the Crown. These varied in format but usually involved granting the owners the right to import and export goods at lower rates of taxation. Yet, before the 1620s, only three of Kent's ships were listed as receiving bounty payments.[31] For Kent's shipowners, therefore, access to the bounty cannot have been the prime mover in encouraging the building of larger ships. There might have been an added stimulus after 1625, for in that year the bounty was revived by a royal proclamation. The revival of this practice, however, was unlikely to produce in one year more than double the number of ships 100 tons and over which operated out of Dover and Sandwich.

Kent's Maritime Community, *c.*1565–1630

Ships needed people to build and operate them and required continual maintenance and repair. Crews needed to be supplied with food and arms to protect themselves, their ship and the cargo. Put simply, building, operating and maintaining merchant ships required a large workforce. Yet, defining Kent's maritime community can be challenging. Viewed widely it would include not just those who operated ships such as mariners and shipmasters, but an array of people including shipowners, shipwrights, carpenters, ropemakers, stevedores, sailmakers and merchants. At its narrowest, it might only include those working directly aboard ships, the 'shipboard community'. Where do we set the geographical limits for Kent's maritime community? Do we include the ferry operators who provided vital services across the riverine networks of Kent? It is worth bearing in mind that, in the sixteenth century, vessels of up to 15 tons could sail inland as far as Bedford, and ships of this size and smaller regularly sailed from Kent across to France, and the Low Countries.[32]

In this period, estuarine and riverine communities were complex. In such places lived many fisher-farmers, people who took to the waterways, but also used the plough. Craftspeople might also own vessels that enabled them to transport the commodities they required for their main occupation. Maltsters

30 TNA, SP 12/156, fols 88v, 119r; E 190/6/8, fols 28r, 71v; SP 12/148, fols 163r, 166r. The other two vessels were the *Ruby* of Dover (140 tons, SP 12/198, fol. 53r) and the *Grace of God* of Sandwich (100 tons, SP 12/198, fol. 5r).

31 The 120-ton *Luke Evangelist* of Erith, 1573; the 240-ton *Mayflower* of Rochester, 1604; the 190-ton *Amity* of Rochester, 1610. See Brian Dietz, 'The Royal Bounty and English Merchant Shipping in the Sixteenth and Seventeenth Centuries', *The Mariner's Mirror*, 77 (1991), 5–20.

32 David Loades, 'The English Maritime Community', in Cheryl. A. Fury (ed.), *The Social History of English Seamen, 1485–1649* (Woodbridge, 2012), pp. 5–26, at p. 5.

and brewers might act as merchants and shipmasters as they transported the barley and malt they needed. Usually, such people only traded coastwise, but they did operate ships of various sizes.[33] The complexity of maritime communities is neatly demonstrated by a 1587 survey of Lydd which shows that several masters and owners of fishing vessels also worked as bakers, husbandmen, blacksmiths, carpenters, tailors and thatchers.[34] In times of emergency, people might be pulled into the maritime community temporarily as they sought paid employment or were pressed into service. Although outside the period of investigation here, in 1372 the *Cog John* of Dover, which undertook a naval patrol to combat 'the malice of enemies', drew over three-quarters of its mariners from places outside of Dover such as Folkestone and Kingston, the latter a village somewhat inland within close reach of Dover.[35] Such recruitment practices probably changed little from the late Middle Ages into the Elizabethan period. Indeed, as Cheryl Fury points out, in the latter the regulation of maritime personnel was never fully enforced, which created opportunities for a multitude of people to work aboard ships temporarily.[36] Bearing in mind the complexity of the maritime community, the following analysis will focus on three areas. First, it will examine the size of Kent's maritime labour force. Secondly, it will investigate the working patterns of Kent's shipmasters, and thirdly it will assess the ages of various members of the shipboard community.

In 1566, a series of surveys were undertaken into the maritime communities of several counties. Fortunately, the one for Kent survives and contains a large amount of detail about the size of its maritime community.[37] It reveals that in twenty ports there were 924 shipmasters, mariners, and fishermen. Given this survey only covers twenty ports, the number in 1566 would have been larger than the survey reveals. It is unlikely that the surveyors paid close attention to the fact that many residents of coastal and riverine settlements had multiple occupations, only some of which were waterborne, a concept known today as the paramaritime.[38] The surveyors were likely concerned with only those people they could 'fix' directly to a ship or boat: the shipboard community. The survey

33 Leanna T. P. Brinkley, *Coastal Trade and Maritime Communities in Elizabethan England* (Woodbridge, 2024), p. 149

34 TNA, SP 12/198, fol. 51r. Also, see Gibson, '1566 Survey', 341–53.

35 TNA, E 101/31/32, m. 2 refers to 'la malice des enemys'.

36 Cheryl A. Fury, 'Training and Education in the Elizabethan Maritime Community, 1595–1603', *The Mariner's Mirror*, 85 (1999), 147–61. See also Geoffrey V. Scammell, 'The Merchant Service Master in Early Modern England', in Geoffrey V Scammell, *Seafaring, Sailors and Trade, 1450–1750: Studies in British and European Maritime and Imperial History* (Aldershot, 2003), pp. 1–22.

37 Gibson, '1566 Survey'.

38 Gérard Le Bouedec, 'La pluriactivité dans les sociétés littorales XVIIe–XIXe siècle', *Annales de Bretagne et des Pays de l'Ouest*, 109 (2002), 61–90; Isaac Land,

of 1582 is the next to provide us with some information as to its potential size. Table 3.8 reconstructs the information provided by the 1582 survey.

According to the 1582 survey, there were some 795 members of the shipboard community. This must be a minimum figure because none of the Kent totals include fishers. The same survey tells us there were 160 fishers in the Sussex port of Rye, so it is safe to assume many more than this lived and worked in Kent's coastal communities. If we take the surveys at face value, the shipboard community of Kent remained relatively stable from the 1560s to the early 1580s. There are some additional musters and certificates dated to the later 1580s that provide information on the shipboard community of Kent, but these only cover the towns of Dymchurch, Folkestone, Hythe, Lydd, Romney, Sandwich and Walmer.[39]

Some seventeenth-century surveys provide information on the numbers of fishers and mariners. For example, in 1623 we are told there were forty-five 'fishermen and seafaring men' in Hythe.[40] In the same year, a survey shows that in Lydd there were eight shipmasters and twenty-one people described as those 'such as usually goe to sea in the fyshinge season with the said masters'. Three of these individuals had been pressed into naval service.[41] A 1626 survey of Walmer reveals a total of eleven shipowners, including one woman, one mariner, and twelve fishermen.[42] The same survey tells us that in Deal there were fifteen people described as pilots, one mariner, twenty fishermen, and twelve sailors. In Ramsgate, there were twenty-one ships owned by forty-one people, including two women.[43] There are more musters dated to 1629–30, one focused on London but which captures several towns in Kent, and a general muster book for the county.[44] Table 3.9 shows the distribution of the named members of the shipboard community and their given occupations.

'Port Towns and the Paramaritime', in Jowitt et al. (eds), *The Routledge Companion to Marine and Maritime Worlds*, pp. 177–201.

39 See TNA, SP 12/198. This records the names of 216 shipmasters, fishers, and mariners.

40 TNA, SP 14/142, fol. 91.

41 TNA, SP 14/142, fol. 111. William Larrance, shipmaster, Thomas Hull, fisher, and Edward Carpenter, fisher.

42 TNA, SP 16/39, fol. 56. The female owner in Walmer was Widow Cocke who part-owned two small boats of 2 tons.

43 TNA, SP 16/39, fols 60–61. The female owners in Ramsgate were Widow Hult (Lult) who part-owned the 8-ton *Greyhound*, Widow Culmen who part-owned the 26-ton *Vineyard*, and Widow Copyn who part-owned the 16-ton *Richard*.

44 TNA, SP 16/132, fols 30–38. The London muster is SP 16/135 and the relevant sections for Kent can be found on fols 5–54r and 105r–163r.

Table 3.8 The shipboard community of Kent, 1582.

Place	Numbers of 'seafaring men'	Shipmasters	Mariners
Whitstable	29		
Herne Bay	4		
Milton Regis	52		
Rainham	24		
Upchurch	13		
Halstow	11		
Sittingbourne	9		
Tonge	2		
Queenborough	18		
Gillingham	35		
Rochester	18		
Maidstone	15		
Dartford	13		
Sandwich		33	109
Deal		5	30
Walmer		3	15
Ramsgate		13	37
Dover		25	80
St Peters		6	24
St Johns		2	6
Ringwould		2	10
Hythe		12	64
Faversham		16	
New Hythe		11	49
Total	243	128	424

Source: TNA, SP 12/156, fol. 102.

Table 3.9 The shipboard community of Kent, according to the 1630 musters.

Place	Number of people	Occupation (number)
Chatham	3	Shipmaster (1)
		Shipmaster/owner (1)
		Shipowner (1)
Deptford	62	Boatswain (1)
		Fisher (3)
		Gunner (2)
		Mariner (30)
		Quartermaster (4)
		Shipmaster (3)
		Waterman (19)
Erith with Woolwich	24	Fisher (5)
		Waterman (19)
Gillingham	38	Fisher (29)
		Mariner (6)
		Shipmaster (1)
		Shipmaster/owner (2)
Gravesend	128	Boatswain (1)
		Gunner (4)
		King's Servant (1)
		Mariner (1)
		Quartermaster (1)
		Sailor (1)
		Shipmaster (1)
		Shipmaster/owner (2)
		Trumpeter (2)
		Waterman (114)
Greenwich	152	Boatswain (3)
		Fisher (14)

Table 3.9 The shipboard community of Kent. (*continued*)

Place	Number of people	Occupation (number)
		King's Servant (9)
		Mariner (10)
		Quartergunner (1)
		Queen's Servant (2)
		Shipmaster (1)
		Waterman (110)
		Unknown (2)
High Halstow	3	Fisher (3)
Lower Halstow	34	Fisher (13)
		Mariner (13)
		Shipmaster/owner (8)
Maidenhead	3	Waterman (3)
Milton Regis	99	Fisher (47)
		Mariner (25)
		Servant (3)
		Shipmaster (2)
		Shipmaster/owner (17)
		Shipowner (5)
Oare	20	Fisher (19)
		Shipmaster/owner (1)
Queenborough	31	Fisher (14)
		Mariner (9)
		Servant (1)
		Shipmaster/owner (6)
		Shipowner (1)
Rainham	16	Fisher (6)

Table 3.9 The shipboard community of Kent. (*continued*)

Place	Number of people	Occupation (number)
		Mariner (6)
		Shipmaster/owner (4)
Seasalter	42	Fisher (17)
		Mariner (15)
		Shipmaster (1)
		Shipmaster/owner (8)
		Shipowner (1)
Sittingbourne	5	Mariner (1)
		Shipmaster (1)
		Shipmaster/owner (2)
		Shipowner (1)
Strood	57	Fisher (43)
		Mariner (9)
		Shipmaster/owner (5)
Teynham	2	Fisher (2)
Upchurch	38	Fisher (30)
		Mariner (4)
		Servant (1)
		Shipmaster/owner (3)

Source: TNA, SP 16/132, fols 30–38; SP 16/135, fols 5–54r, 105r–163r

There are 757 individuals recorded on these musters. Of these, 265 (35 per cent) were watermen and 245 (33 per cent) were fisherfolk. The seabound 'ship-board community', including boatswains, mariners, sailors, shipmasters, quartermasters, gunners and shipowners/masters and trumpeters accounted for 219 (29 per cent) people. Of course, key towns such as Sandwich, Dover, Rochester, Faversham, Folkestone, Margate and Hythe are not included. A certificate for Faversham dated to 1596 reveals there were twenty-seven mariners and thirty-five shipmasters in the town.[45] Dover and Sandwich would have contained more mariners and masters than Faversham. As the above tables show, at least thirty-five to forty settlements in Kent engaged directly in maritime activity. If these places were surveyed in 1630, we might have the names of approximately 1,500 people.

The three key surveys that were undertaken in 1566 (924), 1582 (795), and 1630 (757) reveal a rather static maritime community. As noted, these surveys do not include all coastal and riverine places in Kent. In 1566 only seventeen places were listed, twenty-four in 1582 and eighteen in 1630. Indeed, only five places appear in both the 1566 and 1630 surveys.[46] Moreover, the evidence presented above shows that as we move into the seventeenth century Kent's merchant fleet was expanding. In 1566, it was approximately 3,900 tons, in 1582 it measured over 6,300 tons, and we have a recorded figure of over 7,500 tons for the 1620s–30s. As pointed out above, in 1630 the tonnage of Kent's merchant fleet might have been 9,000. How could the tonnage increase but the maritime community remain static? One explanation is that ships in the seventeenth century had higher labour productivity and other efficiency gains. Musters, certificates and government surveys which show labour-to-ton ratios also come with interpretive problems. For example, there seem to be regional differences in the number of mariners required per ton of ship. Geoffrey Scammell noted how some sixteenth-century ships could have labour:ton ratios of 1:3 while other vessels had ratios of 1:8 or even 1:13.[47] In Poole in 1565, there were twenty-three ships, measuring 419 tons, manned by 193 masters, mariners, and boys; a labour:ton ratio of approximately 1:2.[48] In Bridlington in 1570 there were seven mariners linked with a 35-ton vessel (1:5), and a 30-ton vessel at Whitby had ten mariners (1:3). In Hull, however, crew levels seem to be far lower with ratios of 1:7 and even 1:12.[49] Crew levels were also likely shaped by the economic activity the ship engaged in. Colliers working out of Newcastle, for example, probably required fewer mariners as they transported low value bulk cargo. Indeed, this would explain why a survey in 1587 shows Newcastle ships with labour:ton ratios of 1:8.[50]

Occasionally, we have what seem like crew lists for some of Kent's ships. It is not clear, however, if all the crew were recorded. In 1587, the 50-ton *Grace*

45 KHLC, Fa/CPm 33.

46 Halstow, Queenborough, Upchurch, Milton Regis and Rainham.

47 Geoffrey V. Scammell, 'Manning the English Merchant Service in the Sixteenth Century', *The Mariner's Mirror*, 56 (1970), 131–54.

48 TNA, SP 12/38, fols 44–50.

49 TNA, SP 12/73, fols 35v, 36r.

50 Scammell, 'Manning', p. 132.

of God of Dover had one master and two mariners, while the 12-ton *Peter* was operated by one master and four mariners.[51] In 1629, the 24-ton *Primrose* of Strood had a crew of four and a hoy of 18 tons was operated by a crew of three.[52] There were, of course, bound to be outliers in that some ships for a variety of reasons might be more extravagantly crewed than others. Used carefully, however, the musters, certificates and surveys for Kent allow us to demonstrate that as we move into the seventeenth century fewer mariners per ton were required. Ships in Kent in 1566, for example, required one mariner for every 3 tons. In 1582 Kent's ships required one mariner for every 4 tons. By 1628–29 the ratio was one mariner for every 6 tons. Put simply, a ship sailing in 1629, twice the size of one in 1566, could be operated by the same number of mariners. In 1587, for example, the 32-ton *Mary Flower* of Dover was operated by one master and five mariners, giving a labour:ton ratio of approximately 1:5.[53] In 1629 the 22-ton *Ann* of Gillingham had a crew of three (1:7). In Queenborough, the *Charity* of 35 tons had a crew of five (1:7). In Halstow, the 14-ton *Morning Joy* had a crew of two (1:7).[54] There were of course exceptions. The 20-ton *Thomas* of Milton Regis had a crew of five (1:4) and the 8-ton *John* of Halstow had a crew of three (1:2).[55] Indeed, as pointed out in Chapter 2, there were local differences within Kent. From the 1560s to the late 1620s, Dover and Sandwich vessels went from needing approximately one mariner for every 5 tons to one mariner for every 21 tons. Yet, over the same period, ships from other places in Kent continued to be operated by one mariner for every 3 or 5 tons. Nevertheless, as noted in Chapter 2, the general trend from the 1560s to the 1620s was for labour efficiency savings which meant ships required fewer people to operate them.

It is important to remember, however, that labour:ton information relates to the shipboard community, not the wider maritime community. As trade expanded this could have stimulated growth in subsidiary sectors of the maritime economy. This might be especially so for Kent due to its proximity to the Low Countries, London, and the busy coastal trade networks centred on Essex, Suffolk and Norfolk. Many people would also work on the county's rivers or the east coast coal trade. In 1635, for example, Vincenzo Gussoni, the Venetian ambassador to the Dutch Republic, reported that 20,000 boatmen worked on the Thames between Rochester and Gravesend.[56] Not all these boatmen would be from Kent, but many surely were. There is also the

51 TNA, SP 12/198, fol. 53r.

52 TNA, SP 16/132, fols 31r–v.

53 TNA, SP 12/198, fol. 53r.

54 TNA, SP 16/132, fols 32r, 33r, 34v.

55 TNA, SP 16/138, fols 33r, 35v.

56 Allen B. Hinds (ed.), *Calendar of State Papers Relating to English Affairs in the Archives of Venice, 23, 1632–1636* (London, 1921), 13 April 1635, p. 365. The

paramaritime to consider. Many people working in maritime activities would not be recorded in these surveys, especially women, who played an important role in the fishing industry of Kent. In 1629, Mary Shaw of Milton Regis was named as part-owner of the 14-ton *Violet*.[57] It is likely therefore that across the period covered in this chapter Kent's wider 'maritime community' numbered over 2,000.

In addition to providing us with evidence as to the possible size of Kent's maritime community, the musters of 1629–30 also record the occupations and ages of those listed, allowing us to investigate the average ages of different members of Kent's maritime community.

Table 3.10 Ages of people mustered in Kent, 1629–30.

Occupation	Number	Average age	Youngest	Oldest
Boatswain	5	36	24	50
Fisher	222	29	13	62
Gunner	5	36	22	56
King's Servant	4	41	21	56
Mariner	116	22	15	55
Quartergunner	1	36		
Quartermaster	5	32	25	48
Sailor	1	40		
Servant (aboard a ship)	5	18	15	20
Shipmaster	11	38	22	62
Shipmaster/owner	58	40	24	69
Shipowner	7	45	26	65
Trumpeter	2	24	22	26
Waterman	244	32	17	69

Source: TNA, SP 12/132, fol. 30; SP 16/135, fols 5–54r, 105r–163r. Note: not all those mustered are provided with ages, and the London muster is badly damaged.

full report covers pp. 361–70. From 1632 to 1634 Gussoni was a diplomatic agent in England and was well-placed to provide such information.

57 TNA, SP 16/132, fol. 36v.

The ages probably come as little surprise. That shipowners were, on average, older than mariners is to be expected. Unless shipowners inherited a ship at a young age it would take time to accrue the necessary capital to buy a ship. Of course, some owners could have been 'arm's-length' investors without any prior involvement in the maritime community. This might have been true of gentry families who would often invest in fishing vessels but never operate them. There were also familial links between owners and masters. In 1630, in Milton Regis, Roger Barton senior (65 years old) owned the 30-ton *Prosperous* and Roger Barton junior (42 years old) the 16-ton *Mary*. By 1630, Barton senior had probably retired to the quayside while Barton junior continued to work at sea. Moreover, there was a larger pool of shipmasters/owners than shipowners. This suggests that Kent's shipowners were an active part of the shipboard community. We can see evidence of owners/masters also involving their relatives in the business of shipping. In 1629, William Robinson (aged 55) was the master/owner of the 14-ton *Angel* of Halstow and John Robinson (aged 24) was part of the crew.[58] In 1629, Nicholas Suddall owned and commanded the 24-ton *Primrose* of Strood and Nicholas Suddall (aged 19) and William Suddall (aged 20) were crew members.[59] These linkages show older family members providing opportunities for younger generations to gain the necessary skills and experience to one day own vessels of their own.[60]

The port books also allow us to reconstruct the careers of Kent's shipmasters. This can be done in various ways, such as undertaking enriched biographies of a sample of shipmasters. But first, let us undertake a macro-level analysis of the working lives of shipmasters. Table 3.11 provides information on the number of shipmasters in a selection of ports and reconstructs their service patterns.

Table 3.11 Service patterns of Kent's shipmasters, by port, 1565–90.

Ports	Numbers of masters	Only overseas	Only coastal	Both
Aylesford	5	0	5	0
Broadstairs	23	11	12	0
Dartford	6	1	5	0
Dover	125	34	58	33
Erith	4	2	1	1
Faversham	103	22	70	11
Folkestone	13	3	8	2

58 TNA, SP 16/132, fol. 33r.

59 TNA, SP 12/132, fol. 31v.

60 *Ibid.*

Table 3.11 Service patterns of Kent's shipmasters, by port, 1565–90. (*continued*)

Ports	Numbers of masters	Only overseas	Only coastal	Both
Fordwich	1	0	1	0
Gillingham	9	0	8	1
Halling	7	0	7	0
Halstow (Lower)	4	0	4	0
Harty	7	0	7	0
Herne Bay	4	1	3	0
Hoo St Werburgh	2	0	2	0
Hythe	69	25	32	12
Lydd	3	0	3	0
Maidstone	54	1	50	3
Margate	38	4	31	3
Millhall	36	0	35	1
Milton Regis	77	11	64	2
Minster on Sea	1	0	1	0
New Hythe	31	1	30	0
Northfleet	1	0	1	0
Oare	4	1	3	0
Queenborough	16	4	12	0
Rainham	24	0	24	0
Ramsgate	24	7	10	7
Reculver	2	0	2	0
Rochester	45	2	42	1
Sandwich	163	56	71	36
Sittingbourne	7	0	6	1
Snodland	2	0	2	0
St Mary's Bay	3	0	3	0
Strood	8	0	8	0
Tonge	1	0	1	0
Whitstable	19	1	17	1
Total	941	187 (20%)	639 (68%)	115 (12%)

Source: see above tables.

Up to 1590, a fifth of masters worked solely in overseas trade and over two-thirds worked only in the coastal trade. Not surprisingly, masters from small settlements, such as Halling and Gillingham, tended to sail predominately coastwise. In such places, a single shipmaster might be responsible for most voyages. From 1565 to 1585, Richard Gorham of Gillingham was responsible for forty-two of the fifty-four overseas and coastal voyages that left or entered the port.[61] Apart from three overseas voyages, his career was focused on coastal runs between Sandwich and London, although he undertook a few voyages to Devon and Dorset. In 1571, he commanded the 60-ton *Trinity Richard* when he helped to ship a large cargo of wool out of London.[62] In 1579, he commanded the same vessel when he entered Exeter with a cargo of hops and malt for Richard Pinder of Sandwich.[63] Many of the masters doing coastal runs were involved in the shipment of grain. For example, in February 1580 John Cock skippered the 20-ton *Trinity* of Broadstairs from Margate to Hythe with a cargo of malt.[64] Masters working from smaller ports often also shipped sundry goods across Kent, Sussex and London. In 1565, for example, Robert Cole of Harty commanded the 7-ton *John* to London with a cargo of haberdasheries, hops, and soap.[65]

In other ports, there could be an equal number of masters working in both branches of trade. In Broadstairs, almost half only worked in overseas trade. In Hythe, if we include those in the 'both' category, most masters had experience sailing overseas. Most of Hythe's overseas trade was focused on Calais, Boulogne-sur-Mer and Dieppe. One of the key exports from Hythe was horses.[66] Some shipmasters specialised in the Boulogne trade. From February to September 1574, John Buckland made eleven runs to the French port moving horses. Over the same period, Michael Buckland, presumably a relative of John, was also a frequent visitor, again freighting horses. These two masters also worked regularly with merchants from London, Sussex, and places across Kent such as Canterbury and Saltwood.[67]

61 His voyages are in the following port books: TNA, E 190/1/5; E 190/3/1; E 190/5/6; E 190/6/5; E 190/473/7; E 190/638/1; E 190/639/11; E 190/740/25; E 190/741/19; E 190/741/21; E 190/743/6; E 190/814/8; E 190/815/2; E 190/932/8.

62 TNA, E 190/1/5, fols 1r–2v; E 190/5/6, fols 1r–v.

63 TNA, E 190/932/8, fol. 1r. The name of the vessel suggests Gorham was probably the owner or part-owner.

64 TNA, E 190/741/17, fol. 2v.

65 TNA, E 190/3/1, fol. 36v.

66 See, for example, TNA, E 190/739/25, which shows a significant number of horses being moved from Hythe to Boulogne-sur-Mer.

67 See, for example, TNA, E 190/740/29, which neatly highlights the activity of John and Michael Buckland.

By the Elizabethan period, even larger ports such as Sandwich focused on coasting. As noted in Chapter 2, the increasing focus on coastal trade was driven by the accelerated growth of London in the sixteenth century and the rise of the metropolitan market. From the end of Elizabeth's reign until 1640, London's export volume increased fivefold.[68] This expansion in overseas activity encouraged more coastal trade as demand for materials such as hemp and rope soared. More importantly, the growing population of London needed feeding. In the first four decades of the seventeenth century, the population of the city grew rapidly. In East London land was drained and wharfed which encouraged settlement on a large scale. In 1600, the population of these eastern districts was approximately 21,000; by the end of the century it was over 91,000.[69]

Kent's shippers were ideally placed to benefit from this growth. From May 1565 to August 1587, an incredible ninety-six journeys by Thomas Wheeler of Sandwich appear in surviving records. For two of these voyages, he sailed to Newcastle, one was to Maidstone and one to Christchurch, but for the rest, he sailed to or from London.[70] Often he would move wool, lead and foodstuffs such as figs, herring and vinegar from London to Sandwich and return with products such as butter and wheat.[71] Another prolific Sandwich coaster was William Goldatche. From 1565 to 1570, Goldatche made at least forty voyages with most centred on London. Usually in command of the 20-ton *Matthew*, he frequently shipped cloth into London and returned to Sandwich with wool and foodstuffs.[72] In fact, from 1565 to 1590, three Sandwich shipmasters, Thomas Wheeler (ninety-six voyages), William Cook (seventy-eight voyages) and William Goldatche (forty voyages), were responsible for 48 per cent of coastal voyages to and from Sandwich. Sandwich also attracted shipmasters from other ports. In 1566, Robert Monday and William Lamberd, both from Poole,

68 F. J. Fisher, 'London's Export Trade in the Early Seventeenth Century', *Economic History Review*, 2nd series, 3 (1950), 151–61, at p. 152.

69 M. J. Power, 'East London Housing in the Seventeenth Century', in Peter Clark and Paul Slack (eds), *Crisis and Order in English Towns, 1500–1700: Essays in Urban History* (London, 1972), pp. 237–62, at p. 237. East London is defined by Power as the 'area lying east and north-east of the City of London, comprising the parishes of Stepney and Whitechapel, East Smithfield, the Liberty of Minories and the precinct of St Katherine's Hospital'. Within its boundaries, therefore, were important maritime places such as Wapping, Limehouse and Shadwell.

70 His service record is scattered through the following books: TNA, E 190/4/1; E 190/4/3; E 190/5/4; E 190/6/1; E 190/6/2; E 190/6/5; E 190/6/6; E 190/6/8; E 190/6/9; E 190/638/1; E 190/639/2; E 190/643/5.

71 TNA, E 190/6/5, fols 1v–26, E 190/6/8, fols 19r, 50r; E 190/639/2, fols 2v, 3v, 4v.

72 TNA, E 190/3/1, fols 11v, 52r, 64r, 66r, 70r.

commanded the 25-ton *James* of Sandwich from Southampton.[73] Monday freighted 300 lb of Cornish tin for the Sandwich merchant William Everes, and Lamberd transported tin and cloth for John and Nicholas Capelin and Thomas More of Southampton.[74] In 1576, John Lennan, in command of the 14-ton *Grace of God* of Sandwich, imported 1,000 cwt of hops from Dunkirk into Southampton.[75]

Table 3.12 Service patterns of Kent's shipmasters, by port, 1595–1620.

Ports	Number of masters	Only overseas	Only coastal	Both
Aylesford	1	0	1	0
Broadstairs	15	3	10	2
Chatham	2	1	1	0
Dartford	2	0	2	0
Dover	169	46	67	56
Faversham	72	20	38	14
Folkestone	3	1	2	0
Fulston	1	1	0	0
Gillingham	19	3	15	1
Gravesend	14	0	14	0
Halstow (Low. & High.)	10	0	10	0
Harty	1	0	1	0
Hoo St Werburgh	1	0	1	0
Hythe*	26	11	6	9
Maidstone	39	0	36	3
Margate	45	12	24	9
Millhall	22	0	22	0
Milton Regis	62	7	48	7
New Hythe	13	0	13	0
Oare	1	1	0	0

73 TNA, E 190/814/3, fols 25v, 29r. Both masters sailed from Southampton to La Rochelle.

74 The Capelin family had close ties with Cornwall and were active in the tin trade: see Brinkley, *Coastal Trade*.

75 TNA, E 190/814/10, fol. 24r.

Table 3.12 Service patterns of Kent's shipmasters, by port, 1595–1620. (*continued*)

Ports	Number of masters	Only overseas	Only coastal	Both
Queenborough	15	2	12	1
Rainham	28	0	27	1
Ramsgate	8	3	5	0
Rochester	55	11	43	1
*Sandwich**	119	50	50	19
Sittingbourne	10	1	7	2
Snodland	3	0	3	0
Stoke (Hoo)	3	0	3	0
Strood	13	0	13	0
Teynham	3	0	3	0
Upchurch	2	0	2	0
Whitstable	13	0	9	4
Total	790	173 (22%)	488 (62%)	129 (16%)

Source: see above tables.

*Only books from 1594–1605 were used for this port.

**Due to documentary coverage the sample for Sandwich includes port books from 1594 and 1621–3.

As we move into the latter part of the sixteenth and into the seventeenth century, we can see a small shift in the service patterns of Kent's masters (see Table 3.12). Up to 1590, 20 per cent of Kent's shipmasters only worked in overseas trade, but in the later period, this increased to 22 per cent. In some ports, the service patterns remained largely static. This might be because native shipmasters were more conservative and focused on established routes. Overseas trade at this time was also increasingly dominated by Dutch shippers, which might have encouraged English traders to stick with the routes and commercial networks they were familiar with. In Dover, from 1565 to 1620, the proportion of masters working only overseas remained the same, as it did in Sandwich.

Other ports had sharper differences between the two periods. From the 1590s the proportion of Hythe shipmasters sailing only overseas increased. This can be partly explained by the smaller sample for Hythe in the 1595–1620 period, but events in France might have influenced these patterns. While horses remained an important export from Hythe to Boulogne-sur-Mer, by the mid-1590s firearms were shipped to Boulogne in large numbers. From 3

October 1598 to September 1599, for example, 124 arquebuses were transported in seventeen shipments from Hythe to Boulogne.[76] Indeed, apart from two voyages that exported beer to Dieppe, all Hythe exports in 1598–99 consisted of shipments of firearms to Boulogne. The religious upheaval in France might have intensified this firearms trade. Since the Edict of Boulogne (1573) and the Edict of Nantes (1598) tensions had eased somewhat, but Boulogne was in a region associated with longstanding Huguenot support, where the demand for weapons remained high.[77]

Some of the overseas masters were busy. From 1595 to 1620, Thomas Askey was responsible for 13 per cent of all Faversham's overseas voyages.[78] His principal focus was Dunkirk, but he also sailed to Vlissingen and Calais, mostly in command of the *Mackerel* and the 12-ton *Anne*.[79] From Dunkirk, he imported Flemish cloth, hops and Spanish wines. The main export from Faversham was cloth of various sorts. Some masters, such as Michael Borough from Faversham, operated in coastal and overseas trade. From 1598 to 1612, he worked solely in the coasting trade, principally sailing from Faversham into London.[80] In 1613, however, he switched to overseas voyages, sailing to Vlissingen, Dunkirk, and Calais. From Dunkirk, he transported wheat and hops for Nicholas Barker.[81] From Vlissingen, he freighted coarse canvas for William Clegg. For his Calais trip, he acted as a merchant/master when he imported coal.[82] For most of his voyages, he commanded the 12-ton *Grace of God*, which suggests some form of ownership of this vessel.[83]

As noted above, some shipmasters would work from more than one port, but when doing so, they usually undertook the same types of voyages (coastal or overseas) from these places. In the early 1600s, Thomas Arkinstall sailed out of Rochester and Strood, but he always sailed coastwise.[84] In 1599, William Bensted sailed out of Gillingham and in 1609 he operated a ship out of Rainham, but he only worked in the coasting trade.[85] In the 1580s, John Billinghurst worked out of Maidstone, Millhall, New Hythe and Rochester, but always sailed coastwise, principally between Rochester and London.[86]

76 TNA, E 190/750/14.

77 These wars are complex and occurred over a long period: see Mack P. Holt, *The French Wars of Religion, 1562–1629*, 2nd edition (Cambridge, 2012).

78 He was active from 1616 to 1619: TNA, E 190/651/11; E 190/652/2; E 190/652/9.

79 There are no tonnages for the *Mackerel*.

80 See, for example, TNA, E 190/646/8; E 190/646/10; E 190/647/6; E 190/648/1.

81 TNA, E 190/650/8, fol. 1r.

82 TNA, E 190/653/5, fols 1v, 5r–6r.

83 The vessel was sometimes called the *Gift* or the *Grace*.

84 TNA, E 190/648/15, fol. 3v; E 190/647/10, fol. 2v; E 190/650/2, fol. 6v.

85 TNA, E 190/646/12, fol. 1v; E 190/649/7, fol. 1v.

86 TNA, E 190/642/4, fols 1r–2r; E 190/642/12, fol. 1r; E 190/643/3, fol. 2v.

In the 1590s, Hugh Croome worked out of Rochester and Millhall, but only undertook coastal voyages.[87] Some masters had more complex service patterns, such as William Choppinge. In 1575, he sailed the 8-ton *Grace of God* of Margate to Nieuwpoort and in the following year he commanded the 6-ton *Mayflower* of Broadstairs from Margate to Nieuwpoort. Eleven years later, Choppinge skippered the 24-ton *William* of Dover to Newcastle, and in 1608, he commanded the 18-ton *William* from Vlissingen to Rochester.[88]

The socioeconomic status of Kent's shipmasters is difficult to assess. For other counties, we can use lay subsidy returns to measure their wealth, but the tax exemptions enjoyed by the Cinque Ports mean this is not possible for most of the key ports in Kent. We can use other sources. Surveys, for example, often reveal that many shipmasters also owned vessels. In 1580, in Faversham, of the sixteen hoys recorded thirteen were owned and skippered by the same people.[89] Some people owned multiple vessels. John Skoone, for instance, owned and skippered a ketch called the *Barnaby* and a small dredging-boat called the *Anne*. John Deacon owned and commanded a 12-ton ketch called the *Anne* but also possessed the 16-ton *Susanne*, which was skippered by John Willson. Thomas Quick owned two ketch boats, the 8-ton *Edward* and the 16-ton *Peter*, and a 2-ton dredging-cock called the *Cow Turd* (*Cowe Tourde*). The *Edward* was skippered by Quick's apprentice, Richard Keele. The port books show, however, that Quick took command of this vessel on at least two occasions in 1575 sailing from Faversham to London.[90]

The 1580 Faversham survey is also important in terms of highlighting the linkages between shippers. John Rockens is named as the owner of a 20-ton hoy called the *Michael*. The port books reveal that in 1575 he took command of this vessel at least eleven times.[91] In 1580, his apprentice on the *Michael* was Edward Freeman, aged 17.[92] A later survey of Faversham ships shows that by 1596 Freeman owned a 30-ton hoy called the *Mary*.[93] Thus, from 1580 to 1596, Freeman went from an apprentice to a shipowner. The evidence from the port books shows that he had started to skipper vessels as early as 1587 (at 24 years old) when he commanded the 12-ton *Helen* from London to Faversham freighting various cloths, Gascon wine, sack wine, and grocery and haberdashery wares for George Awsten.[94] In May 1595, he sailed from

87 TNA, E 190/644/1, fol. 3v; E 190/644/2, fol. 2r; E 190/646/7, fol. 2v.

88 TNA, E 190/639/13, fol. 12r; E 190/640/9, fol. 4v; E 190/647/7, fol. 2; E 190/648/15, fol. 1r; E 190/649/6, fol. 1r.

89 KHLC, Fa/CPm 24.

90 TNA, E 190/639/9, fols 4r–4v.

91 *Ibid.*, fols 2v–6v.

92 KHLC, Fa/CPm 24.

93 KHLC, Fa/CPm 33.

94 TNA, E 190/643/6, fol. 2v.

Vlissingen to Faversham in command of the 16-ton *Primrose* carrying 6 butts of sack wine and two barrels of codfish for Thomas Annotte.[95] From 1598 to 1605, he commanded the 12-ton *Jane* on at least twenty-six occasions, making trips to London, Vlissingen, and Dover.[96]

There were often close ties within the shipboard community. Some shipowners/masters, for example, had relatives working on vessels owned by others. John Rockens of Faversham (aged 18) was apprenticed to Henry Edward, owner and master of the 35-ton hoy called the *Mary.* This must be a relative of the John Rockens who owned the *Michael* on which Freeman was apprenticed.[97] In the 1560s and 1570s, Rockens senior commanded the *Michael* on at least twenty-six occasions, mainly sailing coastwise to London moving cloth of various sorts.[98] In 1604, John Rockens commanded the 12-ton *Helen* of Faversham to Vlissingen and Calais freighting bay salt, Gascon wine and hops.[99] Given this is nearly forty years since Rockens senior commanded the *Michael*, this was likely Rockens junior, who, by 1604, would have been approximately 42 years old. In 1604, Richard Quick also skippered the 12-ton *Martha* from Faversham to Vlissingen that May with a cargo of wheat belonging to Anthony Bodill. In June, he returned to Faversham from Vlissingen with a cargo of hops for the same merchant.[100] Richard Quick must have been a relation of Thomas Quick (owner of the *Edward* and *Peter*), further evidence of relatives of shipmasters pursuing careers at sea.

Probate records can also reveal much about the wealth of some of Kent's mariners. In 1524, the mariner Robert Wolluy of Rainham left over £40, including 6s 8d to help repair the church and a silver cross to the church worth £10.[101] Those attending his funeral were to be given one penny each. He left a manor at 'Testarton' to Beatrix, his wife, along with three score ewes with their lambs and a further £10. He bequeathed further property in Rainham to John and Thomas Wolluy, as well as to Christopher Barnard. He gave his daughter Margaret a cow and 25s – and £7 to his daughter Agnes. Other masters were equally wealthy. In 1586, Thomas Woulters bequeathed over £100 in money to various relatives.[102] He gave 20s to the poor people of Sandwich to be shared

95 TNA, E 190/645/3, fol. 1v.

96 TNA, E 190/646/10, fols 1v–6r; E 190/647/6, fols 1r–3r; E 190/648/1, fol. 1v; E 190/648/4, fols 1r–4r;

97 KHLC, Fa/CPm 24.

98 TNA, E 190/638/3, fol. 5r; E 190/639/9, fols 1v–6v; E 190/3/1, fols 17r, 31r, 39v, 47v; E 190/4/1, fols 22v, 49r; E 190/5/3, fol. 2v; E 190/5/4, fol. 3r; E 190/6/8, fols 54r–56r.

99 TNA, E 190/648/4, fols 2r–4r.

100 TNA, E 190/684/4, fol. 2r.

101 TNA, PROB 11/21, fol. 31.

102 TNA, PROB 11/69 (the folio number is too faded to read).

between them. He gave his daughter (Thomason) £60 and a silver gilded cup, a silver salter and a dozen pots and spoons, a feather bed, and various pewter platters, dishes and copper pots. Woulters first appeared in the port books in 1566 when he commanded the *William* from Sandwich to Southampton with a cargo of wheat and malt.[103] In the 1570s, he frequently took command of the 12-ton *Sampson* of Sandwich sailing to and from Vlissingen and Nieuwpoort. His last recorded voyage occurred in September 1577 when he commanded the *Sampson* from Sandwich to Nieuwpoort transporting a cargo of cloth.[104] Curiously, Woulters asked to be buried in Rye, a sign of the interconnectedness of Cinque Port communities. In the 1620s, another Thomas Woulters was working out of Sandwich, probably a relative of the Thomas who died in 1586.[105] In 1589, Richard Woolters, a mariner of East Malling, bequeathed to his son Richard £30 and to Thomas his other son £20 along with a cottage in East Malling. His daughter, Rose, received £30 20s. He gave his mother £5 yearly, with his wife Alice receiving the 'rest and residue of [my] goods'.[106] In 1575, Giles Rage of Lewisham left his three children twenty nobles 'to be paid oute of my shippes parte'. He gave his wife Elizabeth 'all the residue as well as movables as all other apparel', and his brother, William, received 40s. His mother-in-law was gifted a feather bed with three pairs of sheets and pillows.[107] In 1595, John Davis, a mariner of Queenborough, left a house to his wife, Margaery, on condition that it was sold 'to the most advantage that may be for the better mayntence of her'. From the proceeds of the sale, he wished to distribute £80 to various people, including 'John David the eldest son of his son-in-law'.[108]

An important probate record is linked with William Ferrers. As noted above, he was named on the 1572 ship survey as the master of the largest ship then in Kent, the *Luke Evangelist* of Erith. The vessel he took charge of the most, however, was the 55-ton *Trinity* of Erith.[109] His will of 1575 reveals much about his life and his wealth.[110] We learn that he owned the *Trinity*, a vessel

[103] TNA, E 190/814/3, fol. 9v.

[104] TNA, E 190/640/9, fol. 4v.

[105] TNA, E 190/657/14; E 190/656/8; SP 16/34, fol. 181v.

[106] TNA, PROB 11/73, fol. 298v. In the port books Woulters of Sandwich was often spelt Woolters. He was clearly related to the Richard Woolters of East Malling.

[107] TNA, PROB 11/57.

[108] TNA, PROB 11/85, fol. 153.

[109] His service with this ship is recorded in the following port books: TNA, E 190/3/1, fols 68r, 68v, 69r; E 190/4/1, fols 2r, 41r, 54r, E 190/4/2, fol. 153v; E 190/1010/12, fols 3r–4v; E 190/1010/13, fols 3r, 4r; E 190/1010/14, fols 7r, 8v; E 190/1010/23, fol. 2r; E 190/1011/4, fols 7r, 8v; E 190/1011/8, fols 3r–4r; E 190/1011/19, fols 5r, 6r; E 190/1010/23, fol. 1r.

[110] TNA, PROB 11/57, fols 201–202.

he commanded on at least twenty-four occasions. He bequeathed the vessel to his brother Henry and forgave him his debts. William's daughters, Joan and Charity, received 'one half of all or half part of all my shipping unbequeathed with all the furniture and apparel belonging to the said and all thone half and halfe part of the gayne and profit of three viougs'. His wife (Joan) was to have 'the benefit and profit of the said shippes for the viodge that now they be of towards the payment of my debts'. Ferrers' will shows he had interests in multiple vessels. He left his daughters under the care of his partners Thomas Andrewes of London and Peter Hill of Rotherhithe.[111]

Turning to the port books, we can reconstruct the career of Ferrers in some detail. Like most of Kent's shipmasters in this period, he worked mainly in the coasting trade, and so far as we know, he only made two overseas journeys. In 1568, he skippered the *Trinity* on a voyage from Antwerp to London and four years later he entered London from Hamburg in charge of the *Luke Evangelist* which was carrying a large cargo of butter.[112] Yet other than these journeys he spent the rest of his career sailing from London to the southwest of England, principally to the ports of Helston/Helford, Truro, and Falmouth, with two voyages to Bristol. The working life of Kent's coasters was shaped by the county's proximity to London, East Anglia, Essex and Sussex, but Ferrers' career was different. In 1568, he freighted from Bristol to London a cargo of wine and lead for William Gibbons, a merchant of London, but most of his voyages were linked with Cornwall.[113] Ferrers tended to ship haberdashery wares from London to Cornish ports and bring back tin, probably for use in the growing London pewter industry. The mention in his will that Thomas Andrewes was his partner also sheds more light on the connections these two created. In 1579, Thomas Andrewes sailed the 80-ton *Elizabeth Bonaventure* from London to Helston with haberdashery wares and feathers. In 1579 and 1580, Robert Andrewes, in command of the 60-ton *Marigold*, also sailed from London to Helston. For the 1580 voyage, Thomas Andrewes was the only merchant shipping goods. In 1580, Peter Hill, another of Ferrers' partners, commanded the 60-ton *Blessing of God* from Truro to London. Indeed, a search of the port books shows Ferrers, Andrewes and Hill had developed an important stake in the coastal trade between Cornwall and London.

The above 'mariners' are shipmasters and probably shipowners, the 'elite' of the shipboard community. At the other end of the scale were ordinary mariners such as William Peacock of Faversham. In 1574, Peacock lay dying in Vlissingen and made his will. He left his wife 40s still owing to him for

111 TNA, SP 15/22, fol. 12r.

112 TNA, E 190/5/5, fol. 30r.

113 TNA, E 190/1128/12, fol. 8r.

two voyages, and £7 that was owed to him by John Giles.[114] In effect, he left his wife with nothing to collect but debts.

Conclusion

This chapter has examined the size and geographical distribution of Kent's merchant fleet over an important period. From the 1560s to the 1630s, England faced a series of potentially serious perturbations in its political relationship with Europe: the Dutch Revolt in the Low Countries, a long war with Spain, and the religious wars in France. Each of these created obstacles and opportunities for trade. Most of Kent's shipmasters worked in the coastal trade. This might have shielded many of them from the geopolitical challenges. But it is worth remembering that many of Kent's shippers also operated in the illicit economy: trading with the enemy and committing acts of piracy. The shipping capacity of Kent's ports underwent some significant changes in this period. The tonnage increased from 5,868 tons in 1572 to 7,586 tons by 1630. Yet, this must be seen as the minimum because, as argued above, by 1630 the tonnage of Kent's merchant fleet might have measured 9,000 tons.

An increase in the total tonnage of Kent's merchant fleet was not the only significant development. After 1620, Kent's shippers began to invest in bigger ships. According to the 1582 survey, there were no ships 100 tons and over in Dover or Sandwich, the two most important ports in the county. By 1587, there were only two ships of that size, and in the early seventeenth century there were again apparently none, as these presumably had ceased to operate. By the early to mid-1620s, however, this had changed dramatically. By 1626, Sandwich had twelve vessels 100 tons and over. Likewise, by 1622 Dover had five such vessels and ten by 1626. There was also an increase in ships measuring 50–99 tons. Before 1626 Sandwich had a maximum of five ships measuring 50–99 tons; by 1626 this had expanded to fourteen, an increase of 180 per cent. In 1604 Dover had seven ships measuring 50–99 tons; by 1622 there were twelve ships between 50 and 99 tons, an increase of 71 per cent. Some of these figures may be influenced by documentary coverage and survival, but similar increases occurred elsewhere. In 1604–05, Whitstable had four ships measuring 51 tons and by 1630 it had nine ships totalling 117 tons, a 129 per cent increase in tonnage. In 1604–05, Milton Regis had fourteen ships (200 tons) but in 1630 this port had twenty ships measuring 318 tons, a 59 per cent increase in tonnage. The average tonnage of Kent's ships also increased. From 1587 to 1605, the average was 21 tons, by 1630 it was 38 tons, an increase of over 80 per cent. This process can only be explained by an expansion of commercial activity.

114 TNA, PROB 11/56, fol. 36. He does not appear in the port books as a shipmaster.

The gradual increase in Kent's tonnage is in stark contrast to the ever-present decline narrative that is attached to some of the county's ports. It is difficult to know when the supposed rot set in, how long it lasted and when it might have ended. Some scholarship places the blame on the longshore drift.[115] Romney was impacted by this, but the extent to which it affected the maritime trade of other Kentish ports is less clear, as this chapter demonstrates. Much of the literature suggests that the Cinque Ports, which once comprised some of the most important maritime trading centres in the county, had declined in the fourteenth and fifteenth centuries. Such assessments have been challenged. Indeed, it has been pointed out that the reduction in the number of ships the Cinque Ports provided to naval operations was due to the changing strategic needs of the Crown.[116]

As we move into the Tudor period the decline narrative linked with some of Kent's ports continues. In the 1530s or 1540s, John Leland stated that a sunken carrack in the harbour of Sandwich had created a build-up of silt which restricted the town's trade.[117] Then, in 1565, a series of commissions were sent to examine the trade and customs houses at each head port. The return for Sandwich stated the port was decayed due to 'certeyn mershes adioyninge to the said haven'.[118] A decade later William Lambarde agreed with the commissioners by saying Sandwich had declined due to 'the abundance of light sand (wherewith the Sea hath of latter yeeres glutted the haven)'.[119] In the early eighteenth century, Defoe said the harbour was 'choked up' and had fallen into decay. Yet, he then goes on to state the inhabitants had recently built a new and impressive bridge and that the town was a place where shipments of corn, malt, and fruit were sent to London.[120] The town may have begun to suffer by Defoe's time but if, by the 1540s, Sandwich's harbour was choked,

115 See, for example, Susan Rose (ed.), *The Navy of the Lancastrian Kings: Accounts and Inventories of William Soper, Keeper of the King's Ships, 1422–1427* (London, 1982), pp. 28–9; Susan Rose, *England's Medieval Navy, 1066–1509: Ships, Men and Warfare* (Barnsley, 2013), p. 57.

116 For a detailed discussion of the literature which argues for a late medieval decline and a challenge to these narratives, see Lambert, 'Naval Service and the Cinque Ports'.

117 Lucy T. Smith (ed.), *The Itinerary of John Leland in or About the Years of 1535–1543, Parts VII and VIII, with Appendices including Extracts from Leland's Collectanea* (London, 1909), p. 48. There was more than one wreck creating problems; see Clarke et al., *Sandwich*, p. 123.

118 TNA, E 159/350, fols 349r–v.

119 William Lambarde, *A Perambulation of Kent, Conteining the Description, Hystorie, and Customes of that Shire; Written in the Yeere 1570, First Published in the Year 1576, and now Increased and Altered from the Author's Owne Last Copie* (London, 1826), p. 118.

120 Defoe, *A Tour*, p. 143.

why, by the early seventeenth century, did Sandwich shippers invest in more and bigger ships? The answer to this question lies in the way maritime trade was conducted. In 1565, a series of reports and surveys reveal that in some ports ships did not always sail into the harbour and were laden and unloaded 'in the road'. In Southampton, for example, a 16-ton lighter called *Robert* was used to serve ballast and help laden other ships.[121] The 5-ton *Hayne* owned by Robert Carpenter of Langstone did 'sarve to unlade vessells when they come with wares'.[122] We can see this occurring in the Kent port books. In February 1618, a ship which imported a cargo of 500 cwt of currants was recorded in the Sandwich books as in 'le Roade landed apud Deale'.[123] A port book covering 1626–27 shows that most of the ships classified as importing goods into Sandwich did so 'out of the Roade'.[124] Sometimes these vessels arrived, and were presumably unladen, at Ramsgate or Deal, but the trade was classified as belonging to Sandwich. It is likely that large ships arrived off the coast near Sandwich and were greeted by smaller lighters which then unloaded the cargo and transported this into the town.

It is worth stressing that Kent's traders did not passively accept coastal change. In 1565, the commissioners reported that Dover was 'muche decayed by the working of the sea which is not in manns power to helpe without greate charges'.[125] The surveyors were correct in that it would require much expense to deal with the problem, but they also underestimated the tenacity of Dover's residents. Some years after this survey, Dover's traders rose to the challenge set out by the commissioners by undertaking a series of complex and expensive infrastructure projects which, among other factors, contributed to a growth in trade.[126] Of course, there could be periods of decline. As Chapter 5 notes, during the wars of the later 1620s, there is evidence that the tonnage of some ports declined, but such peaks and troughs are common. War could also encourage the building of larger ships, which might help explain why, in the 1620s, there were more ships 100 tons and over. Indeed, from the 1570s to the 1620s, broadly, the tonnage of Kent's merchant fleet increased.

While Kent's merchant fleet expanded over this period, efficiency savings meant the shipboard community (the number of people required to operate the ships) remained largely the same size. It is important to remember, however, that those working aboard sea-going ships were not the only members of Kent's maritime community. If we were to include those working on the Medway and the Thames and those, like female shipowners, who were part of the

121 TNA, SP 12/38, fol. 77r.
122 TNA, SP 12/30, fol. 81r.
123 TNA, E 190/652/6, fol. 2r.
124 TNA, E 190/655/12. This practice is also evident in the 1630s: see E 190/658/11.
125 TNA, E 159/350, fols 349r–v.
126 See Chapter 2, this volume.

paramaritime economy, the maritime community of Kent would be much larger than the government surveys reveal, or the number calculated from labour:ton ratios. Looking at the county, the service patterns of Kent's shipmasters changed little from the 1560s to the 1620s. At a local level, however, patterns could change. Up to 1595, 11 per cent of Margate's shipmasters sailed only overseas; by 1620, 27 per cent of them did so. In Sandwich, the proportion of shipmasters working only in overseas trade increased from 34 per cent between 1565 and 1590 to 42 per cent over 1595–1620. In other places, the story is slightly more complex. In Dover from 1590 to 1620, the proportion of masters sailing only in overseas trade remained relatively static but the proportion of masters working in both coastal and overseas trade increased. From 1565 to 1595, 4 per cent of Rochester shipmasters worked only in overseas trade, between 1595 and 1620 this increased to 20 per cent.

Geopolitical conditions undoubtedly shaped the service patterns of many of Kent's shipmasters. From the 1560s the Low Countries, the location of Kent's key European trading partners, saw an armed struggle with Hapsburg Spain which in 1579 resulted in the formation of the Protestant United Provinces. During these troubles, English ships could be embargoed, as occurred in 1568. In the late 1560s through to the early 1590s, therefore, many of Kent's shipmasters might have felt more secure plying safer and more settled coastal routes, especially as an expanding London and a vibrant east coast coal trade ensured there would be plenty of opportunities. Steadily meanwhile, Kent's merchants realigned their overseas trade by focusing on Vlissingen and Middelburg in Zeeland. Furthermore, as Chapter 2 in this volume shows, after peace with Spain was agreed in 1604, there was a significant increase in tonnage sailing overseas from places such as Dover. This was especially so in the 1620s. The shift to Zeeland might also have impacted shipmaster service patterns in other ports too. From 1565 to 1590, 21 per cent of Faversham's masters only sailed overseas, after 1595 this increased to 28 per cent. From 1576 to 1625, there was a significant increase in the number of voyages Faversham ships made to or from the Dutch Republic. Peace with Spain also encouraged more voyages to and from Iberian ports. This and more settled conditions in the Low Countries probably explains why the proportion of Sandwich's masters working only in overseas trade increased after 1595. In short, while it is no surprise that coastal trade continued to dominate the service patterns of the county's shipmasters, they were also shaped by events in Europe.

The wealth of Kent's shipboard community is difficult to examine. The wills used here probably do not represent all members of the shipboard community. Undoubtedly, many mariners, watermen and fishers were like William Peacock of Faversham. A series of wills from the late fifteenth century for Hythe and Lydd show that many fishers tended to bequeath various sorts of fishing nets to relatives or occasionally shares in fishing boats. Yet, even within fisher communities, some people could accrue wealth. In 1478, Henry Bate of Lydd left over £19 in cash, and in 1479 John Stace senior of Hythe bequeathed over £16. In 1475, William Howgin of Hythe left over £18 and gave to his wife one-quarter of his two boats, *Peter the Great* and *Peter the Less*.[127] In 1474 John Cokke, shipman of Milton Regis, left his son Sampson 'all my ships with their gear', which suggests these vessels were more substantial than fishing boats.[128] Some fishers in Kent, especially those engaged in deep sea fishing, could have substantial possessions, including ships of over 20 tons, and some families used fishing to help future generations of the family climb up the socioeconomic ladder.[129]

We can conclude here by referring to the will of William Ferrers. In his will Ferrers left his partner's son, Lancelot Andrewes, £5 for his education on the condition that he 'studie divinitie and not follow the lawe'. Lancelot must have followed this advice because by 1601 he was Dean of Westminster; in 1605 he was made Bishop of Chichester. By 1609 he was Bishop of Ely, and in 1618 he became Bishop of Winchester. He forged close links with Sir Francis Walsingham and Sir Robert Cecil and published important scholarly books defending the English Crown's supremacy over the church.[130] Lancelot had a natural intelligence, but in part, he owed his rapid rise from a merchant/mariner's son to a leading bishop to the shippers from Kent who sailed to the southwest with haberdashery wares and brought back Cornish tin. These commercial activities created enough wealth to help support future generations, so they did not have to experience the hardships of hauling an anchor in a storm off the Cornish coast. They are characteristic of the entrepreneurial spirit that undoubtedly ran through most of Kent's maritime communities.

127 The wills linked with Hythe and Lydd can be found in Leland L. Duncan, 'Transcriptions of Medieval and Tudor Kent P.C.C. & C.C.C. Wills', *Kent Archaeology Society*, https://www.kentarchaeology.org.uk/news/trascriptions-of-medieval-amp-tudor-kent-pcc-amp-ccc-wills-by-l-l-duncan (accessed 21 August 2024).

128 Arthur Hussey, 'Milton Wills (next Sittingbourne)', *Archaeologia Cantiana*, 44 (1932), 79–102, at pp. 98–9.

129 See, for example, Sheila Sweetinburgh, 'Fishermen in Late Medieval and Tudor Kent', in Jowitt et al. (eds), *The Routledge Companion to Marine and Maritime Worlds*, pp. 202–20.

130 P. E. McCullough, 'Andrewes, Lancelot (1552–1626)', in G. C. G Matthew and Brian Harrison (eds), *Oxford Dictionary of National Biography*, 60 vols (Oxford, 2004), https://www.oxforddnb.com/ (accessed 21 August 2024).

4

The Defence of Kent, *c.*1540–*c.*1640

GARY PAUL BAKER

Defence of the realm was a primary concern for any government, and Kent's geographical position enhanced its strategic importance to the English Crown.[1] This was laid out with clarity by the people of Kent on 3 May 1593, when they petitioned for moderation in the assessment of the county for purveyance for the queen's household because of the burdens placed upon them both financially and militarily on both land and sea, their obligations being 'more charg then any inland cowntie or any other marytime shiere'.[2] The century spanning the last decade of the reign of Henry VIII to the eve of the English Civil War was one of particular significance for Kent militarily, especially concerning its role as a defensive bastion against foreign invasion. The final years of Henry's reign witnessed a building programme of coastal defences in England and Wales on an unprecedented scale, with several new fortifications constructed, principally along the south coast, and in Kent in particular. Nearly half a century later, the Spanish Armada brought the threat of invasion via a landing on the Kentish coast at Margate, and even after that immediate threat had passed, hostilities (and English vigilance) remained until the cessation of conflict with Spain in 1604.[3] Thereafter until the Civil War, Kent's role as a defensive bulwark diminished as the realistic prospect of invasion dwindled, but the county never entirely left the government's defensive cognisance.

As in every other county in England and Wales in the sixteenth century – and as had been the case since the Middle Ages – Kentish men were regularly

1 See, for example, four chapters on the defence of Kent from the Romans to the mid-nineteenth century by Keith Parfitt, Adrian Jobson, Christopher Ware and Andrew Lambert respectively, in Bligh, Edwards and Sweetinburgh (eds), *Maritime Kent*, pp. 85–170.

2 TNA, SP 12/245, fols 105–106. This important Kentish perspective is quoted extensively in the Introduction.

3 Colin Martin and Geoffrey Parker, *The Spanish Armada*, revised edition (Manchester, 1999), p. 31.

mustered by their towns and villages. The purpose of these county musters was to ensure that there were adequate able-bodied men available for local defence in times of crisis, that their equipment was up to standard and to perform perfunctory drills.[4] Although in previous centuries the county musters were primarily for defensive operations within the men's home county or at most within the realm, as the sixteenth century progressed the militia were increasingly used for offensive operations at home and abroad. Those of Kent were no exception.[5] These musters do not represent 'professional' soldiers, but their returns do allow us to glimpse the manpower and equipment available to the Crown should it be required.[6] Unfortunately, none of the nominal countywide musters for Kent have survived from the sixteenth century, with only a handful of returns for individual towns, lathes and hundreds remaining.[7] Nevertheless, from what does survive it is clear that the county could muster a good number of men with a variety of arms and weapons comparable with elsewhere in the kingdom. In November 1545, for instance, a muster of Kent's six most northwesterly hundreds (Axstane, Dartford and Wilmington, Little and Lesnes, Blackheath, Bromley and Beckenham, and Ruxley) named 1,036 men, a combination of archers and billmen, with 39 horses, 40 splint armours, 110 bows, 362 bills, 46 daggers, 423 furnished harnesses, 58 salets, 97 sheaves of arrows and 34 swords.[8] The quality of such troops raised by these musters varied greatly, even after the nationwide introduction of the trained bands in 1572, and little changed in this respect until more professional standards were introduced in the first half of the seventeenth century.

Kent's biggest concentrations of manpower were located within its largest urban centres. The most voluminous survival of musters from any of its towns is for Faversham, especially from 1570–96, and there is also decent coverage in the late sixteenth and seventeenth centuries for New Romney and Lydd.[9] Some of the Faversham musters even list individuals by street. In 1570, the muster of the town taken on 13 August included thirteen men residing on Court Street, twenty-six on West Street and six on Preston Street, furnished with

4 See, for instance, J. J. N. McGurk, 'Armada Preparation in Kent and Arrangements Made after the Defeat (1587–1589)', *Archaeologia Cantiana*, 85 (1971), 71–93.

5 On Kent's contributions in the late sixteenth century, see J. J. N. McGurk, 'Levies from Kent to the Elizabethan Wars, 1589–1603', *Archaeologia Cantiana*, 88 (1974), 57–72.

6 On musters and the mustering process, see Lindsay Boynton, *The Elizabethan Militia, 1558–1638* (Newton Abbot, 1971), pp. 13–52.

7 For a list of these musters, see Jeremy Gibson and Alan Dell, *Tudor and Stuart Muster Rolls: A Directory of Holdings in the British Isles* (Birmingham, 1989), p. 18.

8 TNA, E 101/61/10.

9 KHLC, Fa/CPm 1–21 (Faversham); Ly/4 8/1–21 (Lydd); NR/CPm 1/1–50 (Romney, stretching into the eighteenth century).

forty-six harquebuses.[10] By 1596, the town's trained band numbered 116 men, whilst its general/untrained band numbered 113 individuals.[11] A general muster of Faversham in 1614 revealed 364 men available for service: 147 musketeers, 70 corslets, 73 dry pikes, 6 light horsemen, 9 halberdiers and 59 individuals armed with bills and skull caps.[12] At Sandwich in 1599 the untrained/general band consisted of 158 individuals (44 pikemen, 17 musketeers, 45 calivers, and 45 pioneers alongside 7 officers) of which those armed with firearms – the musketeers and calivers – accounted for just under a third of the force.[13] By October 1614, a muster of the whole town named 506 individuals supplying 85 corslets, 14 pairs of cuirasses, 212 muskets, 125 dry pikes, 11 calivers, 2 head pieces, swords, and daggers, 109 bills and skull caps and 36 halberds. In 1619 there were 277 men in the general/untrained band alongside the 156 soldiers in the trained contingent, with just over 40 per cent of the men brandishing firearms; a reflection of the growing prevalence of these weapons.[14]

Doubtless some of those mustered manned the county's beacons. The 'beacons system' stretched back into at least the early Middle Ages, with the defensive signal fires placed in strategic locations along the coast to warn of the approach of an enemy, with lines of sight between them so that information of an impending attack could be relayed to London, with specific instructions issued by Henry VIII for their siting in 1546.[15] Initially they were probably little more than large bonfires placed upon hilltops and in church towers, but from around the eleventh year of Edward III's reign – according to William Lambarde in his *Perambulation of Kent* – 'it was ordeined, that in our shire they should be high Standards with their Pitchpots'. A map of their locations appeared first in a separate composition by Lambarde in 1585, and was then published in the second edition of his *Perambulation* in 1596.[16] Illustrations of

10 KHLC, Fa/CPm 1.

11 KHLC, Fa/CPm 20, 21.

12 TNA, SP 14/78, fol. 66.

13 KHLC, Do/ZCPW 6/1.

14 TNA, SP 14/78, fol. 43 (fols 44–57 appear to be a draft); TNA, SP 14/108, fols 25–26. The trained band in 1619 comprised nine 'officers' broadly defined (a captain, lieutenant, standard-bearer, clerk, surgeon, drummer, fife player and two sergeants), 63 'armed men' and 84 musketeers. The untrained/general band had seven 'officers' (one sergeant and no fife player), two armed men, 102 dry pikemen, 28 halberdiers, 41 billmen, 89 musketeers and 8 calivers. Just over half of the trained (53 per cent) and just over a third of the untrained troops (35 per cent) mustered with firearms.

15 H. T. White, 'The Beacon System in Kent', *Archaeologia Cantiana*, 36 (1934), 83–4.

16 William Lambarde, *A Perambulation of Kent: Conteining the Description, Hystorie, and Customes of that Shyre. Written in the Yeere 1570, by William Lambarde, of Lincolnes Inne Gent: First Published in the Yeere 1576 and now Increased and Altered after Author's Owne Last Copie* (London, 1596), p. 69 (quotation), p. 6 (map).

these structures can be seen in the coats of arms of several Kentish families, and also in a map of such structures on the coast of Dorset in the sixteenth century.[17] They were unlikely to have been manned all year round but there was an expectation that this would be the case during times of potential invasion. They were also to be used in conjunction with naval forces on occasion. In 1600, a note on 'The manner howe the River of Thames shalbe kept' stated that a pinnace called the *Sun* was to lie at Tilbury Hope that 'shall waye and shoote her ordynance to give the allarem to the fortes and *Victory*'. The *Victory*, stationed between the forts at Gravesend and Tilbury, was in turn to alert another ship, the *Lyon*, riding at Greenhithe, which, finally, was to notify more ships at Blackwall. In addition,

> the beacones of Kent, and Essex sydes be well watched, and that uppon sight of any galley, or certen allarme from the pinnace or shippes ther presently may make their fyerre. That two small katches be contynually plyenth up and downe the sands [sound] and each of them to have one peece or a mynyon or falcon in them to shoote off and give allarem uppon sight of any galley, that both the navye and also the beacones may take notice.[18]

Outside of its manpower, Kent's role as a defensive bulwark against invasion was encapsulated in the policy of Henry VIII. In the first quarter of 1539, with the country facing the prospect of invasion, the king ordered by his own 'device' ('intent' or 'desire') 'for the edificacionem of thre newe bulwerks to be made and newly edefied in the downes and other places upon the fruntures of the see'.[19] Alongside the proposed 'blokhowsys' or 'bulwerks' to be constructed in the Downs there were also to be fortresses built at Camber, Calshot Point and in the Thames. After these initial orders, others clearly followed, for the next year a 'booke of certaine of the kings majesties bullwerks, blockhowses and fortresses which his hieghnes hath caused to be newly made' listed twenty-five such places along the south coast from small earthworks to more substantial fortifications, with another list from the same year naming twenty-nine forts.[20] These newer fortifications added to the county's pre-existing medieval castles such as at Dover, Rochester and Queenborough. Over the next few years further fortifications were ordered such as at Hull in 1542 and seven in Essex in 1543, yet following Henry's

Note that all references in this chapter are to this second, 1596 edition. Lambarde's 1585 map is now in the British Library: BL, Add. MS 62935.

17 White, 'The Beacon System', 92.

18 TNA, SP 12/274, fol. 208.

19 TNA, SP 1/143, fols 188, 192.

20 TNA, SP 1/243, fol. 12; E 101/60/4.

death in 1547, the loss of Calais in 1558 and the subsequent peace treaty with France, several of these bastions fell into disrepair and were pulled down or decommissioned in the following decade.[21] After the construction of the Device Forts, further fortifications were added in Kent itself during the rest of the sixteenth century, especially in preparation for, and response to, the Armada scare, such as gun emplacements at Erith, Greenhithe and Northfleet. Alongside the establishment of the Royal Naval Dockyard at Chatham in 1567, Upnor Castle was constructed further down the Medway to protect the royal anchorage.

As important as Kent's fortifications were for defence, what is often forgotten is the county's role as a base for *offensive* operations. Kent is undoubtedly a gateway into the heart of England, but gates often swing both ways. It also served as the principal embarkation point to the continent, especially after the capture of Calais by Edward III in 1347. For much of the next two centuries until the town was recaptured by the French, numerous English armies made their way onto French soil via Calais on ships sailing out of Kentish ports. For many operations, especially when time was short, it made logistical sense to recruit men from the areas of England nearest to the place they would be fighting. The Kentish military community therefore bore a heavier burden for expeditions launched onto the continent than the English midlands and northern counties, just as the petitioners of 1593 had claimed. Thus, the men sent to Boulogne in 1544 were drawn chiefly from Kent, Middlesex, Surrey, Essex, Hertfordshire, Norfolk, Sussex and Buckinghamshire, because those from elsewhere were deemed too 'farre of'. The following year, when reinforcements were needed at the French town, the southeastern counties again bore the brunt of recruitment because other counties were 'so farre from here and they should come so Late'.[22] Similarly, when men were required for the fateful defence of Calais in January 1558, only those from counties 'nere adjoyning' Dover were to be recruited 'with all possible spede'.[23]

Even after the English gateway was permanently closed in 1558 upon Calais' fall, Kent did not revert to a county on the perennial defensive. English support for the Protestant cause against Catholic Spanish rule in the Low Countries in the last decades of Elizabeth's reign saw a continual flow of men and munitions out of England via Kent. English (and Scottish) volunteers aided their Dutch allies in the capture and garrisoning of Brielle, Fort Rammekens (near Ritthem on the then island of Walcheren) and Vlissingen (Flushing) – in 1572. Such was the importance of these locations that as the Anglo-Spanish War broke out in 1585, all three – known as the 'Cautionary Towns' – were

21 TNA, SP 1/167, fol. 70.

22 John Jeremy Goring, 'The Military Obligations of the English People, 1511–1558' (unpublished Ph.D. thesis, University of London, 1955), p. 56.

23 TNA, SP 11/12, fol. 26.

ceded by the Dutch to Elizabeth I via the Treaty of Nonsuch the same year and would remain under English control until returned to the Dutch Republic in 1616. Kent therefore acted, once again, as the staging post and supplier of English 'forward bases' on the continent.

With such a huge amount of military activity between the last decade of Henry VIII's reign and the eve of the English Civil War it is evidently impossible to focus on all its aspects in detail. This chapter will therefore examine just two important facets of Kent and its population's military role over this century. First, it will look at the county on the defensive – in terms of its fortifications – principally Henry VIII's Device Forts. Second, Kent's role as a centre for English naval operations will be examined, alongside the seaborne trade in ordnance, which were interrelated.

The Kentish Device Forts and Coastal Defence

The Kentish Device Forts were part of a major Henrician defensive building programme in the last years of Henry VIII's reign to defend the English coastline from potential invasion from France or Spain. The Kentish forts were operational by 1540 at the latest, with earthwork fortifications also a major part of the initial building scheme, probably thrown up in a hurry as a temporary measure until more permanent stone structures could be constructed.[24] In all, at their height, Kent boasted at least fourteen Device Forts, bulwarks, and blockhouses at strategic locations along the county's coastline.[25] The Downs, a roadstead (a deep stretch of sheltered water) off the east Kent coast north of Dover, was a particularly vulnerable spot, as this popular anchorage was sheltered inside Goodwin Sands and provided easy access to Deal Beach, a long, flat stretch of land where an invasion force could easily land. Consequently, three Henrician forts – often referred to as castles in contemporary documentation – were constructed there. Sandown was the most northerly and Walmer the most southerly, with Deal – frequently referred to as the 'Great Castle' – serving as the central and largest of the structures. These were connected by a series of earthworks defences, referred to in 1540 as the Great Turf Bulwark, the Little Turf Bulwark, Walmer Bulwark, and Clay Bulwark, though a further structure may have been added by the time a survey was undertaken early in Edward VI's reign, as the Downs defences were described as 'the four greene and the clay Bullwark'.[26] All of these were

[24] Peter Harrington, *The Castles of Henry VIII* (London, 2007), p. 24.

[25] The precise number, including all the earthworks in the total, is difficult to quantify. For a description and location of some of those in Kent and elsewhere, see David James Cathcart King, *The Castle in England and Wales: An Interpretative History* (London, 1988), pp. 178–87.

[26] TNA, E 101/60/4; SP 10/15, fol. 25.

designed to provide flanking arcs of fire for one another, and were connected 'by a ditch or covered way stretching for the 2½ miles of coastline; and presumably there was a defensive exterior bank created from the quarrying of the ditch'.[27] Further down the coast was the great twelfth-century medieval castle at Dover, and a series of further forts were built as part of the Device programme thereabouts to bolster this impressive bastion: Archcliffe Bulwark, the bulwark in the cliff (also known as the Black Bulwark), and Mote's Bulwark. The most southerly of Kent's Device Forts was Sandgate Castle, just south of Folkestone, protecting a vulnerable point of the coast which allows access inland between the Kentish cliffs, while the most northerly were the three blockhouses at Gravesend, Higham and Milton-next-Gravesend on the south side of the Thames Estuary, facing the fort at East Tilbury in Essex on the northern bank.[28]

The Device programme was expensive. The cost to the exchequer of the building works from 1539–47 was *c*.£376,000.[29] In September 1552, it was estimated that a staggering sum of nearly *c*.£3.5 million had been spent on various military expenses in the reigns of Henry VIII and Edward VI.[30] Of this total, the nation's fortifications – largely those resulting from Henry's Device programme – in Kent, Sussex, Cornwall, Hampshire and Isle of Wight, Dorset, Yorkshire, Essex and the Channel Islands (Alderney, Guernsey and Jersey) cumulatively cost £290,662 16s 6¼d, or just over 8 per cent of the total military expenditure in these years. The fortifications of Kent (their construction and the wages of the garrisons inclusive) amounted to over a third (35.8 per cent) of the nation's fortification costs, and nearly 3 per cent of the total military output: a large outlay for a single county (see Table 4.1).

27 Harrington, *Castles of Henry VIII*, p. 25

28 For detailed discussion of the construction and costs of the Kentish fortresses, see Martin Biddle, Howard Colvin and John Summerson, 'The Defences in Detail', in Howard Colvin (ed.), *The History of the King's Works: 1485–1660*, vol. 4 part 2 (London, 1982), pp. 455–65, 477–82, 569–87, 602–6.

29 Ware, 'To Defend the Coast', p. 134.

30 TNA, SP 10/15, fol. 29 (£3,501,471 19s 3¾d). This was equivalent to *c*.£1.6 billion in July of 2024: see The Bank of England, 'Inflation Calculator', https://www.bankofengland.co.uk/monetary-policy/inflation/inflation-calculator/ (accessed 11 September 2024).

Table 4.1 Expenses of construction and wages at Kentish fortifications, 1 March 1539–29 September 1552.

Place(s)	Total under Henry VIII: fortifications: wages:	Total wages under Edward VI	Sum Total
Dover:	£1,496 9s 3¾d	£1,058 10s	£3,613 9s 3¾d
(Archcliffe Bulwark, The bulwark below the castle, The black bulwark in Dover cliff)	£1,058 10s		
Dover Pier	£33,600 2s 10d (wages)	£9,279 18s 8d	£42,880 1s 6d
Maison Dieu, Dover (brewhouse, bakehouse, and mills within)	£3,208 7s 5½d (fortifications)		£3,208 7s 5½d
The Downs:	£27,092 12s 1¾d	£4,635 4s	£36,363 1¾d
(Deal Castle, Walmer Castle, Sandown Castle, The 4 green and the clay bulwark)	£4,635 4s		
Sandgate Castle by Folkestone	£5,587 5s 10¾d £1,095	£1,095	£7,777 5s 10¾d
Queenborough Castle	£2,702 11s 10d £1,874 2s 6d	£381 12s	£4,958 6s 4d
Gravesend Bulwarks	£1,072 £273 15s (wages for 3 years ending Mich. 1546)	£547 10s (for 6 years ending Mich. 1552)	£1,893 5s
Milton-next-Gravesend Bulwarks	£1,072 £273 15s (wages for 3 years ending Mich. 1546)	£547 10s (for 6 years ending Mich. 1552)	£1,893 5s

Table 4.1 Expenses of construction and wages at Kentish fortifications, 1 March 1539–29 September 1552. (*continued*)

Place(s)	Total under Henry VIII: fortifications: wages:	Total wages under Edward VI	Sum Total
Higham Bulwark	£980 £246 7s 6d (wages for 3 years ending Mich. 1546)	£492 15s (for 6 years ending Mich. 1552)	£1,719 2s 6d
Totals	£86,268 3s 5¾d	£18,037 19s 8d	£104,306 3s 1¾d

Source: TNA, SP 10/15, fols 25–26. The wages for the reign of Henry VIII, unless otherwise stated, are for the six years from Michaelmas 1540 to Michaelmas 1546. For Edward VI it is from thence for six years ending Michaelmas 1552.

What made the Device Forts novel was that, unlike their medieval antecedents, they were designed specifically with the use of ordnance in mind. This was the first time artillery fortifications had been built en masse in the country, designed by a combination of native and foreign architects and engineers – with perhaps a level of input from Henry VIII himself – based in part on developments in military architecture on the continent.[31] Rudimentary artillery had been employed on the battlefield and in castles in England since the fourteenth century, but it was only in the late fifteenth that a handful of fortifications began to be constructed specifically for the use of ordnance: Dartmouth Castle, Devon, for example, where a new artillery tower was completed in 1495.[32] Typically, guns were accommodated by amending the defences of existing fortifications, a fusing of innovations in military architecture and medieval design. However, medieval castles, as well as military structures, also tended to act as places of permanent residence and domestic living. The Henrician establishments, Platt argued, 'had few of the comforts that would come to be expected in the residence

31 On the design and development of the forts, see Harrington, *Castles of Henry VIII*, pp. 15–29, although note that David James Cathcart King argues that 'the extreme variation between individual castles is very notable … [indicating] that the whole series was essentially experimental, and not firmly based on any contemporary Continental practice': *The Castle in England and Wales*, p. 176.

32 Harrington, *Castles of Henry VIII*, pp. 9–10; Dan Spencer, *Royal and Urban Gunpowder Weapons in Late Medieval England* (Woodbridge, 2019), pp. 164–8.

of a magnate', and though some did contain living spaces for garrisons they were spartan by comparison.[33]

Although there were architectural idiosyncrasies at every site, and though they may have had, as Creighton explained, the 'architectural trappings of medieval castles – drawbridges, portcullises and crenelation – … [the forts] were also squat in appearance, lacking the visual impact of a lofty donjon of a motte-top tower'.[34] The forts' stocky nature and thick walls were to protect them from incoming artillery fire from enemy ships.[35] They were also tiered, with multiple gunports, enabling different types of ordnance to be stationed at different gunports to allow fire at targets at varying ranges, with splayed embrasures allowing the potential for overlapping angles of fire. Indeed, even though there were more gunports than there were artillery pieces in most forts, the sheer number of pieces was nevertheless impressive, especially in the county's larger castles at the time of their construction. In 1540, the town and port of Dover (though not a Device Fort) boasted a combination of forty-five brass and iron pieces, whilst the fort at Milton-next-Gravesend possessed thirty-six and Gravesend twenty-five, not to mention small arms like bows, arrows, bills, pikes, powder and shot.[36] A far more extensive picture of Kent's ordnance can be found in the survey, commissioned in September 1547, of the possessions of Henry VIII at the time of his death. This shows an increase from earlier numbers.[37] Deal Castle is listed with fifty-seven pieces of ordnance of various types; Dover and its bulwarks with at least eighty-six; Gravesend thirty-nine (of which three were broken); Milton forty-seven (one broken); Higham twenty-two; Queenborough Castle and Sheerness blockhouse on the Isle of Sheppey, eighteen; Sandgate Castle thirty-three (although several were in a bad state); Sandown Castle twenty-nine (not including four which were broken); and Walmer Castle thirty-seven, not including four that had broken firing a salute for a French admiral who had visited England the previous

33 Colin Platt, *The Castle in Medieval England and Wales* (London, 1982), pp. 187–8.

34 Oliver H. Creighton, *Castles and Landscapes: Power, Community and Fortification in Medieval England* (London, 2002), p. 51.

35 The most thorough investigation of a Device Fort to date is for Camber Castle, Sussex, from construction and function to excavation: Martin Biddle, Jonathan Hiller, Ian Scott and Anthony Streeten et al., *Henry VIII's Coastal Artillery Fort at Camber Castle, Rye, East Sussex* (Oxford, 2001).

36 TNA, E 101/60/3, fols 6r, 7r. These totals include harquebuses which, by their description as being made of 'yron', suggests they were artillery pieces rather than personal arms.

37 David Starkey (ed.), *The Inventory of King Henry VIII (Society of Antiquaries MS 129 and British Library MS Harley 1419): The Transcript* (London, 1998), pp. 102–44 for the whole country, Kent at pp. 105–9.

year.[38] It was also noted that the earthen bulwarks in the Downs were much defaced.[39] In total, Kent boasted 368 pieces of ordnance in its inventories at the death of Henry VIII, the most by far of any county in England, with only northeastern England, in particular the heavily-fortified border town of Berwick-upon-Tweed, in any way comparable. This wealth of ordnance emphasises the paramount role Kent played in England's defensive strategy at the end of the reign of Henry VIII.

For the following decades there does not appear to have been a complete survey of all the Kentish fortifications as comprehensive as those undertaken in the late 1540s, at least in terms of accounts which reveal the size and number of pieces of ordnance. A huge survey of the kingdom in 1574, for instance, lists the names of the coastal forts and their captains but not the number of artillery pieces.[40] At best, the documentation from the reigns of Edward VI, Mary I and Elizabeth I illuminates only fragments of the picture. An account from June 1568, for instance, reveals that Sandgate possessed eight ordnance pieces with the same number at Mote's Bulwark and Sandown Castle, seven at Walmer, ten at Deal, and twenty-six at Archcliffe Bulwark.[41] In 1588, shortly after the threat from the Armada had dissipated, the number of brass pieces of ordnance remaining in the castles, forts and bulwarks along the southern coast was 146, of which forty (or just over a quarter) were to be found in the fortresses of Kent.[42] In a similar list compiled in December the following year the number of brass pieces in Kent had risen to forty-five.[43] However, by June 1593, an investigation into the forts revealed that several required new pieces to replace the old, with many described as unserviceable.[44] A decade later in 1603 there were only fifteen brass pieces in Kent (ten at Dover, two each at Sandown and Deal, and one at Walmer) compared to the forty there had been in 1589.[45]

This was still the situation in the early seventeenth century. In 1615, several detailed surveys were conducted of Kent's fortifications that listed not only the number of ordnance pieces there – and whether they were of brass or

38 *Letters and Papers, Foreign and Domestic, of the Reign of Henry VIII. Preserved in the Public Record Office, the British Museum, and elsewhere in England*, vol. 21, part 1 (London, 1908), no. 1384 (pp. 693–7), no. 1530 (pp. 756–7).

39 Starkey, *The Inventory*, p. 108.

40 TNA, SP 12/96, fols 259–264.

41 TNA, SP 12/46, fols 168–172.

42 Brass pieces were more expensive than iron but fired more rapidly and were generally more reliable; Paul E. J. Hammer, *Elizabeth's Wars: War, Government and Society in Tudor England, 1544–1604* (Basingstoke, 2003), pp. 79–80; TNA, SP 12/219, fols 7–9.

43 TNA, SP 12/229, fols 89r–89v.

44 TNA, SP 12/245, fol. 60.

45 TNA, SP 15/35, fols 122–124.

iron – but also where the guns were positioned within each fortress, as well as the other martial equipment present. Dover, for instance, contained thirty-one pieces in total (seventeen brass and fourteen iron), a slight uptick in at least the brass guns from the ten present in 1603.[46] Similarly detailed surveys were undertaken at Deal (sixteen serviceable and five unserviceable/defective pieces), Walmer (seven and four), Sandown (twelve and six), and Sandgate (fourteen serviceable) during August and September the same year.[47] Surveys of the number of ordnance pieces at Archcliffe Bulwark (ten serviceable) and Mote's Bulwark (six) were also taken in 1613.[48] Finally, a far more comprehensive survey of Kent's forts was undertaken in 1623.[49] Dover continued to be the most heavily-armoured fortification in the county, with thirty-two pieces (eighteen brass and fourteen iron), with the other forts ranging from six at Mote's Bulwark to seventeen at Sandown, with a sister survey the same year listing only brass ordnance revealing that Gravesend possessed four such pieces and Upnor Castle eleven; very similar to numbers present in the same forts a decade later in 1633–34.[50]

Therefore, whilst we do not possess a complete picture of the number of Kent's ordnance pieces in the first eighty or so years of the Device Forts' existence, the overall trend is clear. The reigns of the last three Tudor and the first two Stuart monarchs saw the number of artillery pieces in Kent's fortresses fall by two-thirds, from a high point of *c*.370 at the end of Henry VIII's reign to 117 by 1623–24. The explanation for this decline – if we infer that the number of pieces of ordnance at the forts denotes their importance to the Crown – was because of changing strategic considerations. As Mark Fissel pointed out: 'Whereas the southern coastal fortifications received great attention under Henry VIII, the northern border castles became increasingly important under the latter three Tudors', and, after the Unification of the Crowns in 1603, 'Channel defences resumed their precedence, only to see a shift northwards again in 1638', as Charles I's troubles north of the border

46 TNA, SP 14/81, fols 20–21.

47 *Ibid.*, fol. 125 (Deal); fol. 127 (Walmer); fol. 134 (Sandown); fol. 137 (Sandgate).

48 TNA, SP 14/74, fol. 156 (Mote's Bulwark); fol. 165 (Archcliffe). Sandgate (fol. 162), Walmer (fol. 149) and Sandown (fol. 150) had also been surveyed in 1613.

49 TNA, SP 14/157, fols 87–109.

50 The totals are as follows: Dover 32 (18 brass, 14 iron); Deal 16 (1 brass, 15 iron); Sandown 17 (all iron); Walmer 11 (all iron); Sandgate 7 (all iron); Mote's Bulwark 6 (all iron); Archcliffe Bulwark 13 (all iron). The Upnor/Gravesend figures are from TNA, SP 14/152, fols 126–127. The numbers from 1633 are. Archcliffe Bulwark – nine cast-iron pieces (two of which had been unserviceable for twenty years and were thus unmounted), seven sakers, and a demi-culverin and three other sakers which were defective. Dover had eighteen bronze cannons in 1633 and twelve in 1634, with Gravesend four bronze, Upnor eleven bronze, and Deal one bronze: SP 16/231, fol. 6; SP 16/279, fol. 74.

intensified.[51] Indeed, these priorities can be seen in the existence of some of the forts themselves. Whilst some forts continued to be used for centuries, others did not long survive their construction. Milton-next-Gravesend and Higham were both decommissioned in 1553 and demolished between 1557 and 1558 to provide materials for repairs at the Tower of London, and Sheerness does not appear in the records (at least in its Tudor incarnation) after 1552.[52] Elsewhere, artillery pieces in the Kentish forts were either not replaced when they became unserviceable or were reassigned (at least the better brass pieces) to places of greater need.[53] In December 1588, for instance, Sir William Wynter estimated that Kent's forts could spare ten brass pieces of ordnance between them, presumably for the Royal Navy. Again, in March 1635, Gravesend, Upnor and Deal – alongside several fortresses in Essex and Hampshire – had their brass ordnance surveyed for the purpose of placing it on ships, with those taken to be replaced by iron guns.[54]

The fall in the number of ordnance pieces in the Kentish forts overall is an indication of their declining importance to the Crown, and there was a somewhat similar trend in the size of their garrisons (see Table 4.2). Shortly after their construction in 1540 and 1541, the forts were at their strongest numerically, accommodating *c.*140 men across all locations (if we assume the later totals of around nineteen men at Dover were present in 1540, and the nine at Milton-next-Gravesend present in 1540 were also there in 1541). This strength remained until the eve of the decommissioning of the blockhouses at Higham and Milton in *c.*1553. By 1564 the forts' manpower had reached its nadir, with less than half the number of men that had been present a decade earlier. The captains at Sandown, Deal and Walmer were described as 'in penncyon' (thus no longer on active duty), and at the latter the same was true of the gunners: 'for that all the pencione are ded ys therefore unfurnishid of sowldyers in tyme of peace'. At Mote's Bulwark not a single man remained since the 'captayne and gonners at this laste paye beinge the xv of November Anno 1564', after which they had been 'cleare dismissed'.[55] This early Elizabethan decline

51 Mark Charles Fissel, *English Warfare, 1511–1642* (London, 2001), p. 36.

52 Harrington, *Castles of Henry VIII*, pp. 80–1; TNA, SP 12/1, fol. 122; Biddle et al., 'Defences in Detail', p. 603.

53 Until the early seventeenth century most naval guns were made of brass. Even though brass was far more expensive than iron, brass was less prone to leaking and bursting. However, during the seventeenth century the technology for casting iron greatly improved, making iron pieces cheaper to produce and more robust than brass, leading to an extensive Kentish iron industry and trade in ordnance (see below). See J. D. Davies, *Pepys's Navy: Ships, Men and Warfare, 1649–1689* (Barnsley, 2008), p. 83; Jeremy Black, *European Warfare, 1494–1660* (London, 2002), pp. 173–5.

54 TNA, SP 12/219, fol. 5; SP 16/535, fol. 118.

55 TNA, SP 12/35, fols 46Ar, 46Av, 46Br, 47r.

reflects the Crown's aforementioned strategic priorities shifting northwards, but evidently the focus on the southern defences began to ramp up over the following decades, as tensions with Spain intensified with growing conflict in the Low Countries from the late 1560s onwards. By 1574–75 garrison strength had risen to eighty-two, and by the early decades of the seventeenth century numbers had stabilised at *c*.116–124 soldiers. Thereafter, this appears to have been deemed the optimal number (at least in peacetime), as a series of musters in 1664–65 shortly after the Restoration listed 122 men in total.

Table 4.2 Garrison sizes at select Kentish fortifications, 1540–1665.

Fort/castle name	1540	1541	1553–54	1564	1574–75	1616–19	1623	1664–65
Gravesend Bulwark	9	9	9		6			
Milton Blockhouse	9		9	n/a	n/a	n/a	n/a	n/a
Higham Bulwark	8	8	8	n/a	n/a	n/a	n/a	n/a
Deal Castle	28	29	29	16	13	21	22	22
Walmer Castle	19	19	19	1	11	19	19	19
Mote's Bulwark	4	4	4	0	6	13	13	12
Archcliffe Bulwark	8	4	10	6	9	7	13	13
Dover Castle			16	18	17	18	19	18
Sandgate Castle	16	16	17	7	9	19	19	19
Sandown Castle	18	19	19	9	11	19	19	19

Source: (for 1540) TNA, E 101/60/4 (E 101/60/5 is a further copy); (for 1541) E 101/60/6; E 101/62/30 likely relates to a similar period; (for 1553–54) SP 11/11, fols 154–155; SP 12/96, fol. 142v (it is unclear if these numbers represent the full garrison); (for 1564) SP 12/35, fols 46r–47r (total for Archcliffe also includes the 'Blacke bullwarke'); (for 1574–75) SP 12/96, fol. 142v; (for 1616–18) SP 14/88, fol. 154 (Dover, 1616); SP 14/93, fols 104, 106 (Deal and Sandown, 1617), SP 14/99, fol. 211; SP 14/103, fols 11, 14, 29 (Archcliffe, Mote's bulwark, and Sandgate, 1618); (for 1664–65) E 101/67/11.

Wages were paid at standard rates across the period. Regardless of size, each garrison had a captain who received 20d (1s 8d) per day, with the gunners (described also as 'cannoneers' or simply 'soldiers') each earning 6d. At the largest garrisons were also lieutenants (receiving 8d), with both the captain and the lieutenant having individuals designated as 'captain's/lieutenant's men' assigned to them (captains up to four and the lieutenant one), each receiving 6d daily. The functions of these 'captain's men' are not made clear in the accounts, but their rates of pay and documentary designation suggest they formed a body of the officers' support staff, serving as attachés performing tasks as required. At the castles, there were also porters (gatekeepers) and sometimes under porters, receiving daily 8d and 6d respectively. There was also a master gunner at Dover Castle. When this position came into being is not clear, but it was occupied by Richard Kent in 1604 and then from Michaelmas (29 September) 1612 until at least Michaelmas 1626 by William Eldred.[56] This was clearly more than an honorary title for a senior artilleryman, as the daily wage for the post was 1s per day; more than the 8d received by the lieutenants. Moreover, William Eldred was described in the survey of Kent's fortresses in 1623 as 'much recommended by the Lord Warden for a sufficient able man in his calling and held fit … to qualifie him with authority and meanes thereto, to be the Master Gunner of all the castles and forts under his Lordships command in the Cinque Portes'.[57]

As important as these totals of men and cannon are for understanding the strength and importance of the forts – or not – to the Crown, they fail to convey the lived experience of the serving personnel, how diligently or otherwise they performed their duties, and the bricks and mortar condition of the forts themselves. There is also a sense that the neat, regimented accounts of soldiers and pay hide a more organic picture of movement in and out of Crown service. Several musters show replacements of soldiers, such as at Sandgate in 1619 when one of the gunners died. But, the sense that there is more to the musters than meets the eye is confirmed by two surviving documents from Deal Castle covering 1614–15; one compiled on 5 September 1615 is a neat and structured account whilst the other from only six days earlier is a working document and full of amendments.[58] We are fortunate that we have other documentation, especially from *c*.1610–26 (and for some places earlier), with a succession of annual accounts from Archcliffe and Mote's bulwarks, and the castles of Deal, Sandgate, Sandown and Walmer, as well as for Dover Castle. These allow us not only to examine the garrison personnel of several forts over a decade and a half, but also – because of a large amount of extraneous documentation – to assess the calibre of the soldiers and the fortifications'

56 TNA, SP 14/74, fol. 160; SP 16/38, fol. 46.

57 TNA, SP 14/157, fol. 105r.

58 TNA, SP 14/110, fol. 189; SP 14/81, fols 124, 155.

fitness for defence. The purpose of this is to answer two questions: first, how martially potent were the occupants of Kent's fortifications; second, to what extent were the fortifications a viable military deterrent?

In all, at least 328 men are named in the musters for these seven locations from *c*.1604–26, bearing in mind that records do not survive for every location each year.[59] Formal musters at each garrison were conducted annually and usually performed by their captain, although more regular roll calls were probably made. The annual headcounts were taken shortly before or after the end of the accounting year (Michaelmas–Michaelmas) before the Lord Warden of the Cinque Ports – at this time Edward, Lord Zouche – (or one of his deputies), who also served as constable of Dover Castle. An analysis of the names of those serving within the garrisons and the wider documentation relating to these forts reveals several interesting facts about the personnel.

First, the soldiers in the garrison were all to be Englishmen. A list of five 'Needfull considerations in the discipline of the Garrison of Sandgate Castle' from 1609 specified that no soldier was permitted 'to appoint any forren watchman to supplie [i.e. fulfil] his service but by the captaines order & appointment', presumably because of concerns about the loyalties of such persons.[60] No place of origin is given in the musters so it is hard to clarify how far this rule was adhered to. Although, considering the regulations from Sandgate did allow foreigners to serve 'in time of neede', it is possible that some trusted 'foreign' individuals did serve.

Second, while a few men appear only fleetingly, most remained within their garrison over several years. Examples include Thomas Morice, gentleman gunner, at Sandgate Castle from 1609 to 1626, and Lawrence Abbott, ever present at Walmer from 1607 to 1624, serving as a 'captain's man' under three separate officers: George Parkins, William Boughton and Edmund Lisle.[61] Captains also remained in their posts over several years, like Thomas Fineux who commanded Mote's Bulwark for at least twenty-two years.[62] William

59 TNA, SP 14/9A, fols 154, 174; SP 14/28, fol. 131; SP 14/48, fol. 76; SP 14/66, fols 39–40, 179–180; SP 14/70, fol. 152; SP 14/71, fols 13–16; SP 14/74, fols 77, 79, 160–161, 170; SP 14/78, fols 22–24, 31, 33–34, 181; SP 14/81, fols 125, 127, 155–156, 164–165, 181–183, 203; SP 14/82, fols 9–12, 20; SP 14/83, fol. 80; SP 14/88, fols 147–148, 154, 162, 164; SP 14/93, fols 104, 106, 108–109, 119, 121–123; SP 14/99, fols 212–213; SP 14/103, fols 11A, 13, 15, 29–30; SP 14/110, fols 162, 164, 183–187, 190; SP 14/116, fols 178–179, 181 182, 184, 186–187; SP 14/117, fols 10, 12; SP 14/123, fols 51, 59, 67–68; SP 14/133, fol. 81; SP 14/172, fols 90, 97–99; SP 14/173, fols 3–4, 13, 15; SP 16/7, fols 46, 85, 87; SP 16/9, fol. 47; SP 16/37, fols 81, 103, 124, 126, 141; SP 16/38, fols 45, 47.

60 TNA, SP 14/48, fol. 77.

61 Only the first and last instances are given here. Morice: TNA, SP 14/48, fol. 76 (1609); SP 16/37, fol. 103 (1626). Abbott: SP 14/28, fol. 130 (1607); SP 14/173, fol. 12 (1624).

62 TNA, SP 14/9A, fol. 174 (1604); SP 16/38, fol. 46 (1626).

Byng was the longtime captain at Deal Castle with a career spanning at least three decades. Appointed in 1611, he remained there – barring a brief hiatus to the Low Countries in 1618 'for the dispatch of some private busenes' – until 1642 when he was expelled for suspected royalist sympathies. He may have regained his position after the Restoration but had lost it by May 1661, finally passing away in 1669 aged in his mid-eighties.[63]

There was also a small degree of exchange of personnel between fortresses, such as the gunner Charles Crimble, who is noted at Dover in 1615 and then down the coast at Sandgate a decade later in 1625–26, and Dunstan Woodgate, who served as an under porter of Walmer Castle from 1612 to 1621 and then as a gunner at Mote's Bulwark in Dover from 1624 to 1626.[64] Dunstan's experience of serving in two capacities (as under porter and gunner) was not unique. John Crumpe, a gunner at Sandgate from 1609 to 1620 was in the garrison as an under porter in 1624, before he returned to his role as a gunner again in 1625.[65] The overwhelming majority of troops, however, maintained their originally assigned roles throughout their service.

Third, the number of men with the same surnames suggests family connections between soldiers. For example, William and Saunder Berles in the garrison of Deal Castle in 1611, and Thomas Neale (the younger and elder, thus likely father and son) served in the same place in 1614 as one of the castle's porters and a lieutenant's man respectively.[66] Indeed, in 1626, the lieutenant of Sandgate, Sir John Hippisley, requested that his son Thomas replace him as lieutenant.[67]

Fourth, it seems that positions within the garrisons were eagerly sought, with those within appointed by the Lord Warden. A petition by Abraham Mummery in 1618 for the position of gunner in Deal Castle stated that he had 'searved faithfully for many yeares as a sworne watchman' at Deal 'haveinge receaved his breedinge in that Castle and beinge well acquainted with the service', and he thus, 'humbly beseecheth your Lordshipp … to bestowe one of the gonners roomes [i.e. places] that are now voide'.[68] Mummery had indeed served as a 'captain's man' at the garrison since at least Michaelmas 1613, but the petition was unsuccessful as he does not appear again in the castle after

63 TNA, SP 14/96, fol. 39; Peter Lefevre and Andrew Thrush, 'BYNG, William (1586–by 1669), of Wrotham, Kent; later of Deal Castle, Kent', *The History of Parliament Online*, https://www.historyofparliamentonline.org/volume/1604-1629/member/byng-william-1586-1669 (accessed 3 October 2024).

64 TNA, SP 14/82, fols 9, 10; SP 16/9, fol. 47; SP 16/37, fol. 103 (Crimble); SP 14/71, fol. 15; SP 14/123, fol. 59; SP 14/173, fol. 4; SP 16/38, fol. 46 (Woodgate).

65 TNA, SP 14/78, fol. 76 (1609); SP 14/172, fol. 99 (1624); SP 16/9, fol. 47 (1625).

66 TNA, SP 16/66, fol. 179; SP 14/78, fol. 30.

67 TNA, SP 16/36, fol. 143.

68 TNA, SP 14/104, fols 198–199.

Michaelmas 1616.[69] The prospect of a steady income in what may well have been – as we shall see – a less than strenuous occupation was attractive, but financially it was certainly not as appealing as first appears. Gunners received only 6d daily, the same as a medieval mounted archer two centuries earlier. But, whereas 6d a day in 1400 equated to the wages of a skilled tradesman, two centuries later this value had fallen by 80 per cent in terms of purchasing power.[70] It was also a poor daily rate compared to similar jobs in the early seventeenth century. A gunner in a Kentish garrison earned 14s a month in a twenty-eight-day month, far less than a gunner's mate on a first-rate Royal Navy ship in 1626 (£1 2s 6d), and less even than a quarter gunner's mate on the same (18s 8d). Indeed, the Kentish fort gunner earned less than a gunner's mate on a sixth-rate naval ship (18s 8d). The pay disparity for garrison captains was even more stark. They received £2 6s 8d for a twenty-eight-day month; less than 50 per cent of the pay of a captain of even a sixth-rate naval ship (£4 13s 4d).[71] In other words, pay was a minor attraction for Kentish garrison service. Though we cannot be sure what motivated individuals to seek out such service, a potential explanation is hinted at by other petitions for gunners' posts. In 1618, a mariner of Dover, James Cook, petitioned the Lord Warden for a position at Dover Castle or one of its bulwarks since, despite his long service at sea, 'nowe beinge growen in yeres, [he] cannott undergoe his accustomed paines & labor, [and] ys desyrous to leave his imployment at sea'.[72]

Were, therefore, the Kentish garrisons of the early seventeenth century a place for older men, perhaps supplementing their incomes, with their garrison service only a secondary occupation, or even those looking for a 'retirement' income? If this was the case, then we can hardly assume that the garrison troops were potent militarily. The fact that the elderly James Cook's petition was unsuccessful – he did not subsequently appear in any of the Dover garrisons – may be telling, but the failure of a single petition is hardly conclusive proof either way. Nor is the fact that at least six men from the Kentish garrisons in these years died during their service.[73] Comparison with the garrison at Berwick-upon-Tweed in June 1598 may be instructive here, even though we

69 TNA, SP 14/78, fol. 30; SP 14/88, fol. 162. A petition for the same post from Vincent Denn, who at the time was chief porter at Sandown Castle, was similarly unsuccessful: SP 14/104, fol. 186.

70 Based on the purchasing power of 6d in both 1440 and 1600. The National Archives, UK, 'Currency Converter: 1270–2017', https://www.nationalarchives.gov.uk/currency-converter/# (accessed 2 October 2024).

71 Nicholas Andrew Martin Rodger, *The Safeguard of the Sea: A Naval History of Britain, Volume 1: 660–1649* (London, 2004), pp. 501–2.

72 TNA, SP 14/104, fol. 182.

73 For example, Henry Mawcome at Sandown Castle in 1619: TNA, SP 14/110, fol. 162.

are dealing with an earlier period and a different geographical and military context. A Berwick muster contains the names of 900 men stationed around the garrison and town and provides their ages, place of origin, and length of service.[74] Of the fifty-eight specified as being gunners, the average age was 44 years old, with over 55 per cent of the gunners over the age of 40 and a third over 50. The fact that many of the gunners at Berwick were into their middle age does suggest that these positions were occupied by older men. Being older – of course – did not necessarily mean they were less vigorous in the pursuit of their military duties, and it could be they brought more experience. We must also remember that, given the more pressing military concerns and larger garrisoning of the northern border than Kent at that time, and with it the increased potential for younger, more active men being stationed there, an average age of 44 is even more telling.

Ultimately, without evidence of the ages of the Kentish garrison troops, it is impossible to say whether they were collectively a group of martially active younger men, older individuals in their military dotage, or a mix of both. Yet other evidence is suggestive of a less than professional military culture amongst the garrisons' personnel, in particular their very presence – or lack thereof – within the garrisons themselves. Though one might imagine that the troops were permanently, or at least semi-permanently, resident at the forts, the reality was very different. This can be seen by comparing the musters of Kent's garrisons with corresponding general musters taken in the same year and locality. Deal Castle is a prime example, with both a muster for the garrison at the castle and of the town from 1614.[75] Of the twenty-one men present in the castle muster, only five appear in the corresponding town muster, with a further five from the garrison sharing familial names with individuals from the town, and a further man from the garrison who was not present at the town muster noted as supplying a musket for the townsmen. While the crossover of personnel between the garrison muster and the town muster appears low (just under half of those named in the garrison also mustered amongst the townsmen), it must be remembered that the municipal musters were not intended to name every able-bodied man. Rather, those selected for 'service' were often younger men mustered as proxies for, and fulfilling the obligations of, wealthier, older and more socially elevated individuals.[76] Moreover, the town musters self-evidently only capture those resident within the town itself; it is quite possible that those from the garrisons either did not muster in the town – because they were in the garrison – or more likely that

74 TNA, SP 59/37, fol. 79.

75 TNA, SP 14/78, fol. 30; SP 14/107, fol. 94.

76 Steven Gunn, *The English People at War in the Age of Henry VIII* (Oxford, 2018), pp. 96–116.

they resided in the surrounding villages thereabouts and would thus not be named in this case in a muster of Deal.

However, even more damning evidence for absenteeism from Kent's garrisons can be found. A list from Dover Castle from 1614, for instance, contains the names of thirty-four watchmen of the castle, alongside their place of residence, many of whom came from villages outside Dover like Alkham and Guston, with a handful residing as far away as Pluckley (*c*.25 miles) and Faversham (22 miles). This was hardly an ideal situation for men who were supposed to man the castle's defences, even if they were not permanent members of the garrison.[77] More tellingly, the year before at Dover – in a likely unscheduled muster taken shortly after the death of the castle's captain, Sir Thomas Waller, in July 1613 – of the sixteen, permanent, gunners who were supposed to be resident in the garrison, only three were present in the castle on the day of the muster, with a further three in Dover town.[78] The others were listed as living elsewhere, such as Northfleet near Gravesend and Wickham near Canterbury. Even if their duties were being performed by proxies as, for example, were those of David Fidge by 'Titus', the late Sir Thomas Waller's horse keeper, these were circumstances not conducive to effective military operations. Similarly, at Deal in 1618, the garrison's gunners wrote to the Lord Warden stating that 'wee confesse oure selves to bee all giltie of not lyinge in the castell of [i.e. at] nighte, but one our watch night wee never miss'. Things seem to have little improved two years later, with the gunners again reporting that four of their number still 'doe live [away] frome there servish [… but] all the rest of the garison doe there servish in there owne persons'.[79]

Moreover, we do not know to what extent Kent's garrison soldiers in this period were trained in gunnery. Deal's garrison at least did discharge a shot in June 1626 at a Dutch ship which failed to lower its colours upon entering the Downs because 'it was neither the custome nor fit for us for the honor of his Majesty to permitt strangers to weare there flagg in that manner'. Likewise, on 11 October 1639, the Downs castles 'made many shott' at two Dutch ships that ran aground near them during the Battle of the Downs between the Spanish and Dutch fleets.[80] Indeed, the inhabitants of the garrisons on that day believed they were under threat, if a newsletter by an unknown author is to be believed, for Deal,

[77] TNA, SP 14/78, fol. 180.

[78] TNA, SP 14/74, fol. 79. For Waller's career, see Peter Lefevre, 'WALLER, Sir Thomas (c.1569–1613), of Groombridge and Dover Castle, Kent; formerly of Brenchley, Kent', *The History of Parliament Online*, https://www.historyofparliamentonline.org/volume/1604-1629/member/waller-sir-thomas-1569-1613 (accessed 3 October 2024).

[79] TNA, SP 14/103, fol. 8; SP 14/116, fol. 167. See also similar absences at Sandown in 1618: SP 14/103, fol. 9.

[80] TNA, SP 16/31, fol. 11; SP 16/430, fol. 154.

> a town once unfortified, but now fenced with a castle … stood in some danger by the shot at random which flew from the two armadas. A bullet fell into a stable and struck off a horse's head whilst eating his meat in the manger, but … the people were more affrighted than hurt.[81]

Therefore, the gunners in the Downs forts were capable of discharging their ordnance, but their continued and frequent absences, with many living some distance away from their posts, were hardly ideal for men supposed to be manning the defences at short notice, especially if at least some of them were in their military dotage. This is not to say that all those stationed in the forts were negligent or did not want to do a good job. The gunners and soldiers of Mote's Bulwark in 1619, for example, made protestations to the Lord Warden lamenting the constant absence of their officers from the garrison. They claimed that all but two of the rank-and-file 'are and hath beine inhabitinge within the towne of Dover' and thus were able to perform their expected duties.[82] Nevertheless, the balance of evidence leads to the conclusion that Kent's garrisons were largely militarily impotent in the early seventeenth century, a situation compounded by the state of the fortifications themselves.

Several accounts make plain that these were in a poor state of repair by this time. At Deal in 1615, 'A note of the deacaye of his Majesties castle' listed nine defects, including that 'the wall toward the sea is cleane eaten away, in so much that it lies open to winde and weather without any defence or resistance to the sea'; that 'the drawe bridge is so bad, that it can neither bee well drawne up, nor let downe […] the howses of office are decayed, the water cumming into them, so that it decayes the walls themselves'; and, in explanation (and mitigation) for men's absences, 'there is no cabines for soldiers to lye in'.[83] Some of these deficiencies were caused by neglect, though persistent storm damage was also said to be responsible. Such were the problems that an extensive survey of the forts was undertaken the following year, in May 1616, on the orders of Lord Warden Zouche, 'of the most needfull reparrations now presentlie to be done', which revealed that the cost of repair at Deal and elsewhere was £3,194 6s.[84] Whether these repairs were ever undertaken is unclear, but if they were they cannot have been extensive, for complaints were still being made about forts' conditions nearly twenty years later, with estimates for repairs at Sandown, Deal, Walmer and Archcliffe Bulwark in 1634 amounting to £5,322 17s 4d.[85] Dover too needed attention, as in 1638 its reported defects included that 'the steeple of the church in the castle is lately

81 TNA, SP 16/431, fol. 10.
82 TNA, SP 14/110, fol. 222.
83 TNA, SP 14/82, fol. 198.
84 TNA, SP 14/87, fol. 29v.
85 TNA, SP 16/281, fol. 162r.

fallen down [...] all the peeces of ordinance towards the sea except one demi culveryn are dismounted and lye on the ground for want of carriages', and 'the lodgings of the gunners & other officers of the castle who are tyed to reside are also in much decaye'.[86]

It is clear, therefore, given such evidence, that by the later years of Elizabeth's reign, and certainly by the reigns of her Stuart successors, Henry VIII's Device Forts, constructed on a massive scale, at huge expense, were not as militarily potent as some of their impressive remains, such as at Deal Castle, would suggest. Throughout their long history, they experienced peaks and troughs in their usage and utility that were intrinsically linked to the geopolitical relationship between England and her neighbours. At times of national crisis, such as the period immediately following their construction, during the Armada, in the civil wars of the mid-seventeenth century, or periods of tumult in later centuries, the Device Forts – indeed all of Kent's fortifications – often grew in importance. In truth, during relative peace, or when England's strategic considerations were focused elsewhere, it was perhaps expected that the government, perennially short of cash, let standards slip, both in terms of bricks and mortar and the conduct and professionalism of the garrisons. Nevertheless, their overall worth declined over time due to their increasingly antiquated sixteenth-century design amid the proliferation of more modern weaponry. Indeed, from the start of the eighteenth century, more regular and stable funding for the Royal Navy's ships, and dockyards which built and repaired them, meant that – while it was acknowledged that castles and forts still had a role to play in coastal defence – the 'wooden walls' of the navy took precedence.[87]

Perhaps the most pertinent question is how effective the forts would have been had a serious invasion and landing on the Kentish coast ever been made. In July 1545, when an attack did come, it was on the Isle of Wight, and Sandown Castle on the Isle (not to be confused with Sandown in Kent) was still in the process of being constructed, but the attack was on such a small scale it can hardly be considered a serious test of English defences.[88] Even during the Armada crisis of 1588, although the Kentish forts were readied in anticipation of Spanish troops landing in Kent, the viability of the defences was ultimately never tested. Thereafter, James VI and I's reign ushered in an era of relative peace, and though the reign of Charles I saw foreign relations deteriorate once again, these overseas adventures did not require any further reinforcement of Kent's coastal defences.[89]

86 TNA, SP 16/385, fol. 9.
87 Ware, 'To Defend the Coast', p. 142.
88 Biddle et al., 'Defences in Detail', pp. 550–1.
89 Ware, 'To Defend the Coast', pp. 135–8.

It should also be remembered that the Kentish forts were probably never intended as an impenetrable defensive shield against invasion. Instead, 'troops garrisoned in a locality were expected to resist an invasion as best they could so that an army might mobilise to meet the threat', the garrisons inflicting as many casualties as possible before falling back to join with a relief force.[90] There was a method to the seeming madness of allowing fortresses to fall into disrepair, at least if the scholar Thomas Wilson, who composed an insightful study into the realm in his 'The State of England' (1600), is to be believed.[91]

> It is true that in England there is noe great reckning made of Castells and fortresses, for they doe willingly lett them goe to ruine and in stead thereof build them stately pleasant houses and palaces. The reasons they allege are these, that if there should be any invasion the enemy should have no holdes but such as they must be forced to make themselves, & within that meane time will fynd meanes enough to be disturbed therein; and besides they thinke the courage of the people would be the greater, knowinge they have no retyring places, but must needs fight it out att the first brunt.[92]

Even with this, somewhat shaky, justification being the case, the conduct of the garrisons and the state of the forts themselves left much to be desired and should disabuse us of the notion in William Lambarde's *Perambulation of Kent* (1596) that Henry VIII's programme 'for the defensing of this Realme against forreine invasion, is rightly comparable with any thing that either Eadgar or Alfred … bestowed, and meerely incomparable with all that ever any other his predecessours have attempted'.[93]

Kent, the Royal Navy and the Ordnance Trade

The limitations of Kent's coastal fortresses and the geographical reality of a kingdom surrounded by water were such that the defence of the realm fell first and foremost upon the kingdom's ships, with bricks and mortar defences coming in second – even though ideally the two would complement one another. The Royal Navy was, of course, where the largest and most well-armed ships

90 Fissel, *English Warfare*, p. 39.

91 For a biography of this colourful individual, see Virginia C. D. Moseley and Rosemary Sgroi, 'Wilson, Thomas (c.1565–1629), of Westminster and the Castle Gatehouse, Hertford, Herts.', *The History of Parliament Online*, http://www.histparl.ac.uk/volume/1604-1629/member/wilson-thomas-1565-1629 (accessed 30 October 2024).

92 F. J. Fisher (ed.), *The State of England Anno Dom. 1600 by Thomas Wilson* (London, 1936), p. 12.

93 Lambarde, *Perambulation*, p. 171.

could be found, and much has been written on the development of the navy from the reign of Henry VIII onwards.[94] English monarchs before Henry had certainly possessed warships, but it was the increased number and tonnage of the royal vessels and Henry's reordering of the navy's administration and establishment of what would become the naval board which marked a break from the medieval past. Moreover, the changes in shipbuilding techniques, the increasing amount of ordnance on ships, the licensing and incorporation of Trinity House of Deptford Strand (responsible for training in pilotage and the advancement of navigation and commerce), and the founding of several new royal dockyards, saw an acceleration in naval affairs under Henry to the extent that one of the king's leading biographers argued that he 'deserved his traditional title of "Father of the English navy"'.[95]

Kent was at the forefront of the navy's development. 'The county and its main rivers, the Thames and the Medway', Childs suggested, 'became the birthplace of many Tudor warships, and their home when not at sea'.[96] Deptford, on the south bank of the Thames (in present-day southeast London), straddled the Kent/Surrey border in the sixteenth century and was where Henry VII kept his fleet at anchor, though it had been a site of royal shipbuilding for at least a century before the first Tudor monarch paid £5 for the hire of a storehouse there.[97] Production at the site ramped up with the founding of the royal dockyard at Deptford in the reign of his son in 1513, then at Woolwich in 1512, and later at Chatham, which expanded into Gillingham in 1567 with timber brought in from the royal forests in Kent, Sussex, and elsewhere – both inside and outside the realm. The relationship between the Kentish people, the Royal Navy and shipbuilding became indissoluble for the next three centuries.[98] Assessing the number of ships the dockyards produced for the navy – and calculating the navy's size in both the number of vessels and tonnage – is difficult, for the dates of construction, decommissioning, re-naming, interchangeable classification of vessels, loss in warfare and capturing and status of prize ships, and the dates of purchase and sale, make precision problematic. As Tom Glasgow Jr. pointed out, 'no list of royal

[94] See, for example, David Loades, *The Tudor Navy: An Administrative, Political and Military History* (Aldershot, 1992).

[95] John Joseph Scarisbrick, *Henry VIII* (New Haven and London, 1997), pp. 499–501.

[96] David Childs, *Tudor Sea Power: The Foundation of Greatness* (Barnsley, 2009), p. 167.

[97] *Ibid.*, p. 252.

[98] Dates for the foundations from The National Archives, UK, 'Research Guides: Royal Naval Dockyard Staff', https://www.nationalarchives.gov.uk/help-with-your-research/research-guides/royal-naval-dockyard-staff/ (accessed 9 October 2024); David Loades and C. S. Knighton (eds), *Elizabethan Naval Administration* (Ashgate, 2013), pp. xxvii–xxviii, 38–9, 220, 225–6, 476, 664.

ships is likely ever to be compiled of this period which will not be subject to further corrections'.[99] Matters were not helped by the ad hoc recording of the fleet. Even by 1660, Samuel Pepys, serving on the Navy Board, was perplexed that the only accurate list of the fleet was seemingly the one he had compiled himself out of curiosity – a sentiment his Tudor predecessors would have understood.[100] Nevertheless, in broad brushstroke terms, the navy massively increased in terms of the number of ships and tonnage during Henry VIII's reign, and stagnated under Edward, Mary, and in the early decades of Elizabeth's reign. Its scale subsequently began to increase again during the last decades of the queen's reign and into those of the first two Stuart monarchs, with the 49 vessels extant in 1640 comparable with the 58 (42 sailed and 16 oared) that had been present at the height of Henry VIII's navy in 1545.[101] It should be noted, however, that there was something of a slump during the reign of James VI and I, with the 50 vessels in his navy in 1605 – a high watermark for the period – decreasing to 39 at his death in 1625. This decline mirrors the relative lack of attention paid to the Device Forts at the same time, discussed earlier, with the waning in both naval and coastal spending a reflection of James's desire to maintain peace at home and abroad.

But no matter its size or composition, as the Kentish petitioners in 1593 pointed out, the county and the navy were intrinsically bound. The former provided men, money, munitions, and provisions to the king's ships, and the latter security and employment, both as sailors and in the myriad of industries from shipbuilding and iron working to bread baking and ropemaking.[102] We can take as a case study the Armada crisis of 1588 as an example of Kent's contribution to the naval – and land war – effort. Scholarly estimates, based on contemporary records, for the precise number of English vessels at sea to face the Armada in various capacities during the summer of 1588 range from 197 to 208, but it is clear that *c.*77–80 per cent were merchant vessels.[103] Unfortunately, the sources do not specify the home ports of many of the merchantmen, but at least five were from Kent with their crews inflated because of the needs of war: the *Ruben* (or *Robin*) of Sandwich, 110 tons and

99 Cited from Geoffrey Moorhouse, *Great Harry's Navy: How Henry VIII Gave England Seapower* (London, 2005), p. 323.

100 Robert Latham (ed.), *Samuel Pepys and the Second Dutch War: Pepys's Navy White Book and Brooke House Papers*, Naval Record Society, vol. 134 (London, 1995), pp. 212–13.

101 See Benjamin W. D. Reading, *The English and French Navies, 1500–1650* (Woodbridge, 2002), pp. 198–201. The total numbers of vessels: 1500 – 8; 1545 – 58; 1565 – 32; 1585 – 27; 1605 – 50; 1625 – 38; 1640 – 49.

102 See, for example, Andrewes, 'Trade and Industry', pp. 235–52.

103 Martin and Parker, *The Spanish Armada*, pp. 265–8; Robert Hutchinson, *The Spanish Armada* (London, 2013), pp. 255–73.

a crew of 65; the *Elizabeth* of Dover, 120 tons and 70 men; the *John Young* of New Romney (unknown tonnage and crew); the *Grace of God* of Hythe, 50 tons and 30 men; and the *Hazard* of Faversham of 38 tons and 34 men.[104] The county was also estimated to be able to furnish 12,654 men for local defence in January 1588, a combination of the trained and untrained militia armed with a variety of weapons from bows to arquebuses and calivers.[105] The southern counties were also expected to provide mutual aid to one another in terms of men and supplies were the Spanish to land.[106]

The role Kentish people played in victualling the fleet assembled to face the Armada is more difficult to ascertain, but if the petitioners of the 1590s were correct, then perhaps their complaint was in part a reaction to the extensive burdens placed upon them in 1588. Many of the merchant vessels involved were for transport and victualling rather than fighting, and some of Kent's ships may well have served in this capacity.[107] Moreover, in January of that year, the cost of victualling 2,094 men in the queen's royal ships stationed off Queenborough on the Isle of Sheppey for thirty-one days from 13 February to 14 March at 7d per man per day amounted to nearly £1,893 6s 6d, and this did not include payments for victuals for other mariners and soldiers elsewhere in the Narrow Seas.[108] Whilst this account does not specify from where these victuals came or what they were, the fact that they were in Kent would strongly suggest that the county once again bore the brunt of this burden. This is doubly likely when one considers that Kent produced a large amount of grain for the London market. A great deal of this grain found its way into Royal Navy stomachs, as, for example, in September 1576 when Lord Cobham arranged for the collection for the navy of 300 quarters of wheat and 400 quarters of barley from various hundreds in Kent, and again in December 1585 when John Hawkins, treasurer of the navy, acknowledged receipt of Kentish grain in a letter to Lord Burghley.[109]

Yet the English navy was not yet the main source of ships to protect the coast. In 1600, the perceptive Thomas Wilson wrote in his 'The State of England' that the real strength of England at sea was the merchant marine. For, though the navy 'be of great strength yett it is not the 20 part of the strength of England, for unto the very one Ryver of Thames [alone] there belong 2,000

[104] Hutchinson, *The Spanish Armada*, pp. 268, 272–3; Julian S. Corbett, *Drake and the Tudor Navy* (2 vols, Aldershot, 1988), vol. 2, pp. 138–9.

[105] TNA, SP 12/208, fols 29–30.

[106] McGurk, 'Armada Preparation', p. 71.

[107] John Knox Laughton (ed.), *State Papers relating to the Defeat of the Spanish Armada, Anno 1588*, vol. 1, 2nd edition (London, 1895), p. xl.

[108] TNA, SP 12/208, fol. 31.

[109] Loades and Knighton, *Naval Administration*, pp. 575, 588 n. 2. For Kent's trade in the early modern period, see Chapter 2, this volume.

ships the worst thereof is servisable both for fight and merchandise'.[110] English merchant ships, especially the larger ones, were increasingly in possession of their own ordnance by the seventeenth century. These had been requisitioned by the Crown in times of need to supplement the realm's naval forces both for combat and transportation since at least the thirteenth century, and the ships from Kent's ports were often at the forefront of these endeavours. The original Cinque Ports, of which four were in Kent (New Romney, Hythe, Dover and Sandwich, along with Hastings in Sussex), were not as important naval centres by the sixteenth century as they had been before, due to the problem of constant silting of their harbours (despite efforts at Dover to prevent this),[111] and their role by this point 'was more one of defending their privileges than of delivering on their [historic] responsibilities'.[112] Nevertheless, they continued to be called upon for shipping. From the spring of 1512 to the spring of 1514, for instance, 16 per cent of the 198 merchant vessels Henry VIII requisitioned for his wars against France were from the Cinque Ports, with Dover and Sandwich serving as embarkation points, and the Ports also supplied ships which fought against the Spanish Armada at the end of the century.[113] Kent's other ports, be they limbs of the Cinque Ports or not, also continued to provide ships for military service during the sixteenth century, although demands were less frequent and onerous than they had been during the Middle Ages.

Outside of officially sanctioned, state-controlled activity, there was also a good deal of private enterprise at sea. The Channel was far from a peaceful waterway. Especially after 1585, with the unofficial outbreak of war with Spain until its formal cessation in 1604, the Channel was prowled by armed merchantmen, English men-of-war, and others operating as outright pirates, attacking any vulnerable vessel they could find as opportunity allowed.[114] As we will see in the next chapter, some of these incidents at sea illustrate just how important the efforts of private individuals were to England's and particularly Kent's maritime defence. True enough, they were on occasion a headache for the Crown, but they demonstrated to England's neighbours that the English naval forces and merchant marine in the Narrow Seas were not to be trifled with.

Finally, there is also one area of Kent's maritime activity related to the county's military potential for defence: its ordnance trade. The importance of

110 TNA, SP 12/280, fols 36v–37v. Printed in Fisher, *The State of England*, pp. 36–7.

111 Dixon, 'Economy', pp. 3–4, 143.

112 Childs, *Tudor Sea Power*, p. 171.

113 Lambert and Baker 'The Merchant Fleet and Shipboard Community of Kent', p. 90.

114 Kenneth R. Andrews, *Elizabethan Privateering: English Privateering during the Spanish War, 1585–1603* (Cambridge, 1964), pp. 3–21.

this trade reflects the growing militarisation of the county, and its development in Kent specifically was no accident. Kent's abundance of raw materials in the Weald, of both iron ore and wood for charcoal production, and the county's proximity to the huge London market, were ideal conditions for the iron industry to flourish – but it was in ordnance production specifically that Kent excelled. It is well established that the county was the main gun founding area in the country by the first half of the seventeenth century, the product of which was often shipped to London via Rochester along with foodstuffs, timber, copperas, gunpowder, and iron products from the Weald.[115] For this, we can thank the aforementioned establishment of the Royal Naval dockyards in Kent, which helped to create and stimulate a market for both cannon and gunpowder, with the establishment of a gunpowder works at Faversham in *c*.1573.[116] This industry was also important, self-evidently, for the defence of the realm. The very fact that the artillery pieces were produced in Kent – a county often at the forefront of the Crown's defensive planning – made logistical sense, both for supplying newly built and anchored Royal Naval vessels in the county, and also for the London market, from which ordnance could be shipped throughout the realm. In the same way that Kent and the southern maritime counties bore the brunt of recruitment for armies travelling to the nearby continent because of their proximity to the action, to have the ordnance industry elsewhere in the country would have resulted in costly delays in supplying fortresses and ships at critical junctures. The presence of the industry in Kent was therefore of paramount importance for defence.

The scale of the ordnance trade is often underappreciated. The coastal port books from Rochester from 1580–1616 show just how extensive the trade was.[117] Accounts do not survive for every year, but from the records that do survive, we can see that a minimum of 129 voyages left Rochester (107 by English and 22 by foreign ships), and three sailed into the Kentish port (all English ships) trading in ordnance in these years.[118] The majority of the English

[115] Stephen Bull, *The Furie of Ordnance: Artillery in the English Civil War* (Woodbridge, 2008), p. 70; Hodgkinson, 'Ironworks in Late-16th Century Kent'; and Brown, 'Thomas Browne', 6–15, 16–25.

[116] Andrewes, 'Trade and Industry', pp. 237, 243–4.

[117] The figures presented here were compiled by Robert Blackmore during the 'Maritime Kent' project: Craig Lambert, Sheila Sweetinburgh and Robert Blackmore, 'Maritime Kent: Kent's Maritime Communities and Their European Neighbours: Connections and Relations Across the Narrow Seas, c.1450–c.1650' (University of Southampton, 2024): https://maritimebritain.org/maritime_kent/ (accessed 15 October 2024). I would like to offer my gratitude to Dr Blackmore for kindly supplying the figures for this analysis.

[118] TNA, E 190/641/12; 642/1, 4, 12; 643/3; 644/1–2, 9; 645/1, 10; 646/2, 7; 647/1, 7, 10; 648/9, 15; 649/16, 20; 650/2, 9; 651/3, 9.

ships sailing out of Rochester were Kentish vessels. Rochester's ships were responsible for only two of the 129 voyages leaving the port, with vessels from Millhall (near Aylesford) accounting for the majority of journeys at sixty-three, with Maidstone ships twenty-one, New Hythe seven, Strood two, and Dover, Gillingham, Aylesford and Northfleet one each, whilst London ships undertook eight journeys. The remainder were by ships from foreign ports, mostly in the new United Provinces, with eleven by vessels of Amsterdam, three from Dordrecht, and one from Delfzijl, with the Danish city of Aarhus (one), Gdańsk (three), Emden (two), and a single ship from an unknown port accounting for the rest.

In total, the ships that appear in these surviving records carried at least 2,778 iron artillery pieces. Just over half of the accounts specify the types of guns being carried, and these reveal that minions (a type of small cannon) were by far the most prevalent guns being traded, at nearly 700 pieces, double the number of the larger demi-culverins (*c*.320), and sakers (*c*.350). There were also at least 62 falcons, 36 'bastard' culverins, and 80 of the largest cannons, the culverins, as well as an unspecified number of bombards. Nearly all these guns were shipped to London (98/129 voyages) where they were likely mounted in and around the capital or reshipped along the coast. The remaining thirty-one ordnance voyages went to Aldeburgh, King's Lynn, Southampton, Newcastle, Hull, and Ipswich (one each), with the rest to foreign ports, mostly in foreign ships: Amsterdam (nine), Emden (five), Copenhagen (six), Dordrecht (three), and Friesland and Middelburg (one each).

The largest of the ships in this trade was the 160-ton *Priscilla* of London bound for Copenhagen carrying 11 demi-culverins, 20 sakers, and 4 minions in April 1610 for the king of Denmark, Christian IV; the smallest, the 11-ton *Anne* of Strood which was laden to capacity with 32 pieces of unspecified type in December 1581 bound for London.[119] The ordnance on the *Priscilla* for the Danish king was moved at the behest of the (presumably) Danish merchant Ludolph Englested, who freighted cannon on six other voyages between Rochester, London, and Copenhagen, but by and large, it was native English merchants responsible for this trade. The most prominent and frequently involved were John and Thomas Browne, moving at least 630 artillery pieces between them (22 per cent of all pieces traded) on thirty-six voyages, to London on all but one occasion (the other destination being Amsterdam). This is almost certainly Thomas Browne, the queen's founder of iron ordnance and shot, from at least January 1598, though from these records we know that he had been in the ordnance business since at least 1593.[120] It is also probable that John Browne was Thomas's son who, according to scholar Ruth Brown,

119 TNA, E 190/649/16, fol. 1v; E 190/642/1, fol. 1v.
120 TNA, E 190/644/9, fol. 1v.

first appears in the royal ordnance accounts in June 1617, but who (if it is the same man) can be traced back in the ordnance business to at least 1594.[121] Other merchants moving multiple cargoes were John Fearne (7 voyages, 225 pieces), Thomas Johnson (8/188), Robert Sackville (9/165), William Webb (6/88), and the redoubtable Anne, Lady Gresham, the wife of Sir Thomas Gresham, merchant, founder of the Royal Exchange and financier to all of Henry VIII's children. Anne moved at least 182 artillery pieces to London from 1580 to 1582.[122]

Conclusion

Kent was one of the more heavily militarised regions in early modern England with only the Anglo-Scottish border in any way comparable. On both land and sea, the people of Kent were active both in providing personnel for royal armies and defence, but also in bearing the oft-forgotten burden of billeting soldiers from elsewhere in the country before they travelled abroad, and supplying those men, sailors of the navy and the newly established royal shipyards. The construction of these and Henry VIII's Device Fort programme put Kent on an even greater martial footing. After Henry's dreams of European conquest evaporated towards the end of his reign, royal strategy took on a distinctively more defensive tone which was exacerbated by the fall of Calais in 1558. Despite the English acquisition of the Cautionary Towns in the Low Countries late in Elizabeth's reign, her foreign policy was largely defensive, and Kent remained at the heart of government planning.

The picture one receives from governmental ledgers of military spending on land and sea in these years, especially during the reign of Henry VIII, is of well-funded, well-organised military infrastructure. Vast sums were spent, and great effort expended, on building and maintaining Henry's coastal bastions, especially in their early years, with the Royal Navy's infrastructure in Kent adding to this sense of martial might. But one does not have to scratch far below the surface to see that the reality was far different, the image of martial potency a mirage. Many of Henry's Device Forts, envisaged as great defensive bulwarks against invasion, had begun to decay even before the end of his reign, and by the time of the Stuart monarchs, they were in a parlous state. Despite the efforts of some of their garrisons, the quality and conduct of the men also left much to be desired. This was often due to a lack of funding, but as English strategic eyes began to turn northwards – and inwards – during the reign of Charles I, this was also the result of military expediency. This does not mean, however, that Kent became a martial backwater in the early seventeenth century. Kent's trade in armaments, ordnance in particular, was booming.

121 Brown, 'Ordnance Records', p. 23; TNA, E 190/645/1, fol. 3r.

122 TNA, E 190/641/12, fol. 3v; E 190/642/1, fols 1v, 2r.

Kentish guns were shipped throughout England and were prized much further afield than in English fortifications. Similarly, as we shall see in the next and final chapter, the Kentish merchant fleet – who were often called upon during the Middle Ages for royal service – remained robust in their activities in both trading and disrupting foreign shipping in the Channel, epitomising the importance of private enterprise to the county's military endeavours.[123] The activities of private individuals and groups are always the hardest to trace in the sources, but they doubtlessly underlay much of what the government was trying to achieve in the county concerning national defence, building a martial infrastructure on solid local foundations.

We will never know how much resistance a foreign prince would have faced had they ever landed on the Kentish shore in force, but William Lambarde, at least, expected it to be stiff, for, he claimed:

> the communaltie of Kent was never vanquished by the Conquerour … the foreward in al battels belongeth to them (by a certeine preeminence) in right of their manhood … To be short, they be most commonly civill, just, and bountifull, so that the estate of the old franklyns and yeomen of Englande, either yet liveth in Kent, or else it is quite dead and departed out of the realme for altogether.[124]

Sir Walter Ralegh, on the other hand, was more realistic and less idealistic in his assessment. Reflecting on the Armada crisis a quarter-century earlier, he wrote in his *History of the World* in 1614, that England possessed 'no such force as to encounter an armie like unto that, wherewith it was intended that the prince of Parma should have landed in England'.[125] It is hard to escape the conclusion that the English were lucky – given their defences – that a large, well-organised and adequately supplied army of a continental power never made a landing on the English coast.

123 See Chapter 5, this volume.

124 Lambarde, *Perambulation*, pp. 13–15.

125 Quoted in Geoffrey Parker, 'If the Armada Had Landed', *History*, 61:203 (1976), 358–68, at p. 359.

5

Maritime Predation in the Narrow Seas, *c.*1540–*c.*1640

ROBERT BLACKMORE

Mariners and merchants in the sixteenth and seventeenth centuries faced risks and opportunities. Just as a master and crew of a vessel could turn their hand to trade, fishing, or taking passengers, they could equally engage in theft or salvage – and become victims themselves. Attacks at sea or shipwrecks were disasters but also a bonanza for those in a position to appropriate windfall goods. This chapter will explore these activities in the eastern Channel and southern North Sea, the 'Narrow Seas' around Kent, during the so-called 'Tawney's century' (generally expressed as 1540–1640). It will assess the degree of risk involved in maritime trade, evaluate the concurrent opportunities afforded, and assess the overall effect such actions had. Were these much the same on the coasts of southeastern England, the Low Countries or northern France as anywhere, or were – due to their relative proximity – both magnified? Few sea lanes in this period should have been more lucrative. Through one bottleneck, just 21 miles across at its narrowest, passed almost all the maritime traffic between the North Sea or Baltic, and the Atlantic. For much of the sixteenth century, this could include rich targets headed for or leaving the great Habsburg entrepôt at Antwerp. Even after the main centre of commerce shifted to Amsterdam in the new Dutch Republic, the United Provinces, from 1585, practically all sea trade between northern Europe and the rest of the world would still pass by this route. Likewise, the last leg of any journey from Europe to the growing English capital of London, passed by Kent's coast.[1]

The most straightforward way to access this great wealth was to seize ships forcibly and their cargoes at sea: actions often labelled piracy or privateering. Terms such as 'pirate' or 'privateer' for those who did this, N. A. M.

[1] For a summary of the maritime trade of Kent's ports in this period, see Chapter 2, this volume.

Rodger has rightly emphasised, are highly problematic for what was essentially 'private naval warfare' in a lawless frontier zone where 'robbery under arms was a normal aspect of seaborne trade'. The conventional distinction between the two is principally legal, with the former judged entirely criminal, whereas the latter acted under permission of a polity: having gained a commission or letter of marque or reprisal, official authorisations to prey on foreign shipping. The designation 'privateer' for this period is, however, an anachronism, often misapplied to those engaged in reprisal, where responsibility for foreign debts or losses through theft was imposed collectively on the culprits' compatriots, when legal redress through courts was impossible.[2] While in some respects it could also entrench predation into a formal economic feud, it was essentially a 'legal fiction' by the sixteenth century, with fake losses declared to justify predatory action.[3]

Of the considerable and diverse literature produced on piracy and 'privateering' in the sixteenth and seventeenth centuries, remarkably little concerns the Narrow Seas.[4] Most studies are preoccupied with the more famous depredations in the Atlantic, Caribbean and Mediterranean. John Appleby conceded that piracy in the coastal waters of the British Isles was a 'persistent problem even during the Anglo-Spanish war' and 'flourished following the peace of 1604', activities he described as 'opportunistic, unorganized and modest in scale, sometimes undertaken by groups of men operating in small, poorly armed vessels'. But he too placed most of this expressly in the southwest of England, so in the western Channel, and Ireland.[5] This established focus seems strange. Provided the cost or risk to the perpetrator was not too high, one would logically expect a concentration of robbery precisely where victims were most numerous. As J. L. Anderson pointed out, 'ships are easy to intercept as they predictably double capes or negotiate narrow straits and other "choke points" on trade routes'.[6] Indeed, surviving political sources frequently suggest this was the case for the waters near the Dover strait. For example, the 1554

2 N. A. M. Rodger, 'The Law and Language of Private Naval Warfare', *The Mariner's Mirror*, 100:1 (2014), 5–16, quotation from p. 6.

3 Andrews, *Privateering*, pp. 3–4.

4 See David J. Starkey, 'Voluntaries and Sea Robbers: A Review of the Academic Literature on Privateering, Corsairing, Buccaneering and Piracy', *The Mariner's Mirror*, 97:1 (2011), 127–47.

5 John C. Appleby, 'Jacobean Piracy: English Maritime Depredation in Transition, 1603–1625', in Cheryl A. Fury (ed.), *The Social History of English Seamen, 1485–1649* (Woodbridge, 2013), pp. 277–300, at pp. 282–6; there is a similar emphasis in J. C. Appleby, 'Pirates and Communities: Scenes from Elizabethan England and Wales', in J. C. Appleby and P. Dalton, (eds), *Outlaws in Medieval and Early Modern England: Crime, Government and Society, c.1066–c.1600* (Aldershot, 2009), pp. 149–72.

6 J. L. Anderson, 'Piracy and World History: An Economic Perspective on Maritime Predation', *Journal of World History*, 6:2 (1995), 175–99, at pp. 179, 182;

instructions of Mary I to William Tyrrel, her vice-admiral in the Narrow Seas, expressly ordered him to ensure 'none of here Highnes' subjectes be spoylede or robbede by other natyones as heretofore they have bene', and to deal with 'enye pyrates or rovers apon the seas come in hys dangyour'.[7]

Environmental factors aside, what might drive predation? A longstanding model, termed the 'piracy cycle', contends it began with 'small and independent groups of individuals using their boats for piracy as the desperation of poverty dictates or as the opportunity presents'. Through a beggar-thy-neighbour form of capital accumulation, effective actors could equip themselves with increasingly larger, better-armed vessels, and, in turn, engage more ambitious and lucrative targets. If this continued, eventually they became self-organised and autonomous of political power, liable to ally themselves with that power. Yet these structures remained fragile, and the process could easily collapse.[8] This would be largely compatible with David J. Starkey's interpretation of piracy appearing in 'waves of varying duration and amplitude' under the influence of varying efficiencies in the market for maritime labour.[9] In other words, insufficient employment or inadequate remuneration in maritime communities would be a key motive.

While inequality and poverty in Kent were growing (see Introduction and Chapter 1, this volume) and the aforesaid predation opportunities offered by geography were considerable, it is disputable whether individuals or groups consciously 'turned to piracy'. This is an example of the 'implicitly dualist contrast' that Rodger has rightly criticised modern historians for presenting.[10] Instances of predation in the Narrow Seas are too numerous and the respective ports of origin of the ships concerned were too similar to those involved in peaceable exchange.[11] For instance, the 20-ton *Thomas* of Sandwich, owned by a Sandwich merchant, John Maister, had – in November 1536 – just loaded at Ostend with a cargo of herring belonging to Calais merchants valued at £26 6s 8d, when it was captured by a pink out of Nieuwpoort. The same John Maister also reported that another vessel of his had barrels of beer and herring removed en route by three ships, one from Rotterdam and two out of Sluys, of which one was verified to be a Spanish vessel. It didn't matter how petty the target, one was exposed. Around the same time, various fishermen of Deal,

see also Ursula Daxecker and Brandon Prins, *Pirate Lands: Governance and Maritime Piracy* (Oxford, 2021), pp. 19–46, especially pp. 34–6.

7 TNA, PC 2/6, fol. 6.

8 Philip Gosse, *The History of Piracy* (New York, 1932), pp. 1–2; Anderson, 'Piracy and World History', 175–199, at p. 183.

9 David J. Starkey, 'Pirates and Markets', in Lewis R. Fischer (ed.), *The Market for Seamen in the Age of Sail* (Liverpool, 1994), pp. 59–80, quotation at p. 61.

10 Rodger, 'Private Naval Warfare', pp. 5–16, at p. 6.

11 Again, see Chapter 2, this volume.

who worked in a small boat part-owned by the same Maister, reported that warships from Flanders, possibly the same from Sluys, boarded them in the Downs and stole 10s of fresh fish. A few days later they returned, landed at Deal and stole the boat, valued at just 13s 4d.[12]

All parties operating in the Narrow Seas were equally culpable. In 1561, a detailed report of English piracy was compiled in Antwerp by city officials. Of eleven cases presented by Antwerp's mariners, nine specifically mention, or imply, the complicity of those of Kent. Vessels passing out of London, past Margate, or in the Downs were easy targets. The attacks were often very violent. They not only used cannons and small firearms, and even fired arrows, but once captured, in some cases victims were beaten and even stabbed in the face.[13] A somewhat similar account from 1573 detailed ships of Holland and Zeeland that 'have bene taken and spoyled on the costes and in the havens of Englaund by certene Englishe shippes and howe cruelly the men of the said taken and spoyled shippes have been handled and misused'. Of the further eleven cases of malfeasance reported over just six weeks, all but one involved Kent's ports or mariners. Examples of complaints include that of a certain Cornelis Cornelisson, master of the *Dolphin* of Brielle, whose ship was taken into Margate, his cargo of fish, hops and apples was seized and he, his wife and crew held prisoner for six days. Another episode saw the *Flying Harte* of Zierikzee robbed twice in twenty-four hours, once by a ship from Queenborough and then again by one from Faversham.[14]

Such behaviours were deeply rooted in contemporary coastal society. Indeed, in the 1587 edition of his chronicle, Raphael Holinshed recounted 'an old prouerbe in rime' about Kent's Hoo Peninsula, that went: 'He that rideth into the hundred of How; Beside pilfering sea-men shall find durt ynow'.[15] Our many disparate sources suggest a set of socioeconomic connections that was much as Appleby has described, namely that:

> Localized piracy flourished with the cooperation of the inhabitants of widely scattered maritime communities and with the connivance of local admiralty officials. Along the coasts of southern England and Ireland a varied group of supporters, including traders and shipowners, shop-keepers and ale house-keepers, supplied pirates with provisions in return for a share of their spoil at cheap rates of exchange.[16]

12 TNA, SP 1/117, fol. 107.

13 TNA, SP 70/23, fols 114–119.

14 TNA, SP 70/129A, fols 152–154.

15 *Holinshed Chronicles: England, Scotland, and Ireland. Volume 1* (New York 1807, repr. 1965), p. 53.

16 Appleby, 'Jacobean Piracy', pp. 277–300, at p. 282.

Moreover, the presence of piracy could even generate new ancillary on-shore industries. As it was stated in one government document, from 1579, 'it hath bene certified that in diuerse of the maritime countyes wthin this realme there hath bene erected in diuerse creekes brewhouses, slaughterhouses and stoarehouses to no other end, but to mainteyne traffiques wth pyrates wherby they have bene greatly relieved'.[17]

In 1571, Spanish ambassador Guerau de Espés del Valle named Dover as the principal centre of economic activity associated with maritime predation. He complained that stolen goods and hostages were both being sold in the port – in collusion with local and royal officials – on such a scale that 'there cannot be a greater emporium for pirates in all Europe'.[18] To Appleby, these behaviours constituted a progressive redistribution of wealth rather than being simply extractive.[19] Stolen expensive luxuries like wine, sugars or spices sold in local formal markets, or at a discount on informal markets, might become more accessible to less privileged portions of society. Even if necessities, like grain or fish, were sold, this could drive down market rates and amplify demand if the beneficiaries then had surplus income to spend on other goods. One 1578 list discloses examples of the goods captured by a certain 'pirate' called Captain Goore that were subsequently sold in Kent. These included luxuries like sugars, of which five loaves were marketed, alongside soap and wax, but the plunder mainly comprised 220 Holland cheeses, certainly a necessity. Buyers came from Canterbury, Sandwich, Margate, Whitstable and Sholden (near Deal), but also one from London. Those also implicated 'for dealinge with pirrattes' included Richard Crypps, Margate's searcher, and John Powell, that of Sandwich.[20] The same year, the commissioners for piracy in the Cinque Ports wrote to the privy council how they were 'lefte unprovided of suffycient deputies' to tackle all those involved. When they finally reported early in 1579, they revealed ten complicit individuals from Lydd, Romney, Hythe and Folkestone, who still felt able to refuse to pay 36s fines, pleading poverty, or insisting 'that they had bought those goodes laufully'.[21] Beyond the local economy, some stolen goods could also be dispersed much more widely along the networks of coastal trade. Those from one French hoy, the *Hope* of Rouen, captured in Hythe Bay in 1571 by Kentish sailors from Faversham, Queenborough and Sandwich, are one example. The ship was laden with a highly varied cargo including sugar and sugar candy, cotton, camphor, bay berries and leaf oil, brazilin, madder, red lead, pitch, tar and brass kettle

[17] TNA, SP 78/3, fols 30–32, quotation from fol. 31.

[18] TNA, SP 70/120, fol. 36: 'Ut nullum possit esse aluid magis pyratarum emporium in tota Europa'; see also SP 70/119, fol. 106.

[19] Appleby, 'Pirates and Communities', pp. 149–72, at p. 149.

[20] TNA, SP 12/123, fol. 115.

[21] TNA, SP 12/122, fol. 38; SP 12/129, fol. 39.

bottoms. These reportedly ended up in the hands of individuals from Southall (Middlesex), Harwich (Essex), Ipswich and Lowestoft (Suffolk), Great Yarmouth and Norwich (Norfolk), Hainton (Lincolnshire), Hull (Yorkshire) and even Vlissingen in Zeeland.[22]

Maritime predation was so deeply embedded that it is not contradictory to say it both drove and transcended politics. Polities would react to it, but it continued regardless and was even sometimes intensified by political action. Attacks on Dutch shipping by English vessels continued even while both were allies at war with Spain. In 1589, the Dutch complained that more than £200,000 in shipping and goods had been taken in the previous five years, despite an order of March 1585 from Elizabeth I which prohibited the use of letters of reprisal other than with Spanish or Portuguese ships.[23] Meanwhile, the Dutch themselves were hardly an innocent party. Vlissingen established a reputation as a base for predation. After all, the *Watergeuzen* or 'Sea Beggars', Calvinist zealots key to the foundation of the United Provinces, frequently operated out of the town when they attacked shipping.[24] George Gilpin wrote to Francis Walsingham in July 1584, to report the 'daily dyvers prises brought by the men of warre of Fflushing, whereof now and then they meete wth some comyng from our coaste, especially from Sandwiche'.[25] Even in August 1585, as the ink dried on the Treaty of Nonsuch between England and the Dutch which gave the kingdom control of the town, Thomas Pullyson, the Lord Mayor of London, reported to Walsingham of the 'iniury donn me by the fflushingers', as his ships passed along the route from Calais to London round Kent.[26]

Such reciprocal pillaging somewhat counters the view of D. J. B. Trim that in the late sixteenth century reformed Protestants broadly cooperated and interacted transnationally outside of governmental control. The argument being that English, Dutch and French Calvinists worked together with the religiously-motivated aim of control of the sea.[27] Yet this too occurred to some degree. For example, Protestant English and French Huguenots joined together during the Third War of Religion (1568–70) to predate enemy shipping further

22 TNA, HCA 13/19, fols 108r–109r.

23 TNA, SP 84/31, fols 135–139, quotation at fol. 137.

24 See Ivo van Loo, 'For Freedom and Fortune: The Rise of Dutch Privateering in the First Half of the Dutch Revolt, 1568–1609', in Marco van der Hoeven (ed.), *Exercise of Arms: Warfare in the Netherlands, 1568–1648*, History of Warfare Series, vol. 1 (Brill, 1997), pp. 173–95.

25 TNA, SP 83/22, fol. 127.

26 TNA, SP 12/181, fol. 205.

27 D. J. B. Trim, 'Transnational Calvinist Cooperation and "Mastery of the Sea" in the Late-Sixteenth Century', in J. D. Davies, Alan James and Gijs Rommelse (eds), *Ideologies of Western Naval Power, c. 1500–1815* (New York, 2019), pp. 153–87.

to the west: out of Plymouth and La Rochelle.[28] The aforesaid Kentish captors of the *Hope* of Rouen in 1571 claimed to be in the service of William the Silent (1533–84), Prince of Orange, the leader of the Dutch Revolt.[29] English vessels themselves also undertook predatory operations out of Vlissingen in the 1580s. This was at a sufficient scale to prompt French King Henry III (r. 1574–89) to write to Queen Elizabeth in July 1586 to inform her that the English had captured four or five of his subjects' ships in the Channel off Calais. They had been bound for Dieppe laden with Baltic grain but were intercepted and taken to Vlissingen, where their cargo might command a good price.[30]

Maritime predation was, therefore, multidimensional. All the more so because this was not behaviour unique to the region's Protestant societies. On the opposing side in the Eighty Years' War were the Dunkirkers, who operated from the north coast of Flanders, usually with the endorsement of, and acting as proxies for, the Catholic Spanish government.[31] They too had a particular reputation for aggression, as Anglo-Irish traveller Henry Piers wrote of his experience in July 1595 travelling from Kent to the United Provinces on a Dutch man-of-war, the *Hope* of Rotterdam, 'we did hardly escape in oure passadge from the Dunkirks wch did hotely pursue our shippe'.[32] The impact of the Dunkirkers was affirmed in stark terms in the English parliament in December 1601. A session of the House of Commons that month saw one burgess from Yarmouth claim that 'Dunkirk began with two Ships, and are now increased almost to twenty; they be at home at supper, and the next day here with us' with the effect that 'we may compare our sea-men to sheep, feeding upon a fair mountain, in the midst whereof stands a grove full of wolves'. Edward Peake, speaking specifically of the experience in Kent, declared that he must show the house 'how grievously the town of Sandwich (for which I serve) is vexed, and almost undone; insomuch, as that in that town there is neither owner, master, nor mariner that hath not felt it'.[33] Despite the urgent appeals to the Crown for action which accompanied such accounts, the threat of the

28 Rodger, 'Private Naval Warfare', pp. 5–16, at p. 9.

29 TNA, HCA 13/19, fol. 108r.

30 TNA, SP 78/16, fols 58–59.

31 R. A. Stradling, *The Armada of Flanders: Spanish Maritime Policy and European War, 1568–1668* (Cambridge, 1992), pp. 204–28.

32 Brian Mac Cuarta (ed.), *Henry Piers's Continental Travels, 1595–1598*, Camden Fifth Series, 54, Royal Historical Society (Cambridge, 2018), p. 54.

33 Heywood Townshend, 'Proceedings in the Commons, 1601: December 1st–5th', in *Historical Collections: Or, An Exact Account of the Proceedings of the Four Last Parliaments of Q. Elizabeth* (London, 1680), pp. 267–88. *British History Online*, http://www.british-history.ac.uk/no-series/parliament-proceedings-eliz1/pp267-288 (accessed 18 December 2023).

Dunkirkers persisted. Up until 1607 – and Spain's truce with the Dutch – it has been estimated that forty to fifty vessels were taken each year.[34]

After the Eighty Years' War resumed in 1621, the situation appeared to deteriorate even though, in principle, England remained neutral. One account of an encounter with Dunkirkers on a return voyage of one Dover ship from Vlissingen in May 1624 offers an interesting case in point of the ambiguities of merchant status amid contemporary security concerns. The ship involved, a 40-ton barque owned by Nicholas Eaton, James Hugessen the younger, Thomas Tyddiman, Nicholas Roberts and two widows, Mrs Warde and Trasznell, was set upon by a heavily armed frigate between Blankenberg and Ostend, four miles from land, with the demand: 'strike boogers of the kinge of Spayne'. Outgunned, the Dover ship swiftly submitted and the merchant aboard, James Hugessen the younger, the master William Chamblett and the crew of three immediately surrendered. They were taken to Ostend where the ship's cargo and personal effects of those aboard were seized. As this was – technically speaking – still a time of peace between England and Spain, Hugessen then endeavoured, unsuccessfully, to gain redress from the Spanish Habsburg authorities, first of all from the Admiral of Flanders, based on English neutrality and their 'league and amity'. Yet their view was that since the Dutch attacked ships bound for Flanders those who traded with Holland or Zeeland were themselves legitimate targets. Moreover, there were preparations to increase attacks on shipping further. For, during his sojourn, Hugessen observed 'that at Blankenburgh, Bridges, Oastende, Newporte, Dunkerke and Graueling are about 24 fregatts now built' and that 'if wee shoulde have warrs they are like to doe great harme and indangar many places uppon the sea coaste'.[35]

Depredations by Dunkirkers off Kent's coast indeed increased into early 1625, when it was reported how at least seven ships of Dover and Sandwich had been set upon just off the Goodwin Sands. The vessels were looted, and a number were taken to Dunkirk. The crew of a least one ship were tortured in a variety of ways 'to force them to say they were bound for Holland', including by waterboarding: 'by tying a lynnen cloath about some of there neckes and pouring in one bucket of salte water and one bucket of fresh water into their mouthes'.[36] The response to such a heavy-handed attitude to neutrality was to resort again to reprisal. Under articles laid down by the privy council in February 1625, many attained letters to recoup the value of goods lost, both at the hands of ships of the Spanish Netherlands and the United Provinces.[37] By August, it was claimed that, in Dover alone, nineteen vessels with 3,000 tons

34 Stradling, *The Armada of Flanders*, p. 217.
35 TNA, SP 14/165, fol. 159.
36 TNA, SP 14/185, fol. 208.
37 TNA, SP 14/183, fol. 99.

of goods worth at least £300,000 had accumulated under letters of reprisal. Yet, interestingly, such was the intricacy of cross-Channel trade and connections between their communities, some, James Hugessen included, were accused of having conveyed this bounty back to its owners, directly or via Calais.[38]

So private naval warfare had expanded significantly even before another Anglo-Spanish war commenced in 1625. Thereafter conditions deteriorated further, as Hugessen himself had predicted: 154 prizes were declared by Dunkirkers in 1627–28, and, according to Stradling, 'in 1629–30 the Ostend and Dunkirk squadrons between them took over eighty prizes and sank a further 111 Dutch and English vessels'. He conjured the image of Dunkirk as 'a centre of palpable wealth, a cornucopia of all the world's treasure, its quayside studded with capstans of pure gold. Certainly, Dunkirk and its sister-ports battened on the plunder, becoming in many respects storehouses of plenty.'[39]

A survey of Kent's ports in 1626 gives a sense of how well-armed the county's merchant fleet was as open conflict returned. On Dover and Sandwich vessels, there were 99 and 45 pieces of ordnance respectively – interpreted to mean at least medium-sized cannon – 144 pieces in total, but these were unevenly distributed. Of 56 ships of Dover just 12 carried ordnance (21.4 per cent), whilst at Sandwich, just 9 of 36 ships carried the same (or 25 per cent). Whilst this seems a meagre proportion equipped with such armaments, they were concentrated in the larger vessels. Consequently, the proportion of tonnage armed with ordnance was much higher, at 49 per cent in Dover and 45 per cent in Sandwich. They were, admittedly, not all armed to full capacity. The surveys noted that 58 more pieces at Dover and 30 at Sandwich could be added to relevant vessels, meaning these towns' fleets were 63.1 and 60 per cent armed, relative to their potential. But if these documents are believed, and smaller hoys were not expected to carry ordnance, only 16.1 per cent of vessels at Dover and 5.6 per cent at Sandwich were unarmed but could be.[40]

During war, Kent's maritime communities would also actively formalise predation, as is evident in the surviving records for letters of marque. In Dover, twenty-seven letters of marque were acquired for its ships during 1626–28 (the eighth highest among ports in the British Isles, behind London, Bristol, Weymouth, Dartmouth, Plymouth and Topsham), relating to fifteen unique ships.[41] Many of them do not appear in the 1626 survey, suggesting they had been bought or chartered from elsewhere for the purpose. These were often larger vessels, whose owners were high-status officials and merchants. Sir John Hippisley – a subordinate of George Villiers, duke of Buckingham – who

38 TNA, SP 16/5, fol. 106.

39 Stradling, *The Armada of Flanders*, pp. 217–18, 221–2.

40 Dixon, 'Economy', pp. 609–13 (appendix A); TNA, SP 16/34, fols 181–183.

41 For details of the warrants for these letters of marque, see TNA, SP 16/115, fols 10–57.

was then, amongst other roles, burgess MP for Dover, the lieutenant for the castle, as well as a freeman of the town, held letters for four ships during this period, the *Revenge* (300 tons) and *Have-at-all* (100 tons) with its pinnace the *Holdfast* (30 tons), as well as the *John and Fortune* (60 tons), and *Sweepstake* (60 tons).[42] Yet the resources invested in these ventures were still found locally; since Hippisley had, in his own words in August 1625, 'nether monie nor meanes', he relied on the 'credite and labore' of James Hugessen the elder and younger.[43] The Hugessens likewise had letters of marque in sequential years for the *Hunter* (100/140 tons), commanded by Abraham, their younger son and brother. In 1627, James junior held letters for the *Spy* (80 tons) and Abraham for the *Hopewell* (40 tons), commanded respectively by Edward Doves and John Woodgreene, both local Dover mariners from established families. In 1627, Nicholas Eaton (the past and future mayor of Dover) and his associates held letters for the *Africa* of Dover (120 tons) under the command of William Ledgent and Robert Smyth. Ledgent himself involved his ships the *Hercules* and the *Club*. Other notable names include Arnold Brames, who held letters in 1627 with his associates for the *Raven* (100 tons), commanded by Edward Doves, and a co-owner of the aforesaid *Spy* (80 tons) in 1628, now run by Cobham Doves, as well as its pinnace, the *Primrose*. Dover's impressive contingent was not altogether matched by those of Sandwich. The town acquired just seven letters of marque in this period, applying to five unique ships. John Brookshaw and his associates contributed the *Command* (100 tons), Roger Cripps and others, the *Endeavour* (180 tons), Richard West and others, the *Vintage* (150 tons) and Robert Robinson, the *Hestor* (40 tons). Robert Mills and his co-investors held letters in 1627 and 1628 for the *Love* (170 tons), a vessel he commanded, which had been previously recorded as having ten pieces of ordnance, and room for three more. That no other holders of letters but Mills appeared as shipowners in a 1626 survey may reflect a weaker link between merchant capital and predatory ventures in Sandwich than at Dover.[44]

There is some evidence for their efficacy among the records of appraisements of prizes. The sixty-three vessels recorded as taken by ships of the southeast of England during 1626–31 constituted just 8.6 per cent of the total and were dwarfed by the 421 taken by those of the southwest (57.1 per cent) and 144 by those of London (19.5 per cent). That said, Dover so dominated

42 Virginia C.D. Moseley and Rosemary Sgroi, 'HIPPISLEY (EPSLEY), Sir John (–d.1655), of The Mews, Westminster; Bushey Park, Mdx. and Dover Castle, Kent', in Andrew Thrush and John P. Ferris (eds), *The History of Parliament: The House of Commons 1604–1629* (Cambridge, 2010).

43 TNA, SP 16/5, fol. 192.

44 For the 1626 survey and earlier citation of the *Love*, see TNA, SP 16/34, fols 181–183.

the predation in the southeast that, with fifty-seven prizes taken, it was fifth in the long list of ports involved. The only ports that were more successful were London (144 prizes), Bristol (134), Plymouth (70) and Weymouth (69). Appleby pointed out that around 70 per cent of Dover's prizes were actually 'small, poorly-armed French vessels of low value' taken during the Anglo-French War (1627–29) because this 'allowed Dover privateers to take advantage of the geographical situation of the port to make repeated cross-Channel raids on the French coasting trade'. Yet, this was significant enough for the town's residents, who declared that 'the taking of prizes is now our trade'.[45]

The appraisements indicate that Dover's ships captured different goods from those elsewhere. Countrywide, sugars constituted 63 per cent of captured cargoes by value during 1625–31, worth £321,755, taken largely from Portuguese vessels. Just three shipments of sugars were brought into Dover during this time; instead 28.4 per cent of named cargoes were raw materials like iron, 20 per cent were foodstuffs, 16.8 per cent manufactures and 13.7 per cent wines.[46] Prizes were indeed small, and low value – simply because of this lack of sugar – but they were plentiful. The success rate, as measured by the number of prizes taken per venture, was favourable. The southeast of England enjoyed 1.85–1.97 prizes per venture, depending on the calculation of the number of ventures, and the south 1.14–1.25. This was much higher than 0.81–0.87 per venture for the southwest, and 0.37–0.38 for London. This metric reveals the relative efficiency of predation in the Narrow Seas, probably due to the high concentration of maritime traffic. Moreover, two further points would enhance the image of the region as a centre of predatory action. First, because Kent's ships were, on average, far smaller than, for example, London's, this reduced the propensity for local actors to take the largest vessels. Yet bigger ships from London had to pass through the Narrow Seas and could have taken their prizes there. Second, the frequency of prizes taken by smaller local vessels during this period was likely greatly understated. It would be comparatively easy to avoid the appraisal of smaller prizes amid the fog of war, rather than a large Spanish or Portuguese ship. Actors could dispose of their takings, as low-level piracy had always done. Indeed, such pre-war predation must have continued, and these actions are not included in official records.

For those communities around Kent's coast, active commerce or private naval warfare were not the only ways they could tap the great wealth of the Narrow Seas. Shipwrecks on or near the county's shores or the exploitation of ships in distress could provide similarly lucrative opportunities to acquire

[45] J. C. Appleby, 'English Privateering during the Spanish and French Wars, 1625–1630' (unpublished Ph.D. thesis, University of Hull, 1983), pp. 265–6, 313–14 (his tables 4.2–3).

[46] Calculated by the author from *ibid.*, pp. 207–15 (his appendix II).

goods.[47] David Cressy calculated that of documented wrecks in England and Wales during 1550–1750, the 'heavily trafficked coast of the Channel or Narrow Seas from Southampton to the Isle of Thanet saw the greatest number of wrecks', 36 per cent of the total. If one focuses on his named ships from 1559 to 1625, 33.7 per cent of the total were wrecked on the coast of Kent alone. Cressy specifically cited the Goodwin Sands as an 'especially lethal' location.[48] This dangerous marine sandbank is six miles off Deal, situated just beside the vital anchorage in the Downs. Inclement weather there could wreck vessels en masse. In 1545, for example, several large Portuguese and Spanish galleons, having encountered a 'byrage and tempeste of wether was driuen upon theste ende of Goodwyn Sandes'.[49]

Alongside local illicit action, a complex array of rights and privileges dictated who benefited most, yet the presence of the Cinque Ports along the southeast coast of England was critical. The ports had long received the right of wreck from the Crown, which permitted their residents to take the goods and remains of wrecked ships 'in whatsoever coast and arms of the sea adjacent to the ports', and profit from them.[50] The Warden of the Cinque Ports was particularly invested, as the official frequently received a share, which, from the wardenship of William Brooke, Lord Cobham (1527–97), amounted to a third.[51] As Cressy put it, the 'jurisdiction of the Cinque Ports covered the richest of all wreck zones, including the Goodwin Sands offshore from Deal and Ramsgate, where the Warden claimed Admiralty rights and was watchful for his profits'.[52]

Thus, Kent's naturally dangerous coast became an antagonist of ships, akin to predatory human action. Yet the degree to which the salvage of goods constituted predatory behaviour by individuals concerned is somewhat more ambiguous. Oftentimes the rescue of the mariners and merchants in a distressed vessel was negotiated in exchange for a share of the cargoes saved. If this went well beyond a reasonable reward for labour and risk, rescuers were certainly guilty of exploiting another's misfortunes. The boatmen of Deal, for example, had a reputation for this, entrenched by a later description by Daniel Defoe.[53] Much as with private naval warfare, local merchant interests similarly benefited from the handling of windfall goods, both for onward sale

47 A comprehensive overview of shipwrecks and 'wrecking' in early modern England is David Cressy, *Shipwrecks and the Bounty of the Sea* (Oxford, 2022).

48 *Ibid.*, p. 27, also see his appendix at pp. 263–79.

49 TNA, SP 1/445, fol. 68.

50 Graham S. McBain, 'The Charters of the Cinque Ports – Are They Still Needed?', *Review of European Studies*, 5:2 (2013), 90–126, at p. 121.

51 Brindle, 'Cinque Ports', pp. 338–9.

52 Cressy, *Shipwrecks*, p. 104.

53 *Ibid.*, pp. 2, 75–7.

and return to their original owners. Indeed, Cressy thought the same way of shipwreck as Appleby did of piracy, arguing that the 'price was high for the development of a global economy, but English coastal communities were among its beneficiaries'.[54] The full extent of this business is revealed in one surviving 1594 lengthy inventory for goods salvaged from Dutch ships lost on the Goodwin Sands by men of Romney, Walmer, Deal, Ramsgate, Dover, Lydd, Hythe and Dymchurch in November and December 1592. Considerable sums of money and a wide variety of cloth, as well as extensive quantities of wax and copper, were handled by Charles (Carel) Liebaert, a draper and cloth merchant of Sandwich originally from Bailleul in Flanders.[55]

One incident is well documented because some goods brought ashore were recorded in a port book of Sandwich and Deal for 1616, with entries marked 'Le downes a le wracke'. The goods were Dutch in origin, likely from the *Abraham* of Hoorn, the *Jonas* of Enkhuizen or *Peter* of Amsterdam, wrecked on the Goodwin Sands in January of that year.[56] Amid multiple reports of the Deal boatmen's poor behaviour towards the merchants, the ships' goods were gradually brought ashore.[57] Between 21 March and 22 April 1616, 18,212 lb of pepper and 1,780 lb of cloves were recorded in 75 containers, with an official value of £1,962 13s 4d. The merchants who handled these spices were prominent resident aliens. Balthazar Verhulst, a cloth merchant from Antwerp, but then of Sandwich, handled most: 9,552 lb of pepper and 920 lb of cloves worth £1,026. Another prominent merchant involved was Samuel de Vischer, born in Emden but denizened in 1614, who handled 860 lb of cloves valued at £215. One of these wrecks was still salvageable some months later, on 26 July, when another foreigner, one Lawrence Metcher, was recorded bringing five small casks containing 9 cwt of muscovado sugar, valued at £30.[58] Such were the fortunes to be made on the back of the misfortunes of wrecked ships that the practice could, at times, encourage bitter local rivalries, such as that at Dover between the Hugessen and Brames families, both originally strangers.[59] A good example occurred in March 1621, when James Hugessen the younger

54 *Ibid.*, p. 25.

55 TNA, SP 12/249, fol. 232; also SP 13/f, fol. 001 [Case F. Eliz., No. 1]; for Liebaert's background, see Backhouse, 'Flemish and Walloon Communities', I, pp. 98, 101, 254.

56 Cressy, *Shipwrecks*, pp. 132–3.

57 TNA, SP 14/86, fols 3–4.

58 TNA, E 190/651/13, fols 2r–3r, 5r; William A. Shaw (ed.), *Denizations and Naturalizations of Aliens in England and Ireland*, Publications of the Huguenot Society, vol. 18 (Lymington, 1911), p. 21; Christopher Joby, *The Dutch Language in Britain (1550–1702): A Social History of the Use of Dutch in Early Modern Britain* (Leiden, 2015), p. 71.

59 Dixon, 'Economy', p. 155.

wrote to Lord Zouche to explain that he could not dispose of the goods taken from a Hamburg ship, the *Ark Noah*, partly because of 'scandalose information which Mr Brams [Brames] hath informed agaynst me'. The ship, which had laded at Lisbon, was certainly a desirable target. Hugessen recounted its cargo of salt, ninety chests of powdered sugars, as well as pepper, cloves, cinnamon and five barrels of silver Spanish reals, discovered with the aid of six boats of Deal.[60]

Though such reports of maritime predation and shipwreck, discussed in this chapter, feature heavily throughout surviving records about the Narrow Seas, we unfortunately have no reliable quantitative measures to show their impact on trade, or how the region's societies and economies were affected more broadly. We cannot even adjudge the risks a merchant undertook having their goods conveyed along the shipping lanes, nor the risk to a mariner's person and vessel. While it has been estimated that around 5 per cent of ships that set out were lost to shipwreck, this has not been calculated for the waters near England's coasts.[61] If we add the risk of attack, rates of loss were probably higher. Any analysis will, however, remain speculative. One would, nevertheless, expect the overall effect of a high-risk environment to be negative. These threats could have a direct psychological impact. When certain mariners from Dover and Sandwich returned from a trading expedition to Bordeaux in 1622 and filed a petition to Lord Zouche, Warden of the Cinque Ports, they first acknowledged the perennial hazards by declaring they had 'escaped the greedy appetite of the unsatiate sea'.[62] As well as the feared human existential risk, so-stated, when ships were captured or sunk and inventories lost, that destroyed fixed and working capital. These threats could redirect economic actors towards less risky but less profitable commercial endeavours, or even discourage investment and enterprise more broadly and so constrain the prosperity of ports. If we believe the testimony of merchants, the former was always a possibility. According to Nicolas Gillot of Dieppe and his factor Jehan Robin, the English pirates' predation in the Narrow Seas in the 1580s was such that the grain trade between the Baltic and France might become unviable.[63] Yet the purpose of such appeals was to gain recompense and so they might exaggerate. There is certainly a lot of evidence that insurance premiums to cover ships and seaborne cargo would rise considerably during periods of conflict and increased piracy.[64] This would indicate a rise in risk to

60 TNA, SP 14/120, fol. 27.

61 Cressy, *Shipwrecks*, pp. 23–5.

62 TNA, SP 14/127, fol. 106.

63 TNA, SP 78/16, fol. 38.

64 Jeroen Puttevils and Marc Deloof, 'Marketing and Pricing Risk in Marine Insurance in Sixteenth-Century Antwerp', *The Journal of Economic History*, 77:3 (2017), 796–837, especially at p. 802.

shipping and the demand for services that managed that risk. The qualitative evidence above likewise suggests wars increased the level of threat. However, there is an ambiguous relationship between these and the quantity of fixed capital in trade. The tonnage of ships based in Kent's main ports, Dover and Sandwich, broadly rose during the first Anglo-Spanish War (1585–1604), but declined across the board during the wars of the 1620s. Between 1626 and 1628–29, the tonnage of Dover's vessels fell 34.4 per cent, those of Sandwich 43.1 per cent, Ramsgate 24.5 per cent, Broadstairs 43.8 per cent, Hythe 35.1 per cent and Deal 55.6 per cent.[65] To complicate matters further, we have seen how private naval warfare in Dover and Sandwich, as well as the ports of Flanders, actually stimulated investment in ships and ancillary industries.

In 1635, another petition to the lords of the Admiralty indeed complained of general economic deterioration due to predation. With war between the United Provinces, France and Spanish territories, even ships destined for these places would be attacked by their ships in the Narrow Seas and 'pillaged to the great losse and hinderance' of the merchants and mariners of Dover. Allegedly the French would 'daily lye with their small shallops in sight of the harbour' stopping any crossing to Flanders 'to the great preiudice of the marryners, imployment of shipping, the whole towne in generall and his majesty in his customes'.[66] Again, we cannot be sure quite how seriously to take such complaints. Even if accurate, evidently it was not sufficient to impede commerce. This petition was made when the great entrepôt trade through Dover, described by Kepler, was at its height. Around £610,000 worth of goods were re-exported through its harbour between Christmas 1635 and November 1636 alone, one-quarter of which went to Flanders.[67]

Undoubtedly, control of the Narrow Seas by any polity remained weak, yet because predation was generally undertaken, not by outsiders, but by members of the region's maritime communities themselves, rather than being a threat external to the trade system – as is often supposed – it was part of the system. We cannot adjudge how much, or indeed if, it held back economic growth. Many of the goods obtained ultimately ended up in local or regional markets regardless. In this sense theft or salvage were very one-sided forms of exchange. Merchants and mariners were as comfortable engaging their labour and capital in private naval warfare or wreck as in profitable trade. Indeed, Mary Dixon noted that, in the case of Dover, 'most wealth was accumulated from ship-ownership in the seventeenth century by those who owned large ships that were involved in privateering and salvage work. They

[65] TNA, SP 16/34, fols 179–183; SP 16/39, fols 56–58, 60–61, SP 16/155, fols 82r–123v; Dixon, 'Economy', pp. 609–13 (her appendix A); also see Chapter 2, this volume.

[66] TNA, SP 16/293, fol. 39.

[67] Kepler, *The Exchange*, pp. 162–4 (his appendices C and D).

were also the men who appear to have made most from the composition [entrepôt] trade in that period'.[68] Members of Kent's maritime communities would trade, steal and scavenge, seamlessly, in equal measure, as did their continental counterparts in turn. Indeed, their very proximity seems to have made such plundering routine.

68 Dixon, 'Economy', p. 264.

Conclusion

ROBERT BLACKMORE

The grave of James Hugessen the younger – formerly of Dover – lies in the Church of Saints Peter and Paul in Lynsted, Kent. He died on 2 October 1646, and above his and his wife's effigies, beside the memorial, is written this short verse:

> Infancy youth and Age are from ye wombe
> Man's short but dangerous passage to his tomb.
> Here landed (the proceed of what we vent'red)
> In Nature's custom-house this dust is ent'red.
> Christ's all our gaine by whom, in death we live
> And carry hence, but only which we give;
> Almes-deeds are surest bill at sight, (the rest
> On Heaven's Exchange are subject to protest)
> This uncorrupted Manna of the just
> is lasting; store exempt from worms and dust.

Its morbid but witty fusion of piety with aspects of mercantile life offers us a small glimpse of the final thoughts and sentiments of a figure featured in this book.[1] The son of immigrants from Dunkirk, just across the Channel, he was a successful merchant, shipowner and state agent, both a victim and participant in maritime predation – a man deeply enmeshed in Kent's economy, society and politics at the end of the period concerned.

While not all the lives of people featured in this book were as colourful and varied as that of Hugessen, that they all lived and worked in a county intrinsically linked with the European mainland meant their lives shared many commonalities. We have seen, in Chapter 1, how they experienced, at first hand, the political, socioeconomic, cultural and religious changes that

[1] James Hugessen the younger (1575–1646) and his family are mentioned in Chapters 2 and 5.

England – and much of Europe – underwent across the later fifteenth century and early decades of the sixteenth. They did so not as inhabitants of some provincial periphery but were often highly networked and connected with London, the rest of the country and the nearby continent. This, as Chapter 2 shows, continued into the later sixteenth and early seventeenth centuries. The complex sub-structures and super-structures of commercial life in provincial mercantile communities, here discussed, sustained and adapted socioeconomic connections, especially with London and many European ports. In Chapter 3, an investigation of Kent's merchant fleet and maritime communities from the 1580s to the 1630s reveals similar features: a close-knit but highly networked seafaring society, influenced by the growth of London and events in Europe. Chapter 4 reveals the intermittent government investment in defensive infrastructure – in manpower for sure – but especially physical assets, like forts and warships. While this made Kent comparatively militarised, as per contemporary requirements concerning conflicts with European powers, nascent state involvement remained weak and unreliable throughout much of the period. Instead, Chapter 5 offers a view of Kent and the Narrow Seas as a zone of aggression for the 'private sector'. This was a maritime world in which enterprise might include the movement of goods and passengers, or fishing, but also private naval warfare on a considerable scale, as well as exploitation of ships wrecked or in peril.

To conclude that Kent's location – at the fulcrum of the Narrow Seas and just a few miles' 'short but dangerous passage' from Europe – was entirely irrelevant in these matters, would be incongruous. Geography, and the environment more broadly, could influence opportunities and frame the possible. The bottleneck of the Dover strait certainly concentrated and directed seaborne interchange. The proximity of London and the cities of the Low Countries touched people's lives by sheer force of gravity. Yet neither of these things made any aspects of those lives inevitable. As John R. Gillis wrote in *The Human Shore*, 'thresholds are always precarious but seductive places, freighted with dread as well as invested with great expectations'.[2] Such was the setting in which generations of people from the fifteenth to seventeenth centuries were born, lived and died. Their world was one in which they could see the European mainland on a clear day from the White Cliffs of Dover. Equally, if one stood on the huge sand dunes to the north of Vlissingen one could also look back across the Western Scheldt and see the coast of Flanders curving away into the distance. From both vantage points you would see human activity – both cooperation and conflict – concentrated. This must have held some significance. How it shaped the behaviour of those in the past is debatable, but the question in the Introduction to this volume as to

2 John R. Gillis, *The Human Shore: Seacoasts in History* (Chicago, 2012), p. 60.

how Kent and its sea-coast could function as both a prosperous thoroughfare and violently contested region should be abandoned as a false dichotomy. Instead, we should consider this simply as a space where many aspects of life – economic, social, political, and military – were intensified.

One further short example can instead illustrate how the impact of relatively minor human activities in such a locality could impact wider European, and even world history, in a chaotic, unpredictable fashion. There is a cannon, a late sixteenth-century 17- to 18-pounder cast iron culverin, in the maritime museum of the Citadelle de Port-Louis, near Lorient in southern Brittany, France. As it displays the Tudor Rose and the motto of the Order of the Garter, 'Honi soit qui mal y pense', it is very clearly of English origin.[3] Labelled by the museum as being from the wreck of a vessel named the *Mauritius*, the date of its manufacture is given as 1587 and the gun's maker is identified as one John Phillips.

Fortuitously enough, there is an entry for that year in the coastal port book for Rochester, Kent, which translates as:

> In the Mary Thomas of Melhale [Millhall] of the burden of 46 tons John Dionesse Master on 7 August 1587 towards London.
>
> Of John Phillips, native, for 29 tons of iron and 28 pieces of iron guns containing 16 tons.[4]

Given that the dates and name match, there is a strong possibility that one of these pieces of ordnance listed is that which survives today in Brittany. The individual cited in both was most likely a London gun founder, John Phillips, who – local records indicate – ran a furnace in Ashurst in the Kentish Weald around the same time.[5] After its manufacture, the cannon would have been shipped overland to the River Medway to be loaded aboard the *Mary Thomas*, most likely at Millhall (Milhale) to the northwest of Maidstone. It was then carried by water to London via Rochester.

3 Musée national de la Marine de Port-Louis, Citadelle de Port-Louis, Route du fort de l'Aigle, 56290 Port-Louis. Item inventoried as *Dépôt de l'État gabonais*. Inv. PG 26.

4 TNA, E 190/643/3, fol. 2v: 'In le Marie Thomas de Melhale oneris xlvj dolliorum Johanne Dionesse magistro vij° Augusti 1587 versus London. De Johanne Phillipps indigenus pro xxixe dolliis ferri et xxviij° peciis tormentorum ferri continens xvjo dolliis'.

5 Hodgkinson 'Ironworks in Late-16th Century Kent', 6–15. For details on Kent's role in ordnance manufacture, see also Brown, 'Thomas Browne', 16–25.

The VOC-owned 700-ton *Mauritius* sank in 1609 off Cape Lopez in the Gulf of Guinea near Gabon, in west central Africa.[6] When the ship had acquired John Phillips' gun is uncertain, for, as discussed in Chapters 2 and 4, England frequently supplied Kentish arms to the United Provinces during the first Anglo-Spanish War. Between November 1598 and September 1599, for instance, 250 tons' worth of cast iron ordnance were recorded leaving Rochester bound for Amsterdam.[7] Yet from 1602, when the VOC acquired the *Mauritius* soon after the company's creation, we can trace its movements. The ship's first VOC voyage (17 June 1602–12 July 1604) began at Texel in North Holland, and stopped for a few weeks in Plymouth, another point when perhaps Phillips' cannon was taken on board. On this occasion the ship went to Bantam, in Java (now Indonesia), and back again. It left Texel on its second and final voyage on 12 May 1605 and returned to the Far East via its namesake island of Mauritius and the Nicobar Islands, finally reaching the Malacca Strait on 18 August 1606. There the ship took part in the Battle of Cape Rachado (Tanjung Tuan in modern-day Malaysia), a dramatic confrontation between the Dutch and Portuguese in their rivalry for control of the spice trade. After the battle, the ship spent the next few years in the Far East, eventually making its way, via Vietnam, to China. It then returned across the Indian Ocean and around Africa, where it met its end at Cape Lopez on 19 March 1609.[8]

This connection of a Kent cannon to the *Mauritius* illuminates the county's role as a 'marytime contrye', as contemporaries put it.[9] This was a place that, while ostensibly provincial, was in fact a centre of intense activity, with especially multifaceted links with Europe and beyond. One could hardly predict that the actions of London gunsmith John Phillips in the Kentish Weald or Millhall shipmaster John Dionesse on the River Medway might play some part in the future of empires. But then, as Alfred North Whitehead would say, 'the history of the world depends on a lot of little things'.[10]

6 Wendy van Duivenvoorde, 'The Batavia Shipwreck: An Archaeological Study of an Early Seventeenth-Century Dutch East Indiaman' (unpublished Ph.D. thesis, Texas A&M University, August 2008), pp. 62, 186, 252, 255, 263, 266, 273–4, 278–80, 289, 315–16, 319. See also M. L'Hour, L. Long and E. Rieth, 'The Wreck of an "Experimental" Ship of the "Oost-Indische Companie": The *Mauritius* (1609)', *The International Journal of Nautical Archeology and Underwater Exploration*, 19:1 (1990), 63–73; Michel L'Hour, Luc Long and Eric Rieth, *Le Mauritius: la mémoire engloutie* (Paris, 1989).

7 TNA, E 190/646/2, fols 1r–v.

8 Voyage details contained in the Huygens Institute's database: *The Dutch East India Company's shipping between the Netherlands and Asia 1595–1795*, https://resources.huygens.knaw.nl/das (accessed 14 March 2025).

9 TNA, SP 12/245, fol. 106.

10 Whitehead, 'England and the Narrow Seas', 791–8, at p. 793.

BIBLIOGRAPHY

Manuscript Sources

The British Library, London (BL)

Add. MSS 29616, 29618B, 33511, 48009
Egerton MSS 2092, 2093, 2107, 2108

Canterbury Cathedral Archives and Library (CCAL)

CC/FA/5, 7 City Chamberlains' Accounts
CC/OA/1 Wills and Deeds

Corpus Christi College, Cambridge (CCCC)

MS 128 Documents relating to Archbishop Cranmer

Kent History and Library Centre, Maidstone (KHLC)

Do/FCa/1 Dover Chamberlains' Accounts
Do/ZCPW 6 Lord Warden of the Cinque Ports, Militia
Fa/CPM/1–21, 24, 33 Faversham Musters
Ly/FAc/3 Lydd Musters
Nr/CPM/1 Romney Musters
PRC 17 Archdeaconry Court: Registers of Wills
PRC 32 Consistory Court: Registers of Wills
Sa/AC/1–3 Sandwich Year Books
Sa/Fat/12, 16–17, 33 Sandwich Treasurers' Accounts

The National Archives, Kew, London (TNA)

E 101 Exchequer: King's Remembrancer: Accounts Various
E 122 Exchequer: King's Remembrancer: Particulars of Customs Accounts
E 159 Exchequer: King's Remembrancer: Memoranda Rolls and Enrolment Books
E 190 Exchequer: King's Remembrancer: Port Books
HCA 13 High Court of Admiralty: Instance and Prize Courts
PC 2 Privy Council: Registers
PROB 11 Prerogative Court of Canterbury and related Probate Jurisdictions
SP Records assembled by the State Paper Office

Zeeuwsarchief, Middelburg, Netherlands

GIDS103 Tol van Zeeland, 1584–1805

Printed Primary Sources

'A Brief memorial of what hath been done in former times, concerning the making and repairing of Dover harbour, and the present state thereof', *Early English Books Online*. https://name.umdl.umich.edu/A29459.0001.001, *University of Michigan Library Digital Collections*.

Boys, William, *Collections for an history of Sandwich in Kent: With Notices of the other Cinque Ports and Members, and of Richborough* (Canterbury, 1792).

Caley, John and Joseph Hunter (eds), *Valor Ecclesiasticus*, 1 (London, 1810).

Childs, Wendy R. (ed.), *The Customs Accounts of Hull, 1453–1490*, Yorkshire Archaeological Society Record Series, vol. 144 (1986).

Defoe, Daniel, *A Tour Through the island of Great Britain. Divided into Circuits or Journeys*, 8th edition, vol. 1 (London, 1778).

Dorman, T., 'The Sandwich book of orphans', *Archaeologia Cantiana*, 16 (1886), 179–206.

Duncan, Leland, L., 'Transcriptions of Medieval and Tudor Kent P.C.C. & C.C.C. Wills', *Kent Archaeology Society*, https://www.kentarchaeology.org.uk/news/trascriptions-of-medieval-amp-tudor-kent-pcc-amp-ccc-wills-by-l-l-duncan.

Farmer, John (ed.), *Nice Wanton 1560* (London and Edinburgh, 1909).

Froissart, Jean, *Chronicles*, MS Besançon 865, in P. Ainsworth and G. Croenen (eds), *The Online Froissart* (Sheffield, 2013), http://www.hrionline.ac.uk/onlinefroissart.

Gairdner, James and R. H. Brodie (eds), *Letters and Papers, Foreign and Domestic, of the Reign of Henry VIII*, 18 ii (London, 1902).

Gibson, J. M., 'The 1566 Survey of the Kent Coast', *Archaeologia Cantiana*, 112 (1993), 341–53.

Harrington, Duncan and Patricia Hyde (eds), *The Early Town Books of Faversham c.1251 to 1581*, part 1 (Faversham, 2008).

Hinds, Allen B. (ed.), *Calendar of State Papers Relating to English Affairs in the Archives of Venice, 23, 1632–1636* (London, 1921).

Holinshed Chronicles: England, Scotland, and Ireland. Volume 1 (New York 1807, repr. 1965).

Hull, Felix (ed.), *A Calendar of the White and Black Books of the Cinque Ports, 1432–1955* (London, 1966).

Hussey, Arthur (ed.), *Testamenta Cantiana: East Kent* (London, 1907).

—— *Kent Chantries* (1932).

—— 'Milton Wills (next Sittingbourne)', *Archaeologia Cantiana*, 44 (1932), 79–102.

Jenks, Stuart (ed.), *The London Custom Accounts Part II* (Cologne, 2016), https://www.hansischergeschichtsverein.de/london-customs-accounts.

Lambarde, William, *A Perambulation of Kent: Conteining the Description, Hystorie, and Customes of that Shyre. Written in the Yeere 1570, by William*

Lambarde, of Lincolnes Inne Gent: First Published in the Yeere 1576 and now Increased and Altered after Author's Owne Last Copie (London, 1596).
—— *A Perambulation of Kent, Conteining the Description, Hystorie, and Customes of that Shire; Written in the Yeere 1570, First Published in the Year 1576, and now Increased and Altered from the Author's Owne Last Copie* (London, 1826).
Latham, Robert (ed.), *Samuel Pepys and the Second Dutch War: Pepys's Navy White Book and Brooke House Papers*, Naval Record Society, vol. 134 (London, 1995).
Laughton, John Knox (ed.), *State Papers relating to the Defeat of the Spanish Armada, Anno 1588*, vol. 1, 2nd edition (London, 1895).
Letters and Papers, Foreign and Domestic, of the Reign of Henry VIII. Preserved in the Public Record Office, the British Museum, and elsewhere in England, vol. 21, part 1 (London, 1908).
Mac Cuarta, Brian (ed.), *Henry Piers's Continental Travels, 1595–1598*, Camden Fifth Series, 54, Royal Historical Society (Cambridge, 2018).
Rice Holmes, T. (ed.), *C. Julius Caesar, Commentarii Rerum in Gallia Gestarum VII A. Hirti Commentarius VII* (Oxford, 1914).
Rose, Susan (ed.), *The Navy of the Lancastrian Kings: Accounts and Inventories of William Soper, Keeper of the King's Ships, 1422–1427* (London, 1982).
Shaw, William A. (ed.), *Calendar of Treasury Books*, vol. 4, 1672–1675 (London, 1909).
—— *Denizations and Naturalizations of Aliens in England and Ireland*, Publications of the Huguenot Society, vol. 18 (Lymington, 1911).
Smit, H. J. (ed.), *Bronnen tot de geschiedenis van den handel met Engeland, Schotland en Ierland 1150–1585*, vol. 2 (The Hague, 1950).
Smith, Lucy T (ed.), *The Itinerary of John Leland in or About the Years of 1535–1543, Parts VII and VIII, with Appendices including Extracts from Leland's Collectanea* (London, 1909).
Starkey, David (ed.), *The Inventory of King Henry VIII (Society of Antiquaries MS 129 and British Library MS Harley 1419): The Transcript* (London, 1998).
Temple, Richard Carnac (ed.), *The Travels of Peter Mundy, in Europe and Asia, 1608–1667: Volume I: Travels in Europe, 1608–1628* (Cambridge, 1907).
Townshend, Heywood, 'Proceedings in the Commons, 1601: December 1st–5th', in *Historical Collections: Or, An Exact Account of the Proceedings of the Four Last Parliaments of Q. Elizabeth* (London, 1680).
Warner, George (ed.), *The Lybelle of Englysche Polycye: A Poem on the Use of Sea Power* (Oxford, 1926).

Secondary Authorities

Alfani, G., and H. García Montero, 'Wealth Inequality in Pre-Industrial England: A Long-Term View (Late Thirteenth to Sixteenth Centuries)', *Economic History Review*, 2nd series, 75:4 (November 2022), 1314–48.
Anderson, J. L., 'Piracy and World History: An Economic Perspective on Maritime Predation', *Journal of World History*, 6:2 (1995), 175–99.

Andrewes, Jane, 'Industries in Kent, c.1500–1640', in Michael Zell (ed.), *Early Modern Kent, 1540–1640* (Woodbridge, 2000), pp. 105–39.

—— 'The Early Modern Period 1500–1700: Trade and Industry', in Stuart Bligh, Elizabeth Edwards and Sheila Sweetinburgh (eds), *Maritime Kent through the Ages: Gateway to the Sea* (Woodbridge, 2021), pp. 235–52.

Andrews, J. H., 'Two Problems in the Interpretation of the Port Books', *Economic History Review*, 2nd series, 9:1 (1956), 119–22.

Andrews, Kenneth R., *Elizabethan Privateering: English Privateering during the Spanish War, 1585–1603* (Cambridge, 1964).

Appleby, John C., 'Pirates and Communities: Scenes from Elizabethan England and Wales', in J. C. Appleby and P. Dalton, (eds), *Outlaws in Medieval and Early Modern England: Crime, Government and Society, c.1066–c.1600* (Aldershot, 2009), pp. 149–72.

—— 'Jacobean Piracy: English Maritime Depredation in Transition, 1603–1625', in Cheryl A. Fury (ed.), *The Social History of English Seamen, 1485–1649* (Woodbridge, 2013), pp. 277–300.

Backhouse, Marcel F., 'The Strangers at Work in Sandwich: Native Envy of an Industrious Minority 1561–1603', *Immigrants & Minorities*, 10:3 (1991), 70–99.

Baker, Gary P., 'Domestic Maritime Trade in Late Tudor England c.1565–85: A Case Study of King's Lynn and Plymouth', in Claire Jowitt, Craig Lambert and Steve Mentz (eds), *The Routledge Companion to Marine and Maritime Worlds, 1400–1800* (London, 2020), pp. 95–124.

Beeler, John H., 'Castles and Strategy in Norman and Early Angevin England', *Speculum*, 31:4 (1956), 581–601.

Biddle, Martin, Howard Colvin and John Summerson, 'The Defences in Detail', in Howard Colvin (ed.), *The History of the King's Works: 1485–1660*, vol. 4 part 2 (London, 1982), pp. 415–606.

Biddle, Martin, Jonathan Hiller, Ian Scott and Anthony Streeten et al., *Henry VIII's Coastal Artillery Fort at Camber Castle, Rye, East Sussex* (Oxford, 2001).

Black, Jeremy, *European Warfare, 1494–1660* (London, 2002).

Boston, David, 'England's Earliest Painted and Framed Royal Coat of Arms (Edward VI, 1547–53) in St Mary's Church, Westerham: The Work of a Low Countries' Artist Commissioned by the Gresham Family', *Archaeologia Cantiana*, 141 (2020), 84–97.

Bouedec, Le Gérard, 'La pluriactivité dans les sociétés littorales XVIIe–XIXe siècle', *Annales de Bretagne et des Pays de l'Ouest*, 109 (2002), 61–9.

Bower, Jacqueline, 'Kent Towns, 1540–1640', in Michael Zell (ed.), *Early Modern Kent, 1540–1640* (Woodbridge, 2000), pp. 141–76.

Bowers, Roger, 'The Liturgy of the Cathedral and Its Music, c.1075–1642', in Patrick Collinson, Nigel Ramsey and Margaret Sparks (eds), *A History of Canterbury Cathedral* (Oxford, 1995), pp. 408–50.

Boynton, Lindsay, *The Elizabethan Militia, 1558–1638* (Newton Abbot, 1971).

Brinkley, Leanna T. P., *Coastal Trade and Maritime Communities in Elizabethan England* (Woodbridge, 2024).

Broadberry, Stephen, Bruce M. S. Campbell, Alexander Klein, Mark Overton and Bas van Leeuwen, *British Economic Growth, 1270–1870* (Cambridge, 2015).

Brown, R. Allen, 'Royal Castle-Building in England, 1154–1216', *The English Historical Review*, 70:276 (1955).

Brown, Ruth R., 'The Ordnance Records: Thomas Browne', *Bulletin of the Wealden Iron Research Group*, 2nd series, 24 (2004), 16–25.

Bull, Stephen, *The Furie of Ordnance: Artillery in the English Civil War* (Woodbridge, 2008).

Butcher, Andrew, 'The Origins of Romney Freemen, 1433–1523', *Economic History Review*, 2nd series, 27 (1974), 16–27.

—— 'Rent and the Urban Economy: Oxford and Canterbury in the Later Middle Ages', *Southern History*, 1 (1979), 37–44.

—— 'The Function of Script in the Speech Community of a Late Medieval Town, c.1300–1550', in Julia Crick and Alexandra Walsham (eds), *The Uses of Script and Print, 1300–1700* (Cambridge, 2004), pp. 157–70.

Caiazza, Melanie, 'Saints and Weirs: Late Medieval and Early Modern Communities within a Small Island Landscape in North Kent', in Stuart Bligh, Elizabeth Edwards and Sheila Sweetinburgh (eds), *Maritime Kent through the Ages: Gateway to the Sea* (Woodbridge, 2021), pp. 401–15.

Carus-Wilson, E. M., and O. Coleman, *England's Export Trade, 1275–1547* (Oxford, 1963).

Chalklin, C. W., *Seventeenth-Century Kent: A Social and Economic History* (London, 1965).

Childs, David, *Tudor Sea Power: The Foundation of Greatness* (Barnsley, 2009).

Clark, Gregory, *English Prices and Wages, 1209–1914* (2003). https://gpih.ucdavis.edu/files/England_1209-1914_(Clark).xls

—— 'The Condition of the Working Class in England, 1209–2004', *Journal of Political Economy*, 113:6 (December 2005), 1307–40.

Clark, Peter, *English Provincial Society from the Reformation to the Revolution: Religion, Politics and Society in Kent, 1500–1640* (Hassocks, 1977).

Clarke, Helen, Sarah Pearson, Mavis Mate and Keith Parfitt (with contributions from Sheila Sweetinburgh and B. Jones), *Sandwich: The 'Completest Medieval Town in England': A Study of the Town and Port from Its Origins to 1600* (Oxford, 2010).

Clay, C. G. A., *Economic Expansion and Social Change: England 1500–1700* (Cambridge, 1984).

Cleere, Henry, David Crossley, Jeremy Hodgkinson and Bernard Charles Worssam, *The Iron Industry of the Weald* (Cardiff, 1995).

Coleman, D. C., 'An Innovation and Its Diffusion: The "New Draperies"', *Economic History Review*, 2nd series, 22:3 (1969), 417–29.

Collinson, Patrick, 'The Protestant Cathedral, 1541–1660', in Patrick Collinson, Nigel Ramsey and Margaret Sparks (eds), *A History of Canterbury Cathedral* (Oxford, 1995), pp. 159–61.

Colvin, H. M. (ed.), *The History of the King's Works*, vol. iv (London, 1982).

Connor, Meriel, 'The Priory of Christ Church Canterbury and Its Connections with London in the Late Middle Ages', *Archaeologia Cantiana*, 135 (2014), 33–46.

Corbett, Julian S., *Drake and the Tudor Navy* (2 vols, Aldershot, 1988).

Creighton, Oliver H., *Castles and Landscapes: Power, Community and Fortification in Medieval England* (London, 2002).

Cressy, David, *Literacy and the Social Order: Reading and Writing in Tudor and Stuart England* (Cambridge, 1980).

—— *Shipwrecks and the Bounty of the Sea* (Oxford, 2022).

Croft, Pauline, 'Trading with the Enemy 1585–1604', *The Historical Journal*, 32:2 (1989), 281–302.

Davies, J. D., *Pepys's Navy: Ships, Men and Warfare, 1649–1689* (Barnsley, 2008).

Davis, Ralph, *English Overseas Trade 1500–1700* (London, 1973).

Daxecker, Ursula, and Brandon Prins, *Pirate Lands: Governance and Maritime Piracy* (Oxford, 2021).

Dietz, Brian 'The Royal Bounty and English Merchant Shipping in the Sixteenth and Seventeenth Centuries', *The Mariner's Mirror*, 77 (1991), 5–20.

Dimmock, Spencer, 'English Small Towns and the Emergence of Capitalist Relations, c.1450–1550', *Urban History*, 28 (2001), 5–24.

Draper, Gillian, and Frank Meddens, '"There hath not bene any Grammar Scole kepte, Preacher maytened or Pore People releved, other then … by the same Chauntreye": Educational Provision and Piety in Kent, c.1400–1640', in Robert Lutton and Elisabeth Salter (eds), *Pieties in Transition: Religious Practices and Experiences, c.1400–1640* (Aldershot, 2007), pp. 75–91.

—— *The Sea and the Marsh: The Medieval Cinque Port of New Romney*, Pre-Construct Archaeology monograph (London, 2009).

Edwards, Elizabeth, 'Interpretations of the Influence of the Immigrant Population in Kent in the Sixteenth and Seventeenth Centuries', *Archaeologia Cantiana*, 122 (2002), 281–6.

Eldred, Jason, '"The Just will pay for the Sinners": English Merchants, the Trade with Spain, and Elizabethan Foreign Policy, 1563–1585', *Journal for Early Modern Cultural Studies*, 10:1 (2010), 5–28.

Elton, G. R., *England Under the Tudors* (1955, repr. Abingdon, 1991).

Fisher, F. J. (ed.), *The State of England Anno Dom. 1600 by Thomas Wilson* (London, 1936).

—— 'London's Export Trade in the Early Seventeenth Century', *Economic History Review*, 2nd series, 3 (1950), 151–61.

—— 'The Development of the London Food Market, 1540–1640', in E. M. Carus-Wilson (ed.), *Essays in Economic History*, vol. 1 (1954), pp. 135–51.

Fissel, Mark Charles, *English Warfare, 1511–1642* (London, 2001).

Fuidge, N. M., 'CROMER, William (c.1531–98), of Tunstall, nr. Sittingbourne, Kent', in P. W. Hasler (ed.), *The History of Parliament: The House of Commons 1558–1603* (Woodbridge, 1981).

Fury, Cheryl A., 'Training and Education in the Elizabethan Maritime Community, 1595–1603', *The Mariner's Mirror*, 85 (1999), 147–61.

Gibson, Jeremy, and Alan Dell, *Tudor and Stuart Muster Rolls: A Directory of Holdings in the British Isles* (Birmingham, 1989).

Gillis, John R., *The Human Shore: Seacoasts in History* (Chicago, 2012).

Gosse, Philip, *The History of Piracy* (New York, 1932).

Grassby, Richard, *The Business Community of Seventeenth-Century England* (Cambridge, 1995).

Graves, Michael A. R., 'Sackville, Robert, second earl of Dorset', *Oxford Dictionary of National Biography*, https://doi.org/10.1093/ref:odnb/24449.

Grummitt, David, 'Kent and National Politics', 1399–1461', in Sheila Sweetinburgh (ed.), *Later Medieval Kent 1220–1540* (Woodbridge, 2010), pp. 235–50.

Gunn, Steven, *The English People at War in the Age of Henry VIII* (Oxford, 2018).

Hammer, Paul E. J., *Elizabeth's Wars: War, Government and Society in Tudor England, 1544–1604* (Basingstoke, 2003).

Harrington, Peter, *The Castles of Henry VIII* (London, 2007).

Hasted, Edward, *The History and Topographical Survey of the County of Kent: Volume 1* (Canterbury, 1797).

Hatcher, John, *The History of the British Coal Industry: Volume 1: Before 1700: Towards the Age of Coal* (Oxford, 1993).

Henderson, John, *Piety and Charity in Late Medieval Florence* (Chicago and London, 1997).

Hipkin, Stephen, 'The Structure, Development, and Politics of the Kent Grain Trade, 1552–1647', *Economic History Review*, 2nd series, 61:S1 (August 2008), 99–139.

Hodgkinson, J. S., 'Ironworks in Late-16th Century Kent', *Bulletin of the Wealden Iron Research Group*, 2nd series, 24 (2004), 6–15.

—— *The Wealden Iron Industry* (Cheltenham, 2008).

Hogben, Brian, 'Preaching and the Reformation in Henrician Kent', *Archaeologia Cantiana*, 101 (1984), 169–85.

Holman, James, *Medieval New Romney: A Town Shaped by Water*, Canterbury Archaeological Trust monograph (Canterbury, 2020).

Holt, Mack P., *The French Wars of Religion, 1562–1629*, 2nd edition (Cambridge, 2012).

Hope, Andrew, 'Martyrs of the Marsh: Elizabeth Barton, Joan Bocher and Trajectories of Martyrdom in Reformation Kent', in Robert Lutton and Elisabeth Salter (eds), *Pieties in Transition: Religious Practices and Experiences, c.1400–1640* (Aldershot, 2007), pp. 41–55.

Hoyle, R. W., 'Taxation and the Mid-Tudor Crisis', *Economic History Review*, 2nd series, 51:4 (1998), 649–75.

Hutchinson, Robert, *The Spanish Armada* (London, 2013).

Hyde, Patricia, and Michael Zell, 'Governing the County', in Michael Zell (ed.), *Early Modern Kent 1540–1640* (Woodbridge, 2000), pp. 7–38.

Joby, Christopher, *The Dutch Language in Britain (1550–1702): A Social History of the Use of Dutch in Early Modern Britain* (Leiden, 2015).

Jones, Evan T., 'Illicit Business: Accounting for Smuggling in Mid-Sixteenth-Century Bristol', *Economic History Review*, 2nd series, 54:1 (2001), 17–38.

—— *Inside the Illicit Economy: Reconstructing the Smugglers' Trade of Sixteenth Century Bristol* (London, 2012, repr. 2016).

Kamen, Henry, *European Society 1500–1700* (London, 1984).

Karn, Nicholas, 'England's Trade with the Continent in the Early Thirteenth Century: Customs and the Port of Dover', *Journal of Medieval History*, 46 (2020), 306–34.

Kepler, J. S., *The Exchange of Christendom: The International Entrepôt at Dover 1622–1651* (Leicester, 1976).

Kerridge, Eric., *Trade and Banking in Early Modern England* (Manchester, 1988), pp. 5–32.

King, David James Cathcart, *The Castle in England and Wales: An Interpretative History* (London, 1988).

Kowaleski, Maryanne, 'The Expansion of the South-Western Fisheries in Late Medieval England', *Economic History Review*, 2nd series, 53 (2000), 429–54.

—— 'Maritime Trade and Industry in Medieval Kent', in Stuart Bligh, Elizabeth Edwards and Sheila Sweetinburgh (eds), *Maritime Kent through the Ages: Gateway to the Sea* (Woodbridge, 2021), pp. 215–33.

L'Hour, M., L. Long and E. Rieth, 'The Wreck of an "Experimental" Ship of the "Oost-Indische Companie": The *Mauritius* (1609)', *The International Journal of Nautical Archeology and Underwater Exploration*, 19:1 (1990), 63–73.

L'Hour, Michael, Luc Long and Eric Rieth, *Le Mauritius: la mémoire engloutie* (Paris, 1989).

Lambert, Craig, 'Naval Service and the Cinque Ports, 1322–1453', in Gary P. Baker, Craig Lambert and David Simpkin (eds), *Military Communities in Late Medieval England: Essays in Honour of Andrew Ayton* (Woodbridge, 2018), pp. 211–36.

Lambert, Craig and Gary P. Baker, 'The Merchant Fleet and Shipboard Community of Kent, c.1565–c.1580', *Archaeologia Cantiana*, 140 (2019), 89–110.

—— 'An Investigation of the Size and Geographical Distribution of the English, Welsh, and Channel Islands Merchant Fleet: A Case Study of 1571–72', in Richard J. Blakemore and James Davey (eds), *The Maritime World of Early Modern Britain* (Amsterdam, 2020), pp. 79–102.

Land, Isaac, 'Port Towns and the Paramaritime', in Claire Jowitt, Craig Lambert and Steve Mentz (eds), *The Routledge Companion to Marine and Maritime Worlds, 1400–1800* (Routledge, 2020), pp. 177–201.

Lloyd, T. H., *The English Wool Trade in the Middle Ages* (Cambridge, 1977).

—— *England and the German Hanse, 1157–1611: A Study of Their Trade and Commercial Diplomacy* (Cambridge, 1991).

Loades, David, *The Tudor Navy: An Administrative, Political and Military History* (Aldershot, 1992).

—— 'The English Maritime Community', in Cheryl A. Fury (ed.), *The Social History of English Seamen, 1485–1649* (Woodbridge, 2012).

Loades, David and C. S. Knighton (eds), *Elizabethan Naval Administration* (Ashgate, 2013).

Lutton, Robert, *Lollardy and Orthodox Religion in Pre-Reformation England* (Woodbridge, 2006).

—— 'Heresy and Heterodoxy in Late Medieval Kent', in Sheila Sweetinburgh (ed.), *Later Medieval Kent 1220–1540* (Woodbridge, 2010), pp. 167–87.

Luu, Lien Bich, *Immigrants and the Industries of London, 1500–1700* (London, 2005).

Margetts, Andrew, Giles Dawkes, Damian Goodburn, Lucy Allott, Stacey Adams and Alice Dowsett, 'What "Incomparable Jewells Havens, and Sure Harbours Are": The Remains of Late 16th Century Dover Harbour and Their Wider Significance', *Post-Medieval Archaeology*, 57:1 (2023), 177–98.

Martin, Colin, and Geoffrey Parker, *The Spanish Armada*, revised edition (Manchester, 1999).

Mate, Mavis E., *Trade and Economic Developments, 1450–1550 – The Experience of Kent, Surrey and Sussex* (Woodbridge, 2006).

—— 'The Economy of Kent, 1200–1500: The Aftermath of the Black Death', in Sheila Sweetinburgh (ed.), *Later Medieval Kent 1220–1540* (Woodbridge, 2010), pp. 11–24.

McBain, Graham S., 'The Charters of the Cinque Ports – Are They Still Needed?', *Review of European Studies*, 5:2 (2013), 90–126.

McCullough, P. E., 'Andrewes, Lancelot (1552–1626)', in G. C. G. Matthew and Brian Harrison (eds), *Oxford Dictionary of National Biography*, 60 vols (Oxford, 2004), https://www.oxforddnb.com/.

McGurk, J. J. N., 'Armada Preparation in Kent and Arrangements Made after the Defeat (1587–1589)', *Archaeologia Cantiana*, 85 (1971), 71–93

—— 'Levies from Kent to the Elizabethan Wars, 1589–1603', *Archaeologia Cantiana*, 88 (1974), 57–72

Mercer, Malcolm, 'Kent and National Politics, 1461–1509', in Sweetinburgh (ed.), *Later Medieval Kent 1220–1540* (Woodbridge, 2010), pp. 251–71.

Moorhouse, Geoffrey, *Great Harry's Navy: How Henry VIII Gave England Seapower* (London, 2005).

Morley, B. M., *Henry VIII and the Development of Coastal Defence* (London, 1976).

Moseley, Virginia C. D., and Rosemary Sgroi, 'Wilson, Thomas (c.1565–1629), of Westminster and the Castle Gatehouse, Hertford, Herts.', *The History of Parliament Online*, http://www.histparl.ac.uk/volume/1604-1629/member/wilson-thomas-1565-1629.

—— 'HIPPISLEY (EPSLEY), Sir John (–d.1655), of The Mews, Westminster; Bushey Park, Mdx. and Dover Castle, Kent', in Andrew Thrush and John P. Ferris (eds), *The History of Parliament: The House of Commons 1604–1629* (Cambridge, 2010).

Munro, John H., 'Tawney's Century (1540–1640): The Roots of Modern Capitalist Entrepreneurship in England', in David S. Landes, Joel Mokyr and William J. Baumol (eds), *The Invention of Enterprise: Entrepreneurship from Ancient Mesopotamia to Modern Times* (Princeton, 2010), pp. 107–55.

—— 'Usury, Calvinism, and Credit in Protestant England: From the Sixteenth Century to the Industrial Revolution', University of Toronto Working Paper no. 439 (2011), pp. 15–19.

Orme, Nicholas, 'John Cole (c.1467–1536) and the Origins of Education in Faversham', *Archaeologia Cantiana*, 137 (2016), 107–26.

Outhwaite, R. B., 'Dearth and Government Intervention in English Grain Markets, 1590–1700', *Economic History Review*, 2nd series, 34:3 (1981), 389–406.

Parker, Geoffrey, 'War and Economic Change: The Economic Costs of the Dutch Revolt', in J. M. Winter (ed.), *War and Economic Development: Essays in Memory of David Joslin* (Cambridge, 1975), pp. 49–72.

—— 'If the Armada Had Landed', *History*, 61:203 (1976), 358–68

Phelps Brown, Henry, and Sheila Hopkins, *A Perspective of Wages and Prices* (London, 1981), pp. 28–31.

Platt, Colin, *The Castle in Medieval England and Wales* (London, 1982).

Power, M. J., 'East London Housing in the Seventeenth Century', in Peter Clark and Paul Slack (eds), *Crisis and Order in English Towns, 1500–1700: Essays in Urban History* (London, 1972).

Puttevils, Jeroen, and Marc Deloof, 'Marketing and Pricing Risk in Marine Insurance in Sixteenth-Century Antwerp', *The Journal of Economic History*, 77:3 (2017), 796–837.

Reading, Benjamin W. D., *The English and French Navies, 1500–1650* (Woodbridge, 2002).

Richardson, Catherine, 'Household Objects and Domestic Ties', in Cordelia Beattie, Anna Maslakovic and Sarah Rees Jones (eds), *The Medieval Household in Christian Europe, c.850–1550* (Turnhout, 2003), pp. 433–47.

Rodger, N. A. M., *The Safeguard of the Sea: A Naval History of Britain, Volume 1: 660–1649* (London, 2004).

—— 'The Law and Language of Private Naval Warfare', *The Mariner's Mirror*, 100:1 (2014), 5–16.

Rose, Susan, *Calais: An English Town in France* (Woodbridge, 2008).

—— *England's Medieval Navy, 1066–1509: Ships, Men and Warfare* (Barnsley, 2013).

—— 'The Port of Sandwich in the Later Middle Ages', in Stuart Bligh, Elizabeth Edwards and Sheila Sweetinburgh (eds), *Maritime Kent through the Ages: Gateway to the Sea* (Woodbridge, 2021), pp. 371–85.

Rundle, David, *The Renaissance Reform of the Book and Britain: The English Quattrocento* (Cambridge, 2019).

Salter, Elisabeth, 'Some Differences in the Cultural Production of Household Consumption in Three North Kent Communities, c.1450–1550', in Cordelia Beattie, Anna Maslakovic and Sarah Rees Jones (eds), *The Medieval Household in Christian Europe, c.850–1550* (Turnhout, 2003), pp. 391–407.

Scammell, G. V., 'English Merchant Shipping at the End of the Middle Ages: Some East Coast Evidence', *Economic History Review*, 2nd series, 13:3 (1961), 327–41.

—— 'Manning the English Merchant Service in the Sixteenth Century', *The Mariner's Mirror*, 56 (1970), 131–54.

—— 'Shipowning in the Economy and Politics of Early Modern England', *The Historical Journal*, 15:3 (1972), 385–407.

—— 'The Merchant Service Master in Early Modern England', in *Seafaring, Sailors and Trade, 1450–1750: Studies in British and European Maritime and Imperial History* (Aldershot, 2003), pp. 1–22.

Scarisbrick, John Joseph, *Henry VIII* (New Haven and London, 1997).

Shagan, Ethan, *Popular Politics and the English Reformation* (Cambridge, 2003).

Sharp, Buchanan, *Famine and Scarcity in Late Medieval and Early Modern England: The Regulation of Grain Marketing, 1256–1631* (Cambridge, 2016).

Spencer, Dan, *Royal and Urban Gunpowder Weapons in Late Medieval England* (Woodbridge, 2019).

Starkey, David J., 'Pirates and Markets', in Lewis R. Fischer (ed.), *The Market for Seamen in the Age of Sail* (Liverpool, 1994), pp. 59–80.

—— 'Voluntaries and Sea Robbers: A Review of the Academic Literature on Privateering, Corsairing, Buccaneering and Piracy', *The Mariner's Mirror*, 97:1 (2011), 127–47.

Stephens, W. B., 'The Cloth Exports of the Provincial Ports, 1600–1640', *Economic History Review*, 2nd series, 22:2 (1969), 228–48.

Stradling, R. A., *The Armada of Flanders: Spanish Maritime Policy and European War, 1568–1668* (Cambridge, 1992), pp. 204–28.

Sweetinburgh, Sheila, *The Role of the Hospital in Medieval England: Gift-Giving and the Spiritual Economy* (Dublin, 2004).

—— 'Strategies of Inheritance among Kentish Fishing Communities in the Later Middle Ages', *The History of the Family*, 11 (2006), 98–102.

—— 'The Poor, Hospitals and Charity in Sixteenth Century Canterbury', in Robert Lutton and Elisabeth Salter (eds), *Pieties in Transition: Religious Practices and Experiences, c.1400–1640* (Aldershot, 2007), pp. 59–73.

—— 'Eternal Town Servants: Civic Elections and the Stuppeny Tombs of New Romney and Lydd', in Mette Bruun and Stephanie Glaser (eds), *Negotiating Heritage: Memories of the Middle Ages* (Turnhout, 2008), pp. 149–72.

—— 'Hythe's Butcher-Graziers: Their Role in Town and Country in Late Medieval Kent', in Christopher Dyer, Andrew Hopper, Evelyn Lord and Nigel Tringham (eds), *New Directions in Local History since Hoskins* (Hatfield, 2011), pp. 103–13.

—— 'Discord in the Public Arena: Processes and Meanings of the St Bartholomew's Day Festivities in Early Sixteenth-Century Sandwich', in Sheila Sweetinburgh (ed.), *Negotiating the Political in Northern European Urban Society, c.1400–c.1600* (Tempe, AZ and Turnhout, 2013), pp. 85–96.

—— 'Pilgrimage in "An Age of Plague": Seeking Canterbury's "Hooly Blisful Martir"', in Linda Clark and Carole Rawcliffe (eds), *The Fifteenth Century XII: Society in an Age of Plague* (Woodbridge, 2013), pp. 57–77.

—— 'Looking to the Past: The St Thomas Pageant in Early Tudor Canterbury', *Archaeologia Cantiana*, 137 (2016), 163–83.

—— 'Community Care: Civic Charitable Institutions in the Kentish Cinque Ports, c. 1300–c. 1500', *Archaeologia Cantiana*, 141 (2020), 183–98.

—— 'Fishermen in Late Medieval and Tudor Kent', in Claire Jowitt, Craig Lambert and Steve Mentz (eds), *The Routledge Companion to Marine and Maritime Worlds, 1400–1800* (London, 2020), pp. 202–20.

—— 'More Continuity Than Change: Almshouses in Tudor Kent', *Southern History*, 42 (2020/21), 21–45.

—— '"Ready for to go to the Sea": Maintaining Fishing Families in Late Medieval Hythe', in Stuart Bligh, Elizabeth Edwards and Sheila Sweetinburgh (eds), *Maritime Kent through the Ages: Gateway to the Sea* (Woodbridge, 2021), pp. 387–400.

—— 'Neighbours across the Religious Divide: Coping with Difference in Henrician Kent', in Bronach Kane and Simon Sandall (eds), *The Experience of Neighbourhood in Medieval and Early Modern Europe* (London and New York, 2022), pp. 63–77.

—— 'Starting a New Life as Artisans and Traders in Ricardian and Henrician Canterbury', *Archaeologia Cantiana*, 143 (2022), 33–50.

Trim, D. J. B., 'Transnational Calvinist Cooperation and "Mastery of the Sea" in the Late-Sixteenth Century', in J. D. Davies, Alan James and Gijs Rommelse (eds), *Ideologies of Western Naval Power, c. 1500–1815* (New York, 2019), pp. 153–87.

Urry, William, 'The Jubilee of St Thomas, 1420: Billeting and Rationing Problems in the Fifteenth Century', *Canterbury Cathedral Chronicle*, 42 (1947), 23–7.

van Bochove, Christiaan, *The Economic Consequences of the Dutch: Economic Integration Around the North Sea, 1500–1800* (Amsterdam, 2008).

van der Wee, Herman, *The Growth of the Antwerp Market and the European Economy: Fourteenth-Sixteenth Centuries* (The Hague, 1963).

van Loo, Ivo, 'For Freedom and Fortune: The Rise of Dutch Privateering in the First Half of the Dutch Revolt, 1568–1609', in Marco van der Hoeven (ed.), *Exercise of Arms: Warfare in the Netherlands, 1568–1648*, History of Warfare Series, vol. 1 (Brill, 1997), pp. 173–95.

Ware, Christopher, 'To Defend the Coast', in Stuart Bligh, Elizabeth Edwards and Sheila Sweetinburgh (eds), *Maritime Kent through the Ages: Gateway to the Sea* (Woodbridge, 2021).

White, H. T., 'The Beacons System in Kent', *Archaeologia Cantiana*, 46 (1934), 77–96.

Whitehead, Alfred North, 'England and the Narrow Seas', *The Atlantic* (June 1927), 791–8.

Wilkinson, Paul, *The Historical Development of the Port of Faversham 1580–1780*, British Archaeological Reports British Series 413 (2006).

Willan, T. S., *Studies in Elizabethan Foreign Trade* (Manchester, 1959).

William, Neville J., *The Maritime Trade of the East Anglian Ports, 1550–1590* (Oxford, 1988).

Woodruff, C. E., 'An Inventory of the Contents of the Bed-Chamber of Brother Richard Stone, Monk of Christ Church, Canterbury', *Archaeologia Cantiana*, 43 (1931), 103–10.

Wrightson, Keith, *Earthly Necessities: Economic Lives in Early Modern Britain* (New Haven, 2000).

Wrigley, E. A., and R. S. Schofield, *The Population History of England 1541–1871: A Reconstruction* (London, 1981).

Zell, Michael, 'The Prebendaries' Plot of 1543: A Reconsideration', *Journal of Ecclesiastical History*, 27 (1976), 241–53.

—— *Industry in the Countryside: Wealden Society in the Sixteenth Century* (Cambridge, 1994).

—— 'The Coming of Religious Reform', in Michael Zell (ed.), *Early Modern Kent, 1540–1640* (Woodbridge, 2000), pp. 177–206.

—— 'Introduction', in Michael Zell (ed.), *Early Modern Kent 1540–1640* (Woodbridge, 2000), pp. 1–6.

—— 'Landholding and the Land Market in Early Modern Kent', in Michael Zell (ed.), *Early Modern Kent 1540–1640* (Woodbridge, 2000), pp. 39–74.

Unpublished Theses

Appleby, J. C., 'English Privateering during the Spanish and French Wars, 1625–1630' (unpublished Ph.D. thesis, University of Hull, 1983).

Backhouse, Marcel F., 'The Flemish and Walloon Communities at Sandwich during the Reign of Elizabeth I (1561–1603)' (unpublished Ph.D. thesis, University of Southampton, 1991).
Brindle, Graham, 'A Social and Economic Study of the Cinque Ports Region, 1450–1600' (unpublished Ph.D. thesis, University of St Andrews, 1979).
Brodie, Nicholas, 'Beggary, Vagabondage and Poor Relief: English Statutes in the Urban Context, 1495–1572' (unpublished Ph.D. thesis, University of Tasmania, 2010).
Croft, Justin, 'The Custumals of the Cinque Ports c.1290–c.1599: Studies in the Cultural Production of the Unban Record' (unpublished Ph.D. thesis, University of Kent, 1997).
Dixon, Mary, 'Economy and Society in Dover 1509–1640' (unpublished Ph.D. thesis, University of Kent, 1992).
Eastlake, Elizabeth, 'Redressing the Balance: Boxley 1146–1538' (unpublished Ph.D. thesis, University of Winchester, 2014).
Goring, John Jeremy, 'The Military Obligations of the English People, 1511–1558' (unpublished Ph.D. thesis, University of London, 1955).
Kirk, William, 'Development of a Medieval Industry: The Emergence and Decline of Coastal Salt Production in East Kent' (unpublished MA dissertation, University of Kent, 1999).
Lee, Paul, 'Monastic and Secular Religion and Devotional Reading in Late Medieval Dartford and West Kent' (unpublished Ph.D. thesis, University of Kent, 1998).
Palmer, Stuart, 'Politics, Corporation and Commonwealth: The Early Reformation in Canterbury, c.1450–1559' (unpublished Ph.D. thesis, University of Kent, 2016).
van Duivenvoorde, Wendy, 'The Batavia Shipwreck: An Archaeological Study of an Early Seventeenth-Century Dutch East Indiaman' (unpublished Ph.D. thesis, Texas A&M University, 2008).

Web Resources

The Bank of England, 'Inflation Calculator', https://www.bankofengland.co.uk/monetary-policy/inflation/inflation-calculator/.
British History Online, https://www.british-history.ac.uk/.
The Dutch East India Company's shipping between the Netherlands and Asia 1595–1795, https://resources.huygens.knaw.nl/das.
Early English Books Online, https://www.english-corpora.org/eebo/.
England's Immigrants 1330–1550, https://www.englandsimmigrants.com.
The History of Parliament Online, http://www.histparl.ac.uk.
Lambert, Craig, Shiela Sweetinburgh and Robert Blackmore, 'Maritime Kent: Kent's Maritime Communities and Their European Neighbours: Connections and Relations Across the Narrow Seas, c.1450–c.1650' (University of Southampton, 2024), https://maritimebritain.org/maritime_kent/.
The National Archives, UK, 'Currency Converter: 1270–2017', https://www.nationalarchives.gov.uk/currency-converter/#.

The National Archives, UK, 'Research Guides: Royal Naval Dockyard Staff', https://www.nationalarchives.gov.uk/help-with-your-research/research-guides/royal-naval-dockyard-staff/.

Oxford Dictionary of National Biography, https://www.oxforddnb.com/.

van Zanden, Jan Luiten, 'Wages and the cost of living in Southern England (London) 1450–1700', https://hdl.handle.net/10622/VY7UY3, IISH Data Collection, V2.

INDEX

Printed and bound by CPI Group (UK) Ltd, Croydon, CR0 4YY

13/09/2026

14961005-0002